V & ME

Everybody's Favorite Jim Valvano Story

DISCARD

Bob Cairns

foreword by **Roy Firestone**

Alexander Books
Alexander, North Carolina

Publisher: Ralph Roberts
Editors: Philip J. Hawkins, Robert Milks, Pat Roberts
Cover Design: Ralph Roberts
Cover Art: Copyright © 2004 Adam Brill
Interior Design and Electronic Page Assembly: **WorldComm®**

10 9 8 7 6 5 4 3 2 1

ISBN 1-57090-228-3 trade paper
ISBN 1-57090-229-1 hardback

Library of Congress Cataloging-in-Publication Data

Cairns, Bob   1943-
    V & me: everybody's favorite Jim Valvano story /by Bob Cairns; with foreword by Roy Firestone.-- 1st ed.
        p.   cm.
    ISBN 1-57090-228-3 (trade pbk.: alk. paper) -- ISBN 1-57090-229-1 (hardback: alk. paper)
    1. Valvano, Jim. 2. Valvano, Jim--Anecdotes. 3. Basketball coaches--United States--Biography. I. Title: V and me. II Title: Everybody's favorite Jim Valvano story. III. Title.
    GV884.V36C37 2004
    796.323'092--dc22
                                        2004005646

The author and publisher have made every effort in the preparation of this book to ensure the accuracy of the information. However, the information in this book is sold without warranty, either express or implied. Neither the author nor **Alexander Books** will be liable for any damages caused or alleged to be caused directly, indirectly, incidentally, or consequentially by the information in this book.

The opinions expressed in this book are solely those of the author and storytellers and are not necessarily those of **Alexander Books.**

Trademarks: Names of products mentioned in this book known to be or suspected of being trademarks or service marks are capitalized. The usage of a trademark or service mark in this book should not be regarded as affecting the validity of any trademark or service mark.

Alexander Books—a division of *Creativity, Inc.*—is a full-service publisher located at 65 Macedonia Road, Alexander, NC 28701. Phone 1-828-252-9515, Fax 1-828-255-8719. For orders only: 1-800-472-0438. Visa and MasterCard accepted.

This book is also available on the Internet at **abooks.com.** Set your web browser to **http://abooks.com** and enjoy the many fine values available there.

Contents

Everybody's Favorite Jim Valvano Story

DEDICATION

For Pam, Nicole, Jamie, LeeAnn,
and all the Valvano "Family"

ACKNOWLEDGEMENTS

The thanks for these memories go to many people but ultimately to one—Jim Valvano! I know this because V told me so. The first interview I ever did with him was in the spring of 1980. As I turned to leave his office I said, "Coach, do you want to see the article before it's published?"

V said, "Why? All you're going to do is string together my great quotes and put your name on it!"

As I began the research for this book, I reread that article. He was right.

So, V, thanks for all the great quotes, the one-liners, and the incredible memories of your life. This gratitude comes from me and all your friends who remembered what you said or did and were kind enough to share them with me.

Heartfelt thanks from and for *V & Me* go to:

Tom Abatemarco, Joyce Aschenbrenner, Thurl Bailey, Fred Barakat, Mark Bockelman, Jim Boeheim, Linda Bruno, Charlie Bryant, Gary Bryant, Lorenzo Charles, Francis Combs, Chris Corchiani, Bobby Cremins, Ruth Curlee, Vinny Del Negro, Walt Densmore, Dave Didion, George Dixon, Lefty Driesell, Sam Esposito, John Feinstein, Nora Lynn Finch, Mike Finn, Roy Firestone, both Bill Fosters, Terry Gannon, Jim Graham, Jeff Gravley, Mike Gray, Larry Gross, Bob Guzzo, Terry Holland, Sarah Sue Ingram, Ed Janka, Jay Jennings, Art Kaminsky, Pat Kennedy, Tony Kornheiser, Mike Krzyzewski, Frances Lewis, Bob Lloyd, Sidney Lowe, Mike Lupica, Jeff Mann, Jim Marchiony, Ray Martin, Rollie Massamino, Frank McCann, Ed McLean, Cozell McQueen, Greg Miller, Ernie Myers, George Nixon, Dan Patrick, Tom Penders, Max Perry, Rich Petriccione, Jim Pomerantz, Bruce Poulton, Dr. Jerry Punch, Jim Rehbock, Dr. Don Reibel, Harry Rhoads, Johnny Rhodes, Bob Robinson, Les Robinson, Dee Rowe, Jeff Ruland, John Saunders, Don Shea, Dick Sheridan, Dean Smith, Gary Smith, Tubby

Smith, Bob Staak, Dick Stockton, Ken Swartzel, Ray Tanner, George Tarantini, Jerry Tarkanian, Joab Thomas, Mike Tirico, Jamie Valvano, LeeAnn Valvano, Nicole Valvano, Nick Valvano, Pam Valvano, Dick Vitale, Mike Warren, Woody Webb, Frank Weedon, Dan White, Dereck Whittenburg, Graham Wilson, Alex Wolff, John Wooden, and Kay Yow.

A special thanks to the cover's artist, Adam Brill, and to Linda Verigan, Bev Sparks, Bob Milks, Matt Cairns, E.A. Cairns, Ralph Roberts, Pat Roberts, Phil Hawkins, all the good folks at the Jimmy V Foundation For Cancer Research, and my wife, Alyce, who spelled all those great Italian names.

PHOTO CREDITS

KEY TO THE PERSONALITIES
IN THE COVER ILLUSTRATION

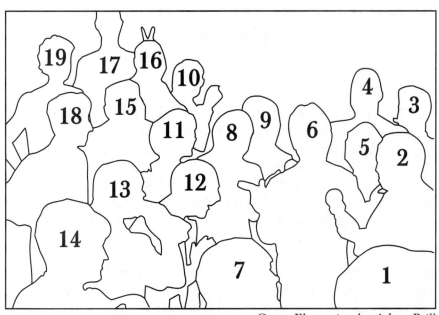

Cover Illustration by Adam Brill

1	The Rest Of Us	10	John Wooden
2	John Saunders	11	Pam Valvano
3	Sam Esposito	12	Tony Kornheiser
4	Dereck Whittenburg	13	Jerry Tarkanian
5	Dick Vitale	14	Bobby Cremins
6	V	15	Dean Smith
7	Lefty Driesell	16	Sidney Lowe
8	Roy Firestone	17	Thurl Bailey
9	Mike Krzyzewski	18	Kay Yow
		19	Terry Gannon

Preface

Those of us whose stories you'll read here all had a similar experience: our first meeting with Jim Valvano. It was one of those momentous occasions, a time we'll never forget. There was the wedding day, the birth of the first child, and V Day, the day we met Jim Valvano.

Sidney Lowe, after sitting through V's first team meeting: "He opened his talk with the national championship. He actually told us we were going to win a national championship. We walked out of there shaking our heads saying, 'Who the hell is this guy?'"

Rich Petriccione, V's manager at Iona College: "I remember as a freshman riding with him for thirty minutes from Iona to Fairleigh Dickinson to scout a game and in that short period of time he told me that he was going to win an NCAA Championship, appear on the *Tonight Show* with Johnny Carson, meet the president of the United States, shake hands with the pope, and oh yes... star in a TV sitcom based on his own character. I thought this freakin' guy is crazy!"

Tony Kornheiser, *The Washington Post* columnist and host of ESPN's *Pardon the Interruption*: "Jimmy was the funniest stand-around guy I ever met . . . and that includes all the comedians."

Gary Smith, author of "As Time Runs Out," *Sports Illustrated*: "Jim Valvano and Dustin Hoffman stand out as the two most fascinating interviews I've ever had. They were the most full of life, full of humor, and full of intelligence."

Kay Yow, NC State women's basketball coach: "All you had to do was see the Room of Dreams if you wanted to meet Jim. He had this thing in his head, a major production, a high-tech multi-media recruiting room that included video, synchronized with lights and music and showcases. And then he made it happen. It was like Disney World's Country Bear Jamboree goes basketball. At every home game we'd have a line of people waiting to go into the Room of Dreams, and when they left that experience they'd met Jim Valvano!"

My first encounter was less dramatic. It came in the early spring of 1980 with an assignment to write a feature on NC State's new basketball coach for the university's *The Stater*, an alumni magazine. Joe Hancock, a senior writer in the NC State news bureau, the resident office curmudgeon, sent me off with his thoughts on my interview. He didn't like this new coach's duck ass hair cut, hated his pointed shoes, and wasn't all that fond of Yankees. Several hours later after the "V experience," I leaned into Joe's office and said, "I don't know if this guy can coach but I'll tell you what, he's the most entertaining S.O.B. I've ever met!"

Those of us fortunate enough to have been "V'd" know that he was entertaining. And a whole lot more.

> *"The best all-around interview I ever had,"* Roy Firestone, host of ESPN's Up Close.

> *"One of the best coaching jobs in NCAA tournament history," John Wooden, former head basketball coach, UCLA.*

> *"He was an English teacher. On our road trips he'd read us poetry, quote philosophers, teach us to diagram sentences," Dan White, former manager.*

> *"A rare visionary, someone who had the creativity to develop a vision and then implement it," Bruce Poulton, chancellor, NC State University.*

> *"One of the most dynamic, engaging, and powerfully persuasive public speakers I've ever heard. You put a microphone in his hand . . . and magic appeared before your eyes," Harry Rhoads, Jr., president, Washington Speakers Bureau.*

> *"A totally different person than I thought he'd be. If I had a son I'd love for my son to play for him," Dave Didion, the chief investigator who oversaw the NCAA investigation of V and NC State's basketball program.*

Like that very first V meeting I know exactly where and how the idea for *V & Me* hatched. Several years after his death I was visiting in my friend Sam Esposito's office in the athletic department at NC

State. Sam is a man of many distinctions–major league baseball player, NC State College World Series coach, bench coach for NC State's 1974 National Championship basketball team. But among these credits, his greatest may be the fact that for V's decade at NC State, Sam was his confidant and very best friend. I had dropped in on Espo because I wanted him to meet my buddy Craig Detwiler, who at the time was the traveling secretary for the Seattle Mariners. Somehow Valvano came up (when didn't he?) and Sam favored us with a story or two. Then George Tarantini, the men's soccer coach–another close friend of Valvano's–wandered in. The stories continued–laughter, tears, moments of respect. Several hours later, when Craig and I walked out into the cold January day, he turned to me and said, "That was incredible. You could write a book!"

Later, in the spring of '99, when I met with V's older brother Nick to get the blessings of the family and that of the Jimmy V Foundation for Cancer Research, we agreed that in the "Spirit of Jim" this book would not be what V would have called an "off-the-rack 40 Regular!" Typically my interviews began like this: You and a friend are having a drink. Your buddy says, "You knew him, tell me your favorite V story, the memory you just can't forget!"

When I was coming down to the finish of this gathering I was in a Raleigh restaurant interviewing Jay Jennings, the WRAL-TV videographer who chronicled the '83 team from Corvallis to the net cuttings at Albuquerque. Jay turned the table on me and asked, "Has your opinion of him changed? What do you think really made him go?" The buzz words of the book's interviews flew through my head. So very diverse, clearly one of God's more complex pieces of work.

My answer: "I think V was what happens when a good guy with incredible talent is driven to become great." I said. "But here's what I know. He did because he could. And he lived for and in the moment. He loved life. V never missed the moment."

Personal observations from those who were with V are salted into an essay called "Living The Moment" (begins on page 21). The idea here is to simply give readers whose memories might need jogging a sense of his career, in story form–from New York to Albuquerque. For those who wish more details (everything from V's personal recollections of games to focused accounts of his *Personal Fouls* days at NC State) I'd recommend V's diary of the '83 season, *Too Soon to Quit* (Coman Publishing); V's autobiography, *Valvano: They*

Gave Me a Lifetime Contract, and Then They Declared Me Dead, with Curry Kirkpatrick (Simon & Schuster); *I Remember Jim Valvano,* Mike Towle (Cumberland House); and *The Gifts of Jimmy V,* Bob Valvano (Triumph Books). Stories that happen to appear in any other book which also appear in *V & Me* were told to me personally, *V & Me* is, by design, what those excellent books are not. This is a storybook voiced by the people who had the pleasure of having experienced those very special and often private V moments.

In the spring of '93 with less than a month left to live, Jim Valvano stood on a national stage in New York at ESPN's ESPY Awards and seized a very special moment of his own. Weak, dying from cancer, and in incredible pain, he summoned up the strength to give us words to live by: "We should all enjoy the moment–take the time each day to laugh, to cry, and to think."

These anecdotal snapshots drop you into the center of the action of a life that ended far too soon and yet at the end proved to be one that was– by all standards–almost impossible to beat. The stories of *V & Me* will come at you like life, in no particular order.

Prepare to laugh, to cry, and to think!

Bob Cairns

Foreword

I'm often asked a question that relates directly to Jim Valvano. People wonder how many interviews I've done and then invariably want me to name the best. Well, there have been more than 5,000 interviews and I have ranked them by categories—intellectual, thoughtful, funny, entertaining, poignant, etc.

In seven of the ten categories Jim Valvano is number one. In the remaining three he's in the top five. He was, in every sense of the word, the most human interview . . . the most human being. So if I had to paste one name up there above the 5,000, the best is Jimmy V.

A number of my favorite V stories from my *Up Close* interviews are included here in *V & Me: Everybody's Favorite Jim Valvano Story*. They show the many dimensions of the man. The thing about Jim was that he was personality driven. So you could very easily mistake him for a wacky guy. But he was so smart and so caring. He had his demons and he wore his heart on his sleeve. He was incredibly open. Always in search of an audience.

There was this great moment in the movie *Mr. Saturday Night*. The brother says to the comedian, the Billy Crystal character, "What do you need, why are you so restless?"

And Mr. Saturday Night says, "Get me an audience!"

That was Jimmy. Get me an audience! He loved to be loved, was a performer at heart, and whether it was entertaining two guys in a bar or a Vegas room of 2,000, he knew how to hold an audience. The guy closed more restaurants on the East Coast than any night watchman.

But with Jim there was so much more. He said one of the most memorable things during our first *Up Close* interview, and it still gives me chills when I think about it. This was at the height of his celebrity, long before he'd been diagnosed with cancer.

I asked a rather broad question, "What do you want people to say when they talk about you?"

And he thought for a second and then came back at me in that raspy voice, "All right, this is it. I read about Lila Wallace, the cofounder of Reader's Digest. In her will she wrote: 'Being of sound mind and sound body . . . I SPENT IT!' And I think that's what I want, when it's all over. I don't care about the money. I'm talking about the whole thing. The energy, the life, the love for life. I want it all spent and when it's all done I want them to be able to say, 'His dance card was filled!'"

Then there was that incredible night in New York, the early spring of '93 when Jim Valvano took the stage for the last time at ESPN's ESPY Awards. Those of us in that audience and millions at home saw that last dance. Here was a guy who was dying, he didn't have a note or a cue card. And as I sat there and listened I was reminded of an old *Twilight Zone* that I'd seen years ago. Ed Wynn played a character called the Pitch Man. The Pitch Man had to keep death at bay. In the show he distracted death by giving his pitch. It was metaphoric, of course, with a little girl dying and the Pitch Man talking, distracting death, keeping her alive and the inevitable away.

That's what I felt we were seeing with Jimmy that night. His final pitch, his final pre-game speech before he went to the ultimate combat. It was the whole life experience, his whole sense of who he was. When the cue card man tried to get him to wrap it up he said, "That screen is flashing up there thirty seconds, like I care about that screen right now? I got tumors all over my body and I'm worried about some guy in the back going, 'thirty seconds'?" There's a famous Dylan Thomas line from "Do Not Go Gentle Into That Good Night" which goes "Rage, rage against the dying of the light." Jim was raging against the dying of the light.

I remember as I left that night saying to Dennis Miller, "We just saw what might have been the first and last authentic moment in television." And to this day, ten years later, it remains the single most extraordinary moment that I've ever seen in real life broadcasting.

That was Jimmy V. Always the Pitch Man, yet so magnificent... so very real.

There's no better way to keep someone alive than to tell his stories. I tell Bob, he tells Terry, and pretty soon people are remembering their own and one story becomes a thousand. Jimmy Valvano was a storyteller, a guy who I'm sure would have loved to have had a shot at adding his personal favorites to the stories of *V & Me*.

I can smell the cigar smoke and hear that raspy voice now, "Hey, don't forget the Greenville story! You gotta tell the Greenville!"

Roy Firestone

My candle burns at both ends;
It will not last the night;
But, ah, my foes, and, oh, my friends—
It gives a lovely light

Edna St. Vincent Millay
"First Fig"
from **A Few Figs from Thistles**

Jim Valvano
Living the Moment

Jim Valvano was a basketball coach with the intellect of an English professor. He had a metaphor for everything. Writing a piece for NC State's alumni publication, I naively asked if his ultimate goal was to win an NCAA championship.

V metaphored me!

"The NCAA is life. You put yourself in a position to win, take your shot. Get into the tournament and then it's a crap shoot. You have to survive and advance! Survive and advance!"

On the Record Early

More than a man with a ready metaphor, he made a career of positioning himself to not only survive and advance... but to win–at basketball, business, motivational speaking, performing, broadcasting, dreaming, and... life!

Like a New York street player he'd get right in your kitchen, tell you before he made his moves. "Head fake, crossover dribble, in-your-face to the hole!"

Nick Valvano: "One of the things that made Jimmy special was that when he was young and I mean even before he was a teenager, he knew what he wanted to do. He had the incredible confidence and determination to go and do it. That's rare. When we were kids he always talked about coaching. He was always able to say what he was going to do and then go out and do it."

At the age of seventeen V put it in writing, etched his goals on a 3x5 index card, and displayed them for all to see. He'd be starting at guard in high school and then in college. The master plan called for the ultimate survive and advance, the big win... coaching a team to an NCAA Division I championship.

Long Island's Seaford High School, check!

Rutgers University, check!

NC State University, check!

While at Long Island's Seaford High, playing for his father, Rocco, V was an academic achiever and lettered in three sports–baseball, basketball, and football. Pam Valvano, then Pamela Levine, recalls the one "game" Jim didn't play much–the dating game.

"It was funny because Jim never dated in high school, he just played sports. I had a boyfriend who went off to college, and so I put the word out that I wanted to go to the prom. So Jim asked me. I think I drove us to the dance because Jim didn't have a driver's license. His father didn't let him drive until he was about twenty years old because he knew that driving would get him in trouble.

"Anyway he took me to the prom and after the dance we went to dinner. I ordered lobster tails. I didn't know it but he didn't have enough money to pay the check. So he left me in the middle of the dinner and slipped to a phone and called his dad and said, 'I can't pay the bill, I don't have enough money, bring me some money. She ordered lobster tails. Dad, I didn't even know lobsters had tails!'

"That was the first date and over the years he told audiences, thousands of people, about my shopping and my spending and having been named All Mall. But he should have known from that beginning. I wasn't going to be a cheap date!"

The Rutgers Run

The post-prom Rutgers run–1964–1967–earned V a degree in English, magical NIT games in Madison Square Garden, and ultimately the Scarlet Knights' highest athletics honor–Senior Athlete of the Year.

Coach Bill Foster remembers V the survivor: "He really just walked on and he was one of those guys who worked so hard that he just kept getting better. And even though he loved to have a good time and was a lot of fun, he was serious about his basketball, a real addition to the team and the program because he was a good player who made us all relax and his teammates play better."

While playing alongside All-America Bob Lloyd, a prolific scorer, V was saddled with the reputation of being the "other guard." Lloyd, who would go on to play pro ball, remembers V as the best defensive player he ever faced. "He always guarded me in practice and we'd really go at it, a lot of bloody lips. He was unbelievably competitive and a much better athlete than you can imagine. He scored more than 1,000 points in three years at Rutgers and that's really saying something–because I had the ball!"

Lloyd recalls V's most hated play: "When we couldn't beat a defense, Coach Foster would call 14 low. Fourteen was my number. I'd get the ball and the rest of the team would have to clear out and go low, run to the base line. I'd take my guy one on one. Jimmy hated 14 low. He'd just run to the corner of the base line and stand with his hands on his hips and pout.

One day Foster said, 'Jimmy, at least look like you're in the game on 14 low, do something to keep your man with you.'

Jimmy said, 'Hey, the only thing I'm going to attract over there is the band, I'm making eye contact with the fat guy playing tuba!'"

Later in his career at NC State, during that incredible run to the national championship, V had the reputation of being very loose with his players. He knew how to make them feel at ease when the game was on the line. That was nothing new, Jimmy was always that way, Lloyd said. "Bill Foster was a young coach at the time, preparing us for the game of our lives. We're getting ready to play Southern Illinois in the Garden and they've got the great Walt Frazier and Jimmy has to guard him. Bill's got us in the huddle and he's really pumped, telling us over and over how it's just another game, to stay relaxed. He was so wired, he just couldn't quit.

Finally he says, 'Just go out there and be Loosey Goosey!'

Jimmy leans over to me and says, 'Hey, you be Loosey Goosey, I'll be Duckie Wuckie!'"

As V advanced there were a number of stops along the coaching learning curve. Each offered lessons that would affect his career. His very first coaching job was at Rutgers, his alma mater. Here, coaching the freshman team, he learned a most valuable lesson–control the enthusiasm.

ESPN's Mike Tirico recalls one of V's favorites, a story he loved to tell around the ESPN studios (and told in his famous ESPY speech): "This was his coaching debut at Rutgers, right before the first game. He was such a Vince Lombardi disciple, a real fan, and so he gets all pumped up before coaching his first game and he runs into the locker room and he goes into his Lombardi act, telling the guys to play as a unit and then he says. 'And neva' eva' forget–this isn't just about you... now let's go out and win this one for God, our families, and the Green Bay Packers!'"

Then there was V the Rutgers Super Scout. Nick Valvano remembers: "I told Jimmy about this kid who played out on Long Island at Roosevelt High, the same league that Seaford played in. He was a 6' 3" center but a great jumper and just a great player. Jimmy goes and takes a look, watches him in a practice, then games, even has a home visit. But he's not convinced. The kid's coach, Red Wilson, and I stayed on Jimmy about him. But for some reason, maybe he didn't like him at the center position, Jimmy goes back to Bill Foster and says that the kid can't play at the Rutgers level. The kid turned out to be a guy named Julius Erving."

Lesson learned. Don't be too quick to size up talent (see "Little Big Man" in "Everybody's Favorite Jim Valvano Story").

It's Academic

In 1969–1970 in his first head coaching assignment, the education continued. V took Johns Hopkins University, a small private institution that was clearly about academics, to its first winning season in twenty-four years. How academic was Hopkins? The Blue Jays' game-day basketball programs read like the table of contents of the American Medical Journal. V loved to tell the story about the secret of his lineup.

"Hey, I had this medicinal offense! Two heart guys underneath, a brain surgeon in the middle, and a couple of gynecologists at the guards!"

Realizing that his medics had never had the opportunity to enjoy playing in a Christmas tournament, the young coach decided to reward the team with a holiday trip to Bridgeport, Connecticut, where they would play in the Sacred Heart Invitational Tournament. Upon hearing about V's "Secret Santa gift" the players called a quick team meeting. The captain delivered a message to the coach that he'd never forget.

"What ever made you think that we'd want to give up our holidays to play basketball?"

Later V recalled the ultimate clue in a story he related to his younger brother, Bobby Valvano: "I remember a bus ride after a loss at Hopkins. I'm sitting up front just fuming and one of the guys in the back shouts up to the front of the bus, 'Hey, Coach, why is winning so important to you?'"

On UConn's Learning Curve

Determined to coach where winning mattered, when Valvano received a call from his old Rutgers teammate, Dick Stewart, saying that an assistantship was opening up at the University of Connecticut, V made his move. Here he would enhance the coaching pedigree under the tutelage of the legendary Dee Rowe, a man who hated losing and had an insatiable passion for the game.

Dee Rowe: "I once left Jimmy a message on his hotel phone after a devastating loss to Georgetown that said, 'I'm on the roof getting ready to jump, don't catch me!'

"I called him James and until the day he died, he called me Coach. His love of the game matched his love of life and he was just so special. There was a magic about him, you just knew that he would accomplish something special," Rowe said.

There was one rather dubious accomplishment. During V's tenure at UConn, "James" held the distinction of being at Rowe's side during the worst of times.

Rowe: "The squad was really bad and finally Jimmy came to me and said, 'Coach, I know why we're so bad. We have a tongue depressor at center, the kid is 6' 7" and maybe a hundred and fifty pounds, and we've got a kid at point guard with three-inch sleeves. But the big problem here is the names. We've got no basketball names, no Hot Rods, no Erasers. We've got kids named Chico, Shark, Snake, Torus, and Electric Man. How can we win with those names?'"

Rowe: "We did lose a lot when Jimmy was with us so when I spoke at the national championship dinner in '83 in his honor I told the audience. 'You think this guy is a great coach? The only two losing seasons I ever had at Connecticut were the two years Jimmy was my assistant.' Then I said, 'But boy, did I need him. He kept me from jumping in the Connecticut River a number of times.'"

Later in a personal eulogy Rowe offered up another message regarding his assistant coach. It reads, in part:

"No matter the trappings, no matter the whirl around him—all I ever saw was the young coach with the incredible love for his kids' game. He was brilliant, an innovator, driven, a genius in his own way. A fierce competitor, he had a truly great mind and that special feel for the game. A master with X's and O's and the chess game, a great coach."

There was a day Rowe recalled when V thought he was going to have an opportunity to show off all those talents. Rowe, sick with the flu, passed out in the locker room at half-time of a big game. V told the story as follows: 'I helped bring him around to coach another day but I always told Dee that before I agreed to help resuscitate that I had to think long and hard. If Rowe goes, I'm the new head coach of the University of Connecticut Huskies!'"

Speaking of Basketball

That position of authority as once again a head coach would come sooner rather than later. In 1972 Bob Latour, the athletic director at Bucknell University in Lewisburg, Pennsylvania, offered V the head basketball coach's job. He'd survived the off-years at UConn and it was time to advance. Coaching in the Mid-Atlantic Conference was a logical step: the league's champions got an automatic NCAA bid. During his few short years there in the rolling hills of Pennsylvania–he was 33 and 42–V fought an uphill battle. As at Johns Hopkins, both recruiting and winning proved to be a challenge. Players and administrators saw the game as, well, a game.

In one of my early interviews with V (at NC State) he explained the difference between a small private and a big time public university. Bucknell was his example. The theme was "at major universities, coaches are at the mercy of the booster clubs." V knew that the power flowed from the money and that it was more than survive and advance, "you had to win first… just to survive!"

"At Bucknell I was treated like the head of the Chemistry Department. 'Jim, you did a nice job with the boys last year. Here's your budget, have fun and good luck!'"

There were other lessons learned at Bucknell. Sam Esposito, V's friend and running mate at NC State, remembers hearing this one from V a time or two. "With seconds left in the game and Bucknell down by a point, a kid by the name of Carter made a steal and immediately called time-out. V said, 'I'm working the clipboard when Carter, who goes about 6' 6" and about 220 pounds, grabs me and starts shaking me, "Give me the ball, give me the ball!" he's screaming. I get in his face pretty good. He's in mine. By the time we're finished screaming at each other I realize that I need another time-out to design the winning play. Problem! No more time-outs. So I lean into the huddle and say, "Get the ball to Carter." Carter hits the winning shot and we win the game!'"

When in doubt and the game's on the line, trust the talent and . . . always go to the guy who wants the ball!

While he was at Bucknell V's speeches weren't confined to the huddle. In an effort to make house payments he supplemented his salary working basketball camps in Pennsylvania's Pocono Mountains. It was in this rare air that he perfected his skills as a public speaker. Making the rounds from camp to camp he gave inspirational speeches that promoted a hustling, dive-for-the-ball kind of play. The kids called him "Camp Man," and "Super Rat." He taught them to be rats, to scratch and to claw, to take charges. His partner and prop was a little stuffed rat on a skateboard set in a position to take a charge. The act grew to include "Super Rat Take The Charge" T-shirts that he gave as a reward to the toughest players in camp.

Pat Kennedy (head coach, University of Montana), whose family owned the Pocono Invitational Basketball Camp in Stroudsburg, Pennsylvania, recalls V's debut. "My brother and I were running my dad's camp and we heard about this Jim Valvano, a coach at Bucknell who was supposed to be a good speaker. We were the number one camp in the country and had national names speaking—Bobby Knight, Rollie Massamino, Chuck Daly—so my brother and I thought, how good can anyone who's at Bucknell be?

"But we got an opening and so we booked him. I introduced him to the kids and went back to the office to do some work. At about the forty-five minute mark I head down to the courts and all of a sudden I hear this chant, 'V! V! V! V!' I look out on the courts, we had like 300 girls in camp that week, and they have Jimmy hoisted on their shoulders and he's got a pair of scissors. They're carrying him from basket to basket. The main court had about fourteen baskets on it and they're chanting and he's cutting down the nets on all of our camp's baskets.

"My brother, who was the bean counter, says, 'What is this maniac doing?' Each net costs about $2.50 and as the nets come down he's doing the math and he's going to dock Jimmy for each net. So I go up to Randy Ayers, one of our counselors (who later became the head coach at Ohio State and then head coach of the Philadelphia 76ers), and said, 'What the hell is going on?'

Randy has this look and he says, 'I've never heard a lecture like that in my life. The guy talked about being a walk-on at Rutgers, realizing his dream to earn a scholarship and then to play in Madison Square Garden, finally to get to the NIT and cut the nets in the Garden. He told them about daring to dream and living the dream at Rutgers, playing against Walt Frazier in the Garden. This guy is the best I've ever heard!'"

In a year V's speeches were legendary in the Pennsylvania camps. In the not too distant future, after he'd come down from the Poconos and his $150-a-pop talks, he had in his arsenal the nuts and bolts—hope, dream, work, enthusiasm—of the $30,000 inspirational speeches that he later delivered to corporate America for the Washington Speakers Bureau.

I Own A College

In 1975 V was on the move again. When the head coaching position at little Iona College came open the question that he wrestled with wasn't whether he could survive there but whether this advance would ultimately be a win. If he stayed Bucknell promised a raise and a full-time assistant. And there was always that guarantee of an NCAA bid for its conference champion. Then there was Iona, a commuter college embedded in the city of New Rochelle, New York. Its basketball tradition was non-existent. But for V the move was a homecoming of sorts, the ethnic student body—Irish, Italian, and Polish kids—was pure New York. But more importantly (perhaps V checked that 3x5 card that he carried in his wallet), he saw Iona as his ticket to take a team to his dream, the 9:00 o'clock game in his beloved Madison Square Garden ... and ultimately to an NCAA tournament.

Like V, Iona's president, Brother John Driscoll, was a dreamer. They both wanted to put the little college on the basketball map. That's what they did. Under the slogan "Daring To Dream" V built himself a program that would take Iona to that 9:00 o'clock game in Madison Square Garden and... to that "crap shoot" on his 3x5 card... the NCAA Tournament.

But to win and advance he had to have the horses. Players like Dave Brown, Lester George, Cedric Cannon were in the stable. One of V's best sales jobs ever was the recruiting of the recruiter, a fast talking New York guy that V called T-man.

Tommy Abatemarco: "I was working at a Division II school, New York Tech, as assistant basketball coach and JV coach, and also teaching third grade in a public school. I read where V got the job at Iona and he's an Italian guy and I think Iona's big time because it's Division I. So I called him up and told him I wanted to talk to him. He kind of blew me off a little bit and said that he really had his staff. But I kept calling him. I was driving the guy nuts and finally it gets to the point where I saw him at this All Star game. We had signed some of the best kids in the game; now a lot of those kids were Division II and didn't have the grades to play Division I–they were New York Tech. But the players we had were much better than the players that he had at Iona and he saw this and he says, 'I think you should come by my office on Monday.' So I go by and now I was making $10,000 a year teaching and coaching. He got me all revved up, convinced me that this was the way for me to get into the business. He convinced me to quit my teaching job and come to work for him for $2,000.

I went home and told Dawn, my ex-wife, 'Good news. I just got a job.'

And she says, 'How much more are you making than the teaching job?'

And I said, 'Well, that's the bad news, I just got an $8,000 pay cut!'

She said, 'That's big time basketball?'

"I was so broke that first year that I didn't have the 75 cents toll that I needed to go over the bridge to get to Iona. And there were plenty of times I'd have to ask V for the money to go home. Our recruiting budget was $2,000 but we started bringing in the players, and it was in those early days that he would hit kids with a line he repeated a million times over the years, 'Hi, I'm Jim Valvano, I own a college.' And these New York kids would say, 'Really, you own a college?'"

While at Iona T-Man and V went over that 75 cent toll bridge a number of times, signing Glenn Vickers and Kevin Hamilton from Long Island's North Babylon High. They picked up Mike Palma, a transfer from Wake Forest, and Joe McCall, a talented junior college player from New York state. Then in 1977 came the big catches, Kevin Vesey and the bluest of blue chips. V beat out the premier programs in the country and landed the Iona franchise, another Long Island kid, 6' 10" center Jeff Ruland.

Ruland: "I was recruited by Indiana, Wake Forest, and Kentucky and I end up staying on Long Island and playing for Jim Valvano at Iona. I remember walking into Rupp Arena at Kentucky with Iona, years later as a graduate assistant. I looked up at that place and said, "I passed on this to play for Valvano at Iona's Mulcahy Center? The man could recruit and he could sell!"

That sale, the signing of Jeff Ruland, put Iona on America's basketball map. Everyone remembers V's run for a hug after winning the NCAA tournament in 1983 but Jim Marchiony, associate director of athletics at the University of Connecticut, recalls the first leg of the race, one that would eventually take V to his national championship.

"Iona was my first job out of college, and I ended up getting there just in time to see Iona go from a very regional team to one that, in my third year there, was ranked nationally. It was November of '78, when that _Sports Illustrated_ hit the news stands, that led to a classic Jim Valvano moment. Iona and Jim Valvano had made the big time. I'll never forget it.

"Along with the preseason rankings, the issue included an article featuring Super Sophomores, including Magic Johnson, and right there with him and all the others was Iona's own Jeff Ruland. Ruland and all of them were pictured wearing tuxedos. When that magazine came to the office, Jim first looked at that article and then turned his attention to the preseason rankings, because we had been told we'd probably be included.

"He started from number twenty and worked his way toward number one. When he saw we were ranked ninth, he picked up the magazine and raced out of the Mulcahy Center, where we played our basketball games. There was a track right outside the gym, and as a small crowd gathered Jim took three laps around that track with the _Sports Illustrated_ held over his head. Then, still in stride, he ran to the president's office. A signature moment in a very special career!"

And the run continued. V's '78–79 team went 23–5 before losing to Penn in Iona's first-ever NCAA tournament. The following year the Gaels, 29–5, bumped off Louisville 77–60 in that 9:00 o'clock game in "The Garden," and V fulfilled one of his greatest dreams, cutting down the nets.

Pat Kennedy, an Iona assistant coach that year, remembers: "V just had to have the 9:00 o'clock in the Garden, and he kept driving Sonny Werblin (who managed the Garden) nuts about bringing Iona to the Garden. Sonny was a Rutgers graduate, so Jimmy thought Sonny owed it to him. That was Jimmy. 'Sonny, you gotta get me the 9:00 o'clock game!' So finally Sonny gets Jimmy the 9:00 o'clock game in the Garden, and Jimmy says, 'I've been dreaming about this forever.' But it's Louisville, and they're ranked like number one or two in the nation, and they're like 19-point favorites. We've got Ruland, Hamilton, and Vickers and we're pretty good but hey, this is Louisville. Anyway, Jim does this great pre-game talk, and the coaches are crying but I'm looking around and the players are yawning, falling to sleep because they've heard it ten million times. It was his, 'This is the dream, this is what you live for, the rats against the big timers and bupp, bupp, bupp!' speech.

"So out we go and Jimmy and I are walking right down the runway of Madison Square Garden, getting ready to take the court, and he stopped and looked at me and said, 'Patty, this is the game!' And I said, 'What? We're 19-point underdogs!' And he said, 'No, this is the one that I've been talking about in all those speeches, at the camps in the summers, before games, this is the big one. We're going to win tonight and I'm going to cut the nets down!' I said, 'Look, I believe in you, I believe in Norman Vincent Peale and I love you dearly, my man, but we are still 19-point underdogs to one of the best teams in the country!' If we beat Louisville it will be one of the greatest upsets of all time. Well, sure enough, with about four minutes to go we're up by like 13 and they're not going to catch us. And then the buzzer goes off, we win, and I stand there just in awe watching Jim cut down those nets he'd been telling those kids about for years."

V's Iona Gaels went on to run the table in the ECAC Tournament and beat Holy Cross in the first round of the NCAA tournament. The 74–71 loss to Georgetown, a heartbreaker, ended it.

Kennedy: "A great game full of runs, and in the end it came down to us fouling Craig Shelton, the Hoyas' big gun. He missed, we got the ball to Glenn Vickers who kind of hesitated because Ruland flashed open under the basket. But Glenn took the shot, missed and we lost. Afterward, when the press asked Glenn about why he hadn't passed the ball he repeated something that Jim had told him a hundred times. He looked at the reporters and said, 'Hey, I was recruited to take that shot.'"

Tough loss, but as predicted, V and Iona had arrived. V had his scissors at the ready; more nets would be coming down.

Rich Petriccione, now a vice-president for advancement-external affairs at Iona, then V's student manager, remembers those heady days.

"Here he is the coach at Iona; nobody knows who the hell he is but him! Big ego and he could back it up. He knew how incredibly talented he was and he knew that he was different. Like most geniuses with incredible drive to be successful, he knew it was going to happen. I'll never forget the day he thought this one up. He screamed at me like he was Archimedes and had discovered the principle of gravity. V had a lot of Eureka moments. 'Hey, Pet, this is it! This is the equation: You plus Motivation equals Success.'"

Career Decision

Six years later—1983—at NC State V plus motivation equaled the ultimate success. There were more wins and advances along the way. But success brought decisions that weren't confined to the X's and O's of a basketball huddle. Other universities had become aware of Jim Valvano and Iona and with the recognition came opportunities at larger, more established programs.

Nick Valvano: "Jim showed his insecurity to very few people. I was one of the few. Before he ever took any job he always called me. I'm not so sure that I really did any more than listen in many instances, but we would go over the pros and cons. When he was at Iona and the Big East was going to start up, Dave Gavitt was calling him. He told Jim that Iona wasn't going to be a part of the Big East and that he should come coach at Providence. Well, we talked about it and I said, 'Jimmy, you're bigger than that. You can get a bigger job than that.' Now as kids we loved Providence and Lenny Wilkins. But I reminded him that Providence is bigger than Iona but that Providence was going to be as big a challenge in that league as Iona was in New York City. So I was coming from a businessman's perspective, not from a coach's. I thought he should go to a bigger job. He waited and that opportunity came with NC State."

During this time there had been discussions between V and his friend Brother Driscoll about a contract that would make him both Iona's athletic director and coach with a clause that would allow him to step down at any time. So when the NC State opportunity knocked there was more agonizing.

Nick Valvano: "NC State was a hard one. He was very torn between NC State, the big job, and his love for Iona and Brother Driscoll, who had been so very good to him. And then there were the players. My God, getting Jeff Ruland to go to Iona put Jimmy in the position to be considered for the North Carolina State job, and he knew that. But he's only thirty-four years old and he has this big decision to make. Two things happened—he had the dynamics of what State wanted to do because people were hammering at them to make an announcement and sitting there in New York he had Iona who had never had a coach leave for a big time program. Jim was caught in the middle trying to do everything that was right for his career and his players and Iona and he had to make the decision in a very short time frame. So when the story got leaked he was 0 for 3. State had a little egg on its face because they had needed an answer. When he agreed to go the people at Iona just turned on him. And then there was Jeff Ruland; Jeff had to feel betrayed. He didn't come to Iona because he wanted to be in New Rochelle. He'd come to play for Jimmy."

Jeff Ruland: "One of the stories about Jim and me that I tried to clear up but for some reason is still floating around is that I was mad because he left Iona after recruiting me. That wasn't it at all, I had no problem with that. In fact I was considering actually leaving with him. What happened was I had signed with an agent [whom V had legal dealings with] and this got us [Iona] in trouble. That's something that I did that was my fault. But the problem that I had with V that we later straightened out was over the fact that he made a phone call shortly after he took the NC State job and said, 'I've got a new job and a new child on the way, please don't say anything about the agent thing.'"

V had no idea that Ruland had signed and when he read the agent's name he realized that he (V) had been offered a deal to shoot a TV commercial by the same man and that this might be misinterpreted by Iona, NC State, and the NCAA.

Ruland: "He hadn't done anything wrong. What hurt me was that he thought he had to call to tell me not to say anything. That was it, not his leaving. That was something that for a long time I just couldn't forgive him for. And obviously now I look back and realize that life is too short to hold grudges like that. So that's what it was all about. And I'd have never said anything, he was a friend and he didn't have to ask that. We patched it up years later."

But still a very unpleasant time. A New York newspaper cartoon of V with a money bag over his shoulder schlepping south echoed the thoughts of many Iona alums. It, however, missed the mark, as the trek to North Carolina wasn't about money at all. It was about the goals on that 3x5 card, the ACC and a head coaching job at a storied program that had won a national championship. And that program was—if V had anything to do with it—about to win another.

Frank Weedon, NC State's senior associate athletic director, recalls the early negotiations:

"The commitment to NC State came in a meeting in Raleigh at the Capital City Club, there on the top floor. I remember Jim being so animated, telling stories, just full of enthusiasm, and even addressing the subject of winning a national championship. When he finally slowed down Willis [Casey, NC State's AD] just came right out and said it, 'You've got the job!' This was followed by a toast and more enthusiasm from V, talk about facilities and recruiting.

"Then, when we got up from the table Willis said, 'There's one thing you forgot. You forgot to ask about the salary!' Jim just looked at Willis and said, 'Oh, I'm not worried about the salary. I can always make money. Don't worry about the salary!'"

Grand Introduction

When NC State introduced their latest salaried employee, V found himself in one of those very rare moments—speechless.

Chancellor Joab Thomas: "I introduced Jim to the public at the press conference at NC State after he'd been hired. The media had speculated wildly about the new coach for weeks and the big story on the front of *The News & Observer* on the morning that we made this announcement was that Morgan Wooten, from DeMatha High School in Washington, D.C., was going to be the new coach. And incidently to this day I have never met Morgan Wooten. I never contacted him. So at the press conference I got up and spoke very highly of the new coach and introduced Jim and he made a few very brief remarks and then opened it up to questions. The first question asked was, 'What does it feel like to be second choice?' And Jim was just speechless. So I stood up and said, 'Coach Valvano, let me answer that question. As many of you are aware the media has offered this job to several people. But I've only offered it to one... and that's Coach Valvano!'"

My take on Chancellor Thomas's first choice appeared in a cover story in *The Stater*, North Carolina State's alumni publication. My lead read: "Jim Valvano, North Carolina State University's new head basketball coach, is a genuine personality—a rarity in today's pressure-packed world of big time basketball. On March 27, 1980, when Valvano eased up to the microphone at NCSU's Case Athletic Center, his Italian name was still subject to southern mispronunciation. (It's Val-van-o.) In the next thirty minutes the Queens, NY, native made an instant reputation for himself by supplying writers with enough sharp one-liners to fill four columns."

He led with, "When I came here for the interview I played very hard-to-get. I told them I wanted a multi-week contract!"

Then he broke out his A material, the shtick about the Hopkins medicinal lineup where he started the heart guys and gynecologists. He followed with local stuff, introducing the line about Dean Smith. "Hey, if I can't beat him, I'll outlive him!" And he closed with, "One of your local radio stations asked if I'd be willing to come in early one morning and read the Raleigh traffic report. I told them I'd be glad to but, folks, I have news for you. You have no traffic in Raleigh!"

Just a few short weeks later V was down in the cafeteria of Case Athletic Center trafficking his philosophy, giving his new charges the word.

Thurl Bailey: "He told us that he was going to win a national championship. If we wanted to come along for the ride we were welcome. That was our choice. Wow, he just came right out and said it. A national championship. At that point I'm not sure what we thought. But later, of course, we figured it out. He meant it!"

My first one-on-one interview in V's office had me nodding like one of those bobble head dolls. Thank God for tape recorders, I couldn't have possibly kept up with the quotes, not with a pad and pencil. This session, plus my earlier impressions from the press conference, became the basis for the cover feature in that alumni publication.

"If anybody doesn't believe I'm busy they should see this," he said, throwing both feet up on his desk, "blue shoes, brown socks, green pants. I don't even have time to dress right." The end of the act was equally as strong. V knew how to leave them laughing. "Hey, just before I left Iona, right after I got this job, an NCSU alum called to wish me well. He asked me if I knew the difference between a Yankee and a damned Yankee. The guy told me that a Yankee is someone who comes south, stays for a few years, and goes back up north. A damned Yankee stays. So I told him, 'Well, NC State just hired themselves a damned Yankee and you can quote me on that!'"

Sandwiched in between the one-liners were all the damned Yankee's hopes and dreams, everything from his love for both academics and athletics to how these two—often diametrically opposed challenges—intertwine. "There's the real and the ideal," he said. "In the real world, I'm expected to win, fill coliseums, and bring in revenue. But ideally, I'm going to do this with athletes who are interested in preparing themselves for their futures."

A line that might be best described as fine. In big time athletics there's very little wiggle room between the real and the ideal. Would he win at NC State? Yes! Would he graduate players at a high level? Questionable! Would he influence young men by preparing them for successful futures? With a few exceptions, a resounding yes!

Charlie Bryant, former head of the NC State Wolfpack Club: "In the spring of 2003, twenty years after the '83 championship and ten years following Jim's death, NC State hosted a reunion. As much fun as Jim would have had reminiscing with the guys about their run in the NCAA tournament, it wouldn't have been his highlight. What he would have

loved to see was just how well-spoken, well mannered, and how successful these guys are. They are all doing so well, players and managers
alike, and to a man they credit Jim Valvano."

Bryant's son, Gary, V's first manager at NC State, is currently CEO
of Bear Rock Cafes. Bryant, named *Triangle Business Magazine*'s Entre-
preneur of the Year in the spring of 2003, echoes his father's thoughts:
"What has been lost in the Jim Valvano story is the relationships that he
had with his players and managers–all the people who worked with
him. A great deal of whatever success that I have today is owed to his
influence. He gave me responsibility, confidence and guidance and anybody that says he wasn't an inspiration didn't know him."

What the NCAA said was, "Lack of institutional control!" What NC
State said was, "See yah!" What players, friends, and associates say is,
"An inspiration to us all!" What the record says is 346–212 in 19 seasons, eight NCAA tournaments, two ACC Coach of the Year Awards,
and a national championship with North Carolina State University in
1983. During his decade at NC State V was 209–114, took teams to the
NCAA's seven times and to the NIT once, and won ACC champion-
ships in 1983 and 1987. But to that national championship, everything
paled in comparison.

Learning Experience

And the road to this national championship at NC State? V remembered Iona and the formula. In order to win and advance you
had to have winners! He inherited blue chippers in Lowe,
Whittenburg, two floor leaders, one a shooter, the other a ball-han-
dling magician who served as a coach on the floor. His third inherit-
ance was Thurl Bailey, the big man who under V's coaching would
prove to be a late, great bloomer. But he needed more talent so he
brought in the recruiters, Ray "Dice" Martin, a classy New Yorker
who had played for Notre Dame, and his old Iona wrangler, T-Man,
to help him round up more horses.

Abatemarco: "When I first got to NC State we sat down and he said,
'This is the master plan. This is the deal. Carolina is the Cadillac. The
only way we can beat them is to beat them on the court. I have respect
for Dean Smith. I want to stay with Dean Smith but we're not going to
beat them with the kids we have now. We need players.'"

V and company went out and signed Terry Gannon, a long-range
bomber from Joliet, Illinois, then filled the paint with Cozell McQueen,

a 6' 11" center, a native of South Carolina, and Lorenzo Charles, a 6' 7" power forward from Brooklyn, New York. The next year, in '82, he filled in with Ernie Myers, a slashing New York scorer.

V was recruiting players, rattling the cage, making changes. I remember V, still in shock, telling me the story of his first "change" presentation to Willis Casey, State's curmudgeon and frugal AD. He'd just come out of Casey's office and still had his tail between his legs.

V: "Our brochures for basketball really stink. So I get a bunch of brochures together from all the other schools in the ACC and I go into see Willis. I say, 'Mr. Casey, here are the brochures that we're recruiting against. Here is ours.' And I save ours until last and put it on his desk. The difference is obvious. He says, 'What's your point?' and I say, 'Well, how can we recruit against schools like this with what we've got here. I'm running in doing back flips, and Dean just flips off the lights and shows the kids these great highlight films, then drops one of these slick brochures on the kid and his family.' Then Willis looks down over those little glasses of his and says, 'If I get you a new brochure can you guarantee a national championship?' And of course I say, 'Well, not really.' So he says, 'Jimmy, get the hell out of here. That's why I hired you. You ARE our brochure!'"

And the record shows that before that '82–83 season V was no more than that: NC State's new brochure, just another young coach struggling to keep his head above the treacherous waters of the ACC. Wolfpack fans are very good at keeping score and by their count, in his first two years he was 0–6 against Carolina.

ESPN friend John Saunders remembers a V story about how serious this Carolina thing got. "A State fan wrote Jim a letter telling him that if NC State didn't beat Carolina that he would kill Jim's dog. Jim wrote back and said that he appreciated the fan's support for the program and dislike of Carolina but that the Valvanos didn't own a dog. The next week a box arrived at Jim's house, he opened it, and there was a puppy inside with a note around the pup's neck that said, "Don't get too attached... beat Carolina!"

Tough losses to Carolina but there were so many more turns (and lessons learned) in the road that would eventually take V to Albuquerque: Frank Weedon recalls an early "awakening" during V's very first year that would serve him well in March of '83 when the Pack found itself on the line—game after game. Never, ever mention the negative.

"As good as Jim was he was still young when he came to NC State and I remember we were playing Maryland his first year and we've got a nice lead but they keep cutting into it. With less than a minute left we still had a three-point lead. So Jim calls a time-out and tells our guys, over and over, not to foul. Well, there's an old saying, don't ever mention a negative because that's what kids will run right out and do. And that's what happened. Craig Watts fouled Buck Williams and we end up in overtime and getting blown out 82–75.

"Now, the very next week we go to the Holiday Tournament in the Garden and beat Iona and then play St. John's for the championship. Here it comes again, we're up by ten with the game winding down and I was right behind the bench reminding V, 'Remember Maryland, Remember Maryland!' We won—64–55—and after they cut down the nets Jim came over, handed me the trophy, and put the net over my head. 'Frank, I remembered Maryland,' he said."

The 1981–82 team, in its own way, set the stage for the following year. V saw basketball as a game of runs. And in '81 as the Pack tipped it off against Rice in the championship game of the Hawaiian Classic, State was on a run, 9–0 with the promise of going into the New Year undefeated. But Rice threw a "Flex" offense at the Pack, held the ball, and won 51–47.

V rang in 1982 in a dark mood, with a record of 9–1.

In his autobiography, he articulated the importance of that loss. "Know the difference in being 10–0 and 9–1 at the end of December? Only this. Hardly anybody's 10–0 and there are about thirty f*&#ing teams that are 9–1!"

That season was notable for other reasons. The game wouldn't be blessed by the three-point arc and shot clock until the following season. Coaches were still letting the air out of the ball and games typically went ugly early. It was a frustrating time for fans, coaches, referees, and players.

Terry Gannon remembers one of these gut wrenchers, a 36–39 loss to Virginia that typified the "action" that year.

"We're playing Virginia at home, a win we've gotta have. V's game plans were always going to put the lid on the other team's big scorer. So he comes up with a plan to stop Sampson that was simply this: Chuck Nevitt, our 7' 4" guy, behind him and everybody else collapsing on Ralph when the ball came down low.

"He was really adamant about making their shooters beat us from the corner, a shot that he didn't think they'd want to take. So normally Scotty Parzych, our wing guy, would go to the corner to pick up any shooter. But V runs this 'Don't go to the corner defense' at practice and then sits Scotty down before the game and says, 'Scotty, we're collapsing on Ralph. When they kick it to the corner stay inside, front Ralph, don't go to the corner!' This was pre-shot clock, one of the slow down games and we're trying to keep the score low. Which happened. It ended in the thirties.

"The sandwich job on Ralph was working but in the first half, just out of habit, Scotty is still going to the corner. Now at half-time V makes this his theme—and Scotty agrees that he won't go over there again. Second half, ball goes to the corner, Scotty chases, ball comes inside, and Ralph scores. This happens about three times and now there's a foul or something or a time-out and V just goes crazy. He's in Scotty's face and we're all standing there in the huddle watching and finally Scotty says something that we don't hear. Buzzer, game starts, and those of us on the bench who were close enough heard [Coach] Marty Fletcher say to V, 'What the hell did Parzych say?' 'That he had to go to the corner,' V said. Marty asks what V told him and we all heard V say, 'I said, "Well, Scotty, if you have to go then just go ahead and go to the f&*#ing corner!"' That was the game that ended with Jeff Jones mugging Whitt and the ref calling it a jump ball. We lost at the buzzer and I remember that it wasn't just Scotty, we all kept our distance from V after that one."

For the Pack, things didn't get much prettier. There were two good wins—Notre Dame and Duke—and a "cupcake" win against Loyola. Then the wheels were off again, with V watching the season that had begun with such promise end with losses to Wake Forest and Maryland.

In the first game of the ACC tournament the Pack went ugly again with a win that V would call "the worst game in the ACC. The worst post-season game in history." This slowdown affair had all the annoying bells and whistles. Fans booing both teams, Lefty kicking a chair. But when the 40–28 agony finally ended State had its 22 wins. The Pack would lose to Carolina in the ACC tournament but the '82 season wasn't over. V had won enough to advance. He had his NCAA bid.

This, unfortunately, was another learning experience. State played what V called a hyphen team, Tennessee-Chattanooga, to the sound of one hand clapping in a half empty arena in Indianapolis, Indiana. What V took from this 58–51 loss came up a time or two in '82–83, most notably in the huddle as his Pack struggled to get past Pepperdine in round one of the '83 tournament. "You have to win if you want to advance!"

Bob Staak, V's long-time friend whom V had coached at UConn, was now coaching Xavier. Staak remembers that Tennessee-Chattanooga loss: "After that loss Jimmy and I sat up half the night and had a few back at his hotel. I consoled him for a while and then finally said, 'Look, what I really think is that your team stunk tonight and Xavier could have beaten you, and we're six and twenty.'"

Fitting the Glass Slipper

So that loss resonated with V and would stay with him well into the following season. But for the NC State Wolfpack '82–83 would be a new day, one defined by the three-point line, a 24-second shot clock, and a team that came equipped with a coach's dream–chemistry.

Alex Wolff, senior writer, *Sports Illustrated*, recalls the mix: "The team was a delicious collection of basketball personalities. You had these two chunky guards in Dereck Whittenburg and Sidney Lowe, they could have been linebackers. Terry Gannon and Ernie Myers, two scorers. Then in the front court you had Thurl Bailey and Cozell McQueen, who were nice ballplayers but kind of skinny, especially McQueen. And then of course there was the power forward Lorenzo Charles, who we all remember took the air ball and turned it into a championship-winning basket."

Long before *SI*'s basketball writer made his assessment, V had liked this team and its chances. He took them into the season with a V philosophy featuring what he called "must-wins." Of these must-win games he lost to Louisville and Memphis State. He beat Michigan State at home, and then lost to Notre Dame in Reynolds. But an early win over West Virginia in the Meadowlands was a confidence builder. This was a model of sorts. After the loss to Tennessee-Chattanooga on a neutral court the year before, V knew that no matter how talented this team was that they had to learn to win big games against big teams in unfamiliar environs. To say he was a bit pumped for this one would be an understatement. One of V's rules for players and coaches was one that Yogi Berra would have certainly approved of: "You don't say it's over until it's over!"

Ed McLean, V's bench coach and X's and O's man: "He was a fanatic about not announcing a win before it was over, almost superstitious. He'd say, 'We play these things from tap to buzzer, I don't care if we're blowing them out. You haven't won until the buzzer goes off.' So we're playing West Virginia in the Meadowlands and it's about the two-minute mark and we're up by four. West Virginia is good, they could have very easily beaten us. All of a sudden Tommy Abatemarco, one of our assistant coaches, jumps up on the bench and shouts, 'It's over!'

"Now this game is on national televison and I don't know how the cameras missed it because when Tommy screamed 'It's over!' Jim was so wired that he turned and all of a sudden he jumped on him and down they go. V takes him right to the floor. V's on top of his assistant coach right there in front of the bench. Now here's a national TV audience and I'm thinking oh man this is going to be a first, a dead lock for ESPN's *Sports Center*. And the game's going on and here's V sitting on top of Tommy cussing him and finally we pulled him off of him."

Forget the big outside-the-conference games. The ACC was the ultimate grind with every play, every game a dress rehearsal for the NCAA tournament. And right in the middle of this tough season came the biggest L of all. In a wide open, three-point, run-and-gun loss to Virginia at Reynolds, Dereck Whittenburg, V's shooting guard—who had scored 27 points in the first half—went down with a broken foot.

Then the Pack showed its coach championship caliber. The loss of Whitt started what V called the "season within the season," the fourteen games that developed the players who would help take NC State to its national championship. And the one player who defined this movement was Ernie Myers. The freshman guard came up big in game after game.

Ernie Myers: "The thing about V was that he treated you like a man. I was a freshman but he let me know what my role was and he expected me to fill it!"

But it wasn't just players stepping up; there was another little wrinkle in this most unusual season, one that Chancellor Bruce Poulton, who had succeeded Joab Thomas, remembers as one of V's defining moments. "He was extremely audacious, willing to say or ask or confront any kind of a situation. In 1982, a couple of days after the Virginia game, the one where Dereck Whittenburg, the team's shooting guard, was injured, I got a call from Jim asking me if he could get an appointment. I had no idea what this was about. He came in and we made some small talk and then I said, 'Jim, what can I do for you?' And he said, 'I'd like to have a ten-year contract.' I said, 'A ten-year contract? Jim, your record this year is really just so-so, isn't it?'

"His response was, 'Well, it's pretty good but my real problem is this thing with Whittenburg. With Whitt gone the team has become demoralized. They need a shot in the arm and if they were to read in the paper that I was given a ten-year contract it would really bring them around.'

"And I'm sitting there thinking what player is going to be excited about a ten-year contract for a coach? I said, 'Jim, that's interesting. That's kind of a long time frame for a contract isn't it? How about a three-year?' No, he wasn't interested. 'Then how about a five?' Still no. Not enough to turn the team around. So I said, 'Jim, ten years!' And he said, 'Well, I won't hold you to it but it's important because Carolina just gave Dean Smith a ten-year contract.' I said, 'Jeeze, Jim, Dean just won a national championship.' So he says, 'Oh, that's okay, I'm going to win one too!'"

He got that contract and made good on his promise a few short months later. If there was a second "omen" game (along with the West Virginia win) during the regular '82–83 season it came late in Reynolds. V finally got his W against Carolina. He went into that game 0 for 7 against the boys in blue. McQueen, who hit two key free throws late in the game to turn the blue tide and put the Pack up 66–63, remembers: "A couple of seconds before I went to the line we were in the huddle and Coach said, 'Can't anybody hit a free throw around here?' And I said, "I can!'" Then they fouled me and I made them both."

When V's Carolina drought ended with a between-the-legs pass from Lowe to Bailey and the game ending dunk, the applause meter in Reynolds hit a ten on the Richter Scale. The fans mobbed the court. Great foreplay for the Wolfpack crowd, unaware it would have a lot more to cheer about before this season ended.

Following that win over Carolina V had one of those really tough decisions that most coaches would love. Ernie Myers had heroically stepped into the shoes of Dereck Whittenburg. Now Dereck's foot had healed.

Dereck Whittenburg: "When I broke my foot it was sad at the time but I think it really helped our basketball team. Other guys had to step up. Sidney Lowe stepped up his scoring, Thurl Bailey stepped up. Ernie Myers, a freshman, came off the bench and took my place and played terrific. Terry Gannon came off the bench and started hitting threes. Cozell and Lorenzo did the job inside. And so although we struggled a little bit while I was out, they recovered, got better, got on a winning streak, and then I came back. And that's when Jimmy reminded me that now I had to fit in with the team because they had adjusted without me and so now if I could come in and add to the mix that we could make a nice run. And that's just what we did."

At first blush the results of his decision to work Whittenburg back into the lineup looked like V's run might be headed to a dead end. State beat Duke then lost to Virginia and Maryland. When Wake came into Reynolds for the final game of the season the Pack's NCAA bid was on the line. Here's how V put it to his coaches, "Gentlemen, we're about one loss from dusting off the golf clubs because our season will be over!" There was never a time in his career when those words—survive and advance—had more meaning. Which is just what the Pack did. In that last game in Reynolds they cranked up the three-point machine for an ACC season high of 130 points and blew Wake out by 41.

Cinderella Run

Dereck Whittenburg recalls the ACC tournament and how V's pre-game speeches dangled the old win and advance carrot: "When we got to the ACC tournament, Jimmy told us that we probably needed to win at least one game to get the NCAA bid. We were 17–10 and on the bubble. Now in the first round we had to play the Wake team that we'd just blown out in Reynolds. We were fortunate in that we beat them again, this time at the buzzer in a really tough one, 71–70."

Sidney Lowe, who stole the pass that set up Lorenzo Charles and the game-winning score: "There were times that those younger guys, Cozell and Lorenzo, just did things that won games. We were tied at the end and I stole the ball and we called time-out. Now we're running the clock down, I penetrate, pass the ball to Lorenzo and he gets fouled and he goes to the free throw line and he misses the first one but he makes the second one. That's a big play for a young guy, he stepped up and won that ball game. And a lot of his confidence came right down to him, to all of us in fact, from Jim Valvano. You see, V allowed you to play. And that gave you the confidence to go out there and do it."

Whittenburg: "After the Wake game we come into the locker room happy and V says, 'Okay, this puts you in a pretty good position [for an NCAA bid], and then we go out and beat Carolina, and after we beat them he says, 'I guarantee you guys for sure, that if you win the next game, you're in.'"

So now the NCAA bid was a matter of a win over Virginia, a team that V's State team had never beaten, a Ralph Sampson team that had been ranked—off and on—number one in the nation that season.

If there was ever a game that exemplified V's descriptor of basketball as "a game of runs" it was the 1983 ACC tournament championship game. State came out of the blocks with a 12–1 lead, Virginia and Ralph Sampson thundered back in the second half to go up 59–51. Then it was State's turn again. The Pack took a lead late in the game. Terry Holland's team fouled, State missed, and with six seconds left, from out of nowhere a most unlikely player, a little guard, made the defensive play of the game.

Terry Gannon: "We were up by three and Sampson went up for a shot and I happened to be in the right place at the right time and just stepped in and stripped the ball. If he'd have scored and been fouled it would have been a tie game."

That was the turning point and in a matter of seconds the Wolfpack was the ACC champion. V knew he had his coveted NCAA bid. What he didn't know was just how crazy this March Madness would be. His first clue came as the new ACC champs' flight landed at Raleigh Durham Airport.

Jim Rehbock, the Pack's trainer: "Jimmy busted my balls about this one for years. What happened was this: the pilot got the word that there was a huge crowd gathered at the airport. Someone came to me and asked me if we wanted them to land on a back runway and get the team into vans and sneak out the back way. I made the mistake of taking that message to V, who said something like, 'Are you kidding me? I want you to get me a parachute and drop me right into the middle of that crowd!' And so we went right up to the gates and walked into that crowd. And it was unbelievable, a mob, thousands of fans, an incredible experience."

That Sunday night V and Pack learned that their next flight would be to a place called Corvallis, Oregon, to play a team that V said sounded more like a toothpaste than a basketball team—Pepperdine!

Nick Valvano recalls the traditional phone call that came to "Jimmy" at NCAA time: "Our father [V's high school coach] had this thing with Jimmy about going all the way in the NCAA tournament. Every year at tournament time he'd call and say, 'Jimmy, I've got my bags packed!'"

Of course this time they would both (Jimmy and Rocco) need several weeks in changes because Rocco's son and his NC State Wolfpack were going to be on the road for three thrill-packed weeks.

Don Shea, a WTVD-TV sports reporter (who later headed up JTV Enterprises, V's business), remembers Corvallis and the first clues that this tournament was going to be something special: "The team was picked up by a double-decker bus owned by the hotel and when we got to the place Jimmy said, 'I like this decor. What is it, Early Whorehouse?' The walls were velour and the pictures on the walls were, I swear, those satin Elvis and the toreador fighting the bull. V had this Jacuzzi that you could put the whole team in. I'm telling you this room, the whole place was really tacky, and wide open. You could have the keys to the bar and go into the bar anytime during the day or night. What we learned later was that Jimmy was right. This place really was a former brothel. I guess we should have known right there when we came flying into that hotel on that double-decker bus that this NCAA tournament was going to be a pretty wild ride!"

Interesting diversion, but V's mind was elsewhere. Pepperdine, the university that he'd jokingly referred to as a toothpaste, was exactly the kind of team that he hated to play—an unknown quantity with no name recognition. His darkest fear was that he couldn't get his team, the players who had just beaten powers like Carolina and Virginia, up to play a Pepperdine. He couldn't shake the memory of the first round Tennessee-Chattanooga loss from the previous season.

And then they played. The game was everything he feared it would be, an "I've got it you take it" affair with the Pack missing its first 12 shots right out of the chute. It would end tied 47–47 in regulation. When Pepperdine went up 57–52 in the first overtime the Pepperdine bench erupted.

Dr. Don Reibel, the team's orthopedic surgeon: "I was on the NC State bench and there was a moment in overtime when it looked like we didn't have a prayer. One of our assistant coaches showed V that the Pepperdine players were jumping up and down celebrating. He stopped his chalk talk in our huddle and said, 'There's something I want you to see. They think they've won this game. Do you?'"

Later V admitted that Pepperdine had every reason to cheer. "We couldn't hit our rear ends with a flashlight," he'd said. Sidney Lowe fouled out in the first overtime, and this very ugly attempt to survive and advance ground painfully on—fouls, missed shots, missed foul shots. After Cozell McQueen tipped in a Whittenburg missed foul shot and sent it to double overtime, it finally ended—a most merciful ending with State winning 69–67. The Cardiac Pack had begun the race to race hearts. V had made it past the first round, he'd squeezed by the toothpaste school. The Cardiac Pack somehow managed to survive to advance!

Dick Stockton, the CBS announcer who called that game: "I was a part of that championship miracle season. When we did the Pepperdine game, the very first of that incredible run for the championship, well it looked like NC State was going down to defeat. And our producer said start to talk about winners and losers in the game. And so he was showing shots of the bench and so we commented on what it might mean for Jim Harrick from Pepperdine to be moving on and what a great valiant season it was for Jim Valvano and the Wolfpack, overcoming injuries and now here they were suffering their final defeat, Sidney Lowe playing his final college basketball game.

"So we started that, and then I don't know, someone hit a shot for NC State and I said, 'Wait a minute, this game isn't over yet. You can't count this team out, it's too early.' In television they always want you to wrap it up, tie the strings before it's over. And of course to use a cliche, the rest is history—NC State won it in double overtime, and then went off on that run that incidentally was covered by CBS, every game along the way. The Virginia game and Las Vegas were both won at the buzzer. And then of course that incredible final game, the end of a magical ride . . . but I'll never forget Jimmy and that Pepperdine game . . . and to be a part of it and to be the one who saw something coming and put the brakes on the idea of writing that team off, well that is very special to me."

Later that night Terry Gannon and his teammates watched a tape of that game back at the hotel: "When Dick Stockton said, 'Sidney Lowe has fouled out of his last college game,' we all screamed and threw our pizza at the TV set!"

The next hurdle was a very tough Nevada Las Vegas team. My personal TV memory here (please indulge me) was that at the eight-minute mark my seven-year-old son Matt couldn't take the pressure any longer (he'd been brought to tears the Friday night before when Sidney fouled out in that first overtime against Pepperdine) and headed to the driveway to shoot hoops and await the news of State's loss.

But out in Corvallis V had "neva given up," he was pressing and fouling, "putting his team in a position to win." I remember being crouched in front of our TV and watching Bailey hit a jumper with the clock winding down to bring the Pack within one. Then V fouled again, Vegas missed, and now with seconds remaining Whitt cut loose a bomb that caromed into the hands of Bailey, who tapped, missed, somehow caught his own rebound, and then put it up and off the glass for the win. What V remembers (in his autobiography) is seeing that last shot, tap, and then shot in slow motion. What I remember was Matt's face when I walked into our driveway, kissed one off the garage backboard, and shouted: "Three seconds left, Bailey shoots and scores. Wolfpack wins, 71–70!"

Sweet Sixteen

The following week when the team arrived in Ogden, Utah, the Cardiac Pack wasn't just a national story, they were an inspiration to fans all over the country. Thurl Bailey, the hero of the Nevada Las Vegas win, remembers: "When we were on our run to the Final Four—we'd won a couple of games but we weren't really aware yet of what we were doing or the impact that this was having on people—we started getting this fan mail and it kept coming in. And V started reading some of that mail to us. And I'll never forget this one letter from a lady whose husband was in a coma. And this was the moment that we all realized—probably for the first time—just what this all meant and what we could accomplish. Her husband was in the coma and she wasn't a big basketball fan but her husband was. He couldn't watch us play but what she would do was turn the TV on in the hospital room in hopes that maybe he might be able to hear it. She wrote that she had a decision to make as to whether to keep her husband on the respirator or to unplug it. Because we had given her hope and a reason to believe, she had decided to keep her husband alive as long as she could. Now we were just college kids listening to this, and we didn't realize what this all meant. We saw it as basketball and that the impact was on the local or regional level back in North Carolina. But now here comes this letter from somewhere maybe in California. And when Coach Valvano read that to us we knew for the first time that we were touching lives everywhere. He knew it, of course, but it wasn't until he read that letter that we became aware of just how important every game that we'd played and would play had become."

If there was a breather in this breathless run to the national championship it came against a most unlikely team. Utah, a team that had upset UCLA, was now playing what V saw as essentially a home game. The Utes, only about an hour away, bussed in from Salt Lake City to Ogden.

But the home court proved to be little advantage as NC State took target practice (no three-pointers in the NCAA tournament), coming at the Utes with long-range twos. The game ended 75–56, which was a laugher by State's play-'em-to-the-buzzer standards.

Terry Gannon recalls: "I remember that Whitt had a great game and we shot something like 60 percent in the first half. I don't think they thought we could keep it up, but we just kept hitting what would have been ACC threes and just went lights out in the second half, shooting almost 80 percent."

The '83 NCAA tournament had not been a great run for what V called "America's Guests," the "working" press. They'd pronounced the Pack dead against Pepperdine, wrote them off against Vegas, and then predicted that if V had his druthers he'd rather not play Virginia, a team that he'd gone one for three against back in the ACC wars.

Wrong again! Coach Ed McLean: "Jimmy liked the idea of playing against personnel that we knew. Virginia had great talent, including Ralph Sampson, but he knew them and knew how to play them."

Play them V did, albeit once again right down to the wire. At the end a Sampson dunk followed by a Whittenburg jumper tied it at 61. V had the Pack foul Othell Wilson, who made the first shot and missed the second. Suddenly State, trailing by one and just seconds away from a trip to the Final Four, was on the line—literally.

Whittenburg had passed inside to Lorenzo Charles, Lo went to the basket, and Sampson fouled. In an attempt to ice Charles, Terry Holland, the Virginia coach, called a quick time-out.

Lorenzo Charles remembers two foul shots that were, perhaps, even bigger than the championship dunk: "Everybody remembers the dunk that won the national championship, but the game that got us to the Final Four ended with the two foul shots that I hit. Some of the credit goes to V again because he just gave me so much confidence. When we were in that huddle he didn't say, 'Now if Lo makes these shots here's what we'll do.' He said, 'When Lo makes these shots.' And then he simply gave us the defense and I went out and hit them both."

Dr. Don Reibel recalls overhearing what V said after Lorenzo left that huddle: "I was right there listening to this and when the team was in the huddle he's looking at Lorenzo, talking to him, telling him that he's going to walk out there and do exactly what he does in practice every day, 'You make a hundred of these every day in practice. Now you're going to go out there and make these two shots!' I mean nothing but positives and he's only talking to Lorenzo, nobody else, giving him that can't miss philosophy. Finally the horn blows and as the players race out to the foul line, V grabs Sidney by the arm says, 'When he misses the damned foul shot … foul the first S.O.B you see!'"

Lo hit the shots. Virginia called another time-out.

Tommy Abatemarco remembers this all-important huddle: "When we were in our practices or pre-game meetings everybody would tell V what he thought. Nobody would B.S. him. So he'd say something and I'd say, 'I don't like that!' And he'd say, 'Tommy, just shut the f*#& up!' This was our relationship. So we'd be on the bench and the first play or two would go wrong and I'd say, 'I told you. I didn't like that!' And he'd be like, 'T, just shut the f*#& up!' So now here we are playing Virginia to go to the Final Four. Lorenzo has hit two foul shots and with about maybe sixteen seconds left we're up by one. Terry Holland calls time-out. And I have a picture of this on my wall at home. In our huddle V said, 'I'm gonna chase on Wilson and we're going to put a man in front and in back of Sampson in the diamond and one.' I said, 'They're gonna get a wide open shot on the left side!' And he said, 'Shut up. I don't care. I want the guy to take that shot, it's gonna be Mullen!' So sure enough they take the ball out of bounds and we got a guy on Wilson and Wilson starts to penetrate, and I guess Sidney helped off the triangle and they kick it to Mullen, who's wide open, left-handed on the left side, and he shoots and he misses. Sampson can't get the ball because V has him sandwiched in, Cozell in back and maybe Gannon in front. So we win and go to the Final Four. The guy just had an amazing feel for the game and what he wanted to do. Always with confidence and that confidence went right through to the players. He said it, they did it, it worked, and we were in the Final Four!"

Finally... The Final Four

If the Pack's run was going to come to a screeching halt, it looked like it might come in the Georgia game, at least for a period of time in the second half. The Bulldogs had upset Carolina by running and banging the offensive boards, but when they hit the high altitude of Albuquerque they hit the wall. The Bulldogs shot like dogs and at the end of the first half the Pack was up 33–22. Then in the second half V made an admitted mistake (one that perhaps influenced his ultimate decision not to put the brakes on against Houston) and let the air out of the ball. The game uglied up and finally ended mercifully with the Pack winning 67–60. Now State's players became spectators as they awaited the winner of the Houston-Louisville game, which would be the team they'd play on Monday night for the national championship.

It has been well documented that the Houston-Louisville game was a "Last Dunk Standing" wins event. In retrospect, V wished he'd taken his team back to the hotel, that they'd never seen this game. "They dunked everything that wasn't tied down," he said. NC State Chancellor Bruce Poulton, an eyewitness to this air circus, remembers cocktail conversation that followed: "After we beat Georgia Jim did something that may be routine but wasn't the best idea in the world. He kept the team after our game in the arena to watch Houston play Louisville. I was sitting fairly near them and the game was pretty even for a while, and then in the beginning of the second half Houston was playing this guy Anders, and Anders teamed up with Clyde 'The Glide' Drexler, and the speed of those two guys led to a whole series of slams. They got the ball down the court at warp speed and they were dunking all over the place. And Louisville started doing the same thing and I think there were like fourteen or fifteen power slams in that game. And when it was just about all over our guys got up and left the arena and I could tell by the looks on their faces that they were in shock. Heck, most of the people in the arena, all the fans were shocked, even the press, it was an unbelievable display.

"And afterwards, back at the hotel, everyone is hanging around, and I see Jim and I get him in the corner and I mean I've got a question that I have to ask. I pull him over and say, 'Jim, that was just awesome. What in the world are you going to do to stop Houston?' Now this was a Saturday and we were going to play Houston for the championship on Monday. So I'm standing there wondering if he has a plan and he says, 'No problem. I told Cozell that all he has to do is get the tip-off to Sidney. Then Sidney will dribble it until Tuesday!' That was Jim Valvano. And I believed that's what he was going to do. So did the national press and so did Houston!"

Of course V would repeat his comments to his chancellor for the national press at the Sunday press conference: "If we get the opening tap we may not take a shot till Tuesday morning."

Here's what Dereck Whittenberg said into a bank of microphones that day: "We saw them dunking and everything but they are going to play NC State Monday night and we are not going to lie down."

Fifty million fans watching the final game on CBS TV heard this pre-game repartee between V and Guy Lewis, the Houston coach:

V: The offense is important; we've got to control tempo. We've got to take good shots and be sure that the game isn't in the 80s and 90s—it's got to be more in the 50s.

LEWIS: I'm sure that they will try to slow it down. On the other hand we'll try to speed it up a little bit. It will be a battle of the tempos, whether it's slow tempo or fast tempo. But I'd say the odds are in his favor as far as the tempo because it's easier to slow it down than it is to pick it up.

V: We don't have the kind of club that we can come back on them. Fans, if you're watching and we get down like 14–2, it's going to be very difficult for our team to come back.

LEWIS: I'd like to get ahead very quickly and stay ahead the entire ball game.

V: We've been an outside shooting team all year and lived and died with the jump shot. I don't think I'm going to say, "Fellows, I've got a great idea, let's throw it inside."

LEWIS: We'll put a little pressure on the ball and we'll try to contain their good scorers and we'll try to move them up and down the floor.

V: Hopefully we can draw some fouls because we need them to get in some foul trouble, to be honest with you.

LEWIS: Usually the team that wins the rebounding war wins the game. We have one other slogan, though, that we add to that: the team with the most dunks wins the game!

V: We're so close to having a game that could go blowout city!

LEWIS: We may be from the country but we're not easily conned!

Perhaps Lewis couldn't be conned but the press bought V's underdog "won't shoot till Tuesday" story and was cranking out copy that made NC State a snowball rolling slowly toward hell. There were many nay sayers, but the newspaper lead that would make V's locker room wall belonged to Dave Kindred of *The Washington Post*:

"Trees will tap dance, elephants will ride in the Indianapolis 500, and Orson Welles will skip breakfast, lunch, and dinner before State finds a way to beat Houston."

V's posted choice as the runner-up was: "Rain would make it perfect. It always rains at an execution!"

Of course while millions of Americans were chuckling over an elephant taking the flag at the 500 and waiting to see the hangman double knot State's loop, V—behind closed doors with his coaches—was putting together a game plan that would help Dumbo pick up his checkered flag and make a slip knot of the noose.

Gamers

Terry Gannon remembers the pre-game moment to end all V's pre-game moments. "When we came into the locker room before the game, he erased the entire scouting report and said, 'If you think we're going to hold the ball in front of fifty million people for the national championship you're out of your mind. We're going to go out there and kick their ass.' It was like we were going to take the fight to the puncher. Everybody thought he was going to dance and he came out swinging."

Sidney Lowe not only got the message—we're going to play, not be played—but saw an entire team get so fired up that they wanted to run through the locker room wall: "The thing that V did was cross them up. He crossed us up, he crossed everyone up. Because prior to the game he talked about slowing the game down. And everyone believed it. Hell, I believed it. And obviously we'd just seen that incredible Slamma Jamma game. So I'm standing in that locker room when he starts to talk thinking I've gotta go out there and control the ball for forty minutes.

"All of a sudden here it comes, he's walking around that locker room looking at us shouting, 'Do you think we came all this way not to play? Do you think we're going to hold the ball with millions of people watching? This is what we've been fighting for.' And we're getting wide-eyed and more and more fired up. And this is news to us and it's great news. Now we're not nervous about playing for a national championship. We can hardly wait to get out that door and stick it to them. Now we know that we were going to actually 'play' for the national championship. He got us so pumped up and we could hardly wait to get at them. No more control tempo.

"I'll never forget this, when they announced the starting lineups—I've only told this to two people, my mom and my wife—but when they announced the starting lineups, just when they were about to call my name, something hit me. I don't know what it was, if it was spiritual, like the Lord was telling me, you are going to win this game. And as I'm going out there this smile just came over my face. And now when I watch the film I can see it, that smile, and it was the weirdest thing, I just had this wonderful feeling that we were going to win this game. I never worried, never panicked, I had no turnovers, played the whole game. Even hit some big shots in the second half to keep us in the game."

Dereck Whittenburg looks back on the championship game as one that the Pack went into with more confidence than most people imagined. "The ACC was one of the strongest conferences in the country that year. North Carolina and Virginia had both been number one in the country during the year and we'd been playing those guys all year. I think we surprised them [Houston], because once we got the rebound, we pushed the ball a little bit, and when we had shots, we took the opportunity. But we weren't trying to get into a running game, just control the tempo."

State went on an early tear and at the half led by eight. The game plan was working, and to make matters better for the Pack, Clyde Drexler, Houston's ace, picked up a third foul. Bailey was hot but Whittenburg equally cold.

Whittenburg: "During that year one of us would carry the first half or the second half. And Thurl was hot in the first half and so we continued to run our two offense, and I think they may have underestimated Thurl's ability to shoot the ball from the outside. He was very accurate from twelve to fifteen feet and we continued to look for him.

"Even though I was well covered in the first half, I was going to continue to shoot, and I never lost my confidence; I just had to wait for more opportunities. I think they were doing a good job of concentrating on me, not giving me a free shot. In the second half I knew I would get some opportunities, I just had to be ready for them, and luckily they came in transition and we took advantage of some opportunities in the fast break."

A Half to Hell and Back

The second half again proved V right. Basketball was a game of runs. Houston came out smoking and in the first 10 minutes of the second half outscored State 17–2. Suddenly the Wolfpack was down 42–35. Then in an attempt to rest his players, Lewis made a coaching decision that he'd live to regret. He switched to a zone on defense, then held the ball on offense.

In an ESPN special honoring V and the '83 Pack, Clyde Drexler defended Guy Lewis's slow-down decision: "I'd never second-guess Guy Lewis, and the reason he did that was, think about all the things that we had overcome in that game. We'd overcome a slow start, we'd overcome a key player in serious foul trouble, and we'd taken back the lead. And now that we had that lead, the guys who'd helped to get it were exhausted. That altitude in Albuquerque had Akeem, he couldn't breathe at the time, so when he went for a rest the idea was that we would come back and finish strong, so a pretty good move at the time."

Whittenburg: "I thought it was an excellent move at the time because they had the lead and there was no shot clock. We were really susceptible to backdoor [plays] and for them to maybe get some dunks off the spread, so we just kept them in front of us, got some steals, and some baskets in the transition."

Jim Rehbock remembers NC State's take on the rare air of Albuquerque: "Before the game, in the locker room, Jimmy told the team that if they needed any oxygen to see me and that I'd take care of them. And I had to say, 'No oxygen!' Well, you didn't want to contradict Jimmy, especially at a time like this. So he says, 'Why?' And I tell him that a friend of mine who was the Louisville trainer had given his guys oxygen in the Houston game on Saturday and it had an adverse effect on them, worked in reverse. So he says, 'Okay,' and goes on. Now, during the game, in the second half, some of our guys are really running out of gas, and I'm realizing that now I've got to tell him that I'm going to go ahead and give them the oxygen. So just as I'm getting up to give Jimmy the word, all of a sudden Guy Lewis, the Houston coach, slows it down and starts to hold the ball. I sit back down and our guys start to get their wind back. That's how close we came to doing something that may have affected the outcome of the championship game."

Crunch Time

Whittenburg on State's comeback: "I was getting some open looks, Sidney got a couple of steals there, and we ran on the fast breaks, and that was the only way we could do it, on the break. I got those shots in the transition, they were doing so well on me in the half court. And Jimmy kept preaching, you have to take these opportunities in the transition."

Then came crunch time and an easy decision for V. If Houston wanted a national championship, they'd have to win it. V put them on the line.

Whittenburg: "We had no choice but to foul–they had the lead and they were going to spread their offense, which was an excellent coaching move. And we fouled Clyde and he made his first two free throws, we knew we had to foul somebody else other than Clyde. Jimmy's plan was to concentrate not just on fouling but to have the opportunity to be on offense."

And with one minute and five seconds remaining the score was tied at 52. V lay back and waited for the right man to foul. Houston moved the ball back and forth on the left side. When Drexler, the proven shooter, flashed open on the right side Bailey dashed out and fronted him.

Billy Packer, the CBS color commentator: "Jimmy Valvano is going to foul, put somebody on that line."

Houston continued to move the ball, State packed back in their zone, waiting for the ball to get into the hands of the right man. Then they'd foul. The ball went to Franklin at mid-court. This was the guy, a freshman who shot 63 percent from the foul line. Whittenburg blew out and reached around him to make the steal. The whistle blew. Franklin would go to the line.

V's 'Put 'em on the line' ploy worked. Franklin missed, McQueen came down with the ball. And with his hands on the rebound, he tight-rope-walked the end line before flipping the ball back into the capable hands of Sidney Lowe.

Once again, V was right where he wanted to be . . . in a position to win. With the clock ticking, Lowe brought the ball down the court, dribbling slowly toward history.

V called time-out!

Lorenzo Charles: "I remember just before we broke that last huddle Coach looking at me and saying, 'Lo, you haven't been playing up to your level. Wake up!'"

There would be another wake-up call for the Pack. State had anticipated man-to-man pressure. V's thinking was that Lowe would penetrate and dish off to Bailey or find another open man for the winning basket. But Houston came out in a half-court trap and aggressively pressured the ball. The trap was working. The Pack moved the ball around the perimeter with trepidation as they slowly milked the clock. Gannon curled in from the right wing, his back to the basket, to take release passes. Only his cat-like quickness saved one pass and the game from going Houston's way.

Packer on the CBS telecast: "It's a half-court trap. Jim Valvano might not have anticipated this. He'll probably call that time-out."

Around the ball went . . . in and out of the hands of V's offense.

CBS's Gary Bender called the play-by-play: "State with three guards, Gannon, Whittenburg, and Lowe, down to fourteen seconds now . . ."

Then the moment. Drexler dove at Whittenburg, slapped the ball to the top of the key, Whittenburg–somehow– recovered. And then it happened. Whitt turned and fired up the prayer heard around the world!

Bender: "Whittenburg, oh, it's a long way!"

The crowd erupted!

Packer: "They won it. On the dunk!"

All hell broke loose. V was in heaven. But suddenly the man who had spent a lifetime positioning himself to win found himself out of position!

Remembering his ESPN *Up Close* interview shortly after the championship, Roy Firestone recounts V's interpretation of "the run for the hug": "As we watched the video on the program, I asked him, 'Jimmy, when you were running around the court what was going on? You look like a maniac there.' And he said, 'You know, it's one of those moments that when a coach wins a national championship they button their coats, they shake hands with the opposing coach, you gotta understand what was going through my head. I was down in the locker room before that game and I had this nervous stomach so I had to go to the little boys' room and this is a big game so the guy from the NCAA comes and he says, 'Coach, I thought you'd like to know that if you win this game you'll be one of twenty-nine coaches in the history of the game to win this tournament.' So now I'm more nervous and I go back to the little boys' room again. And now a guy from CBS says, 'Hey, this is going to be the most watched game in the history of televised basketball.' Now I say, 'How many will be watching?' and the guys says, 'Oh at least 50 million.'

"So now when that shot left Whittenburg's hand, I can see the ball was short. But most people don't know this–I did not want to play Houston in overtime. . . . Now I'm sharing that with you here on the show, but most people don't know that I didn't want to play them in regulation time either. So all of a sudden Lorenzo grabs it and dunks it. In that moment what did I do? I thought of two things. I had the ring, a big moment, 50 million people watching. So I'm going to do something great. All my life I'd grown up watching Wide World of Sports. Remember the agony of defeat? How about the joy of victory? I wanted to be the joy of victory on Wide World of Sports. So I go out there and I'll find one of my players and I'll hug Dereck Whittenburg because Dereck's won nine games in a row. But Dereck's hugging Sidney Lowe. I'm running around and I've got no one to hug. I'm an Italian kid from Queens all by myself. I got the joy of victory and the agony of defeat all at once because there's no one to hug!"

Moments after the hug run, when V talked to Brent Musburger and those 50 million people watching in on CBS, he couldn't have been more serious. V: "Our kids have never quit in a game down the stretch all year long, and I knew we wouldn't today. We couldn't get any offense generated, the ball would not go in, but we talked all year about being in a position to win, and if you are in a position to win you have a shot at winning, and under four minutes we put ourselves in a position to win by putting them on the foul line."

MUSBURGER: *You had to tell them to go foul them!*

V: *No question, we played to win this game, we don't want anybody to beat us by laying back. You have to do good things to beat us. We would have put them on the line eight, nine times.*

MUSBURGER: *This is the happiest man in America about to celebrate what in my opinion will go down as one of the greatest coaching jobs in the history of this tournament! Go cut down those nets!*

Jay Jennings, WRAL-TV's cameraman, recorded the cutting of the nets, a videotape that hundreds of thousands of North Carolinians would run and rerun on their VCRs for years to come.

"When Lorenzo made the dunk I was at courtside running around, jockeying for position. All I could see was the flow of the game moving down the court. I could see red uniforms and was ducking trying to get a shot but just couldn't, and when Whitt took the shot and I heard the crowd, I thought he'd made the basket. I knew State had won because the crowd went nuts, but I couldn't see, and the person standing right in front of me was huge. I screamed, 'What happened?' and he turned around and it was Chancellor Poulton. He said, 'Lorenzo dunked. We won!'

"So when everyone else was racing around in that wild scene–Cozell and Ernie Myers crawling up on the backboard, V chasing, looking for his hug—I ran to the other end of the court and got up in the stands and into a position where I could shoot down on the basket. I knew that V would be coming to that basket to cut the nets. When he held up the scissors I had the best angle for the shot that I'll always remember as one of my best. Not as good as Lorenzo's but a great shot of a great V moment."

Dee Rowe, the man whom V simply called Coach, recalls his very special moment after those nets had been cut: "The locker room was wild, just like you'd expect. But when we left that locker room it was just the two of us, Jimmy and me. We waited outside in that parking lot after that game, waiting for Jimmy to go into the press conference. And it was a beautiful time we had there together, just the two of us in the heat of that parking lot. We just looked at each other and it was like, WOW, and a very special conversation between the two of us, a moment I'll never forget."

At that post-game press conference V shared some of those emotions: "This is a dream for me and my players for sixteen years and it's so awesome and I'm so tired. Everyone says I'm loose and I am, but I'm almost speechless. I have no funny lines. I'm just in great awe to be a part of the national championship. I think Albuquerque, other than New York, where I was born, Albuquerque is the greatest city that the Lord has ever made. Oh, one more thing, my wife is pregnant. Well, she doesn't know it yet, but she's going to be. And we are going to name our kid Al B. Querque!"

Dick Vitale: "I was sitting next to Rocco Valvano, Jimmy's father, at that post-game press conference. And he was so proud. Jimmy was just wowing them with the Al B. Querque line, claiming to have designed the air-ball play that led to Charles's dunk. And Rocco leaned over to me and said, 'Dick, my boy has them right in the palm of his hand.' And he did, you know, for that moment and his entire life really, that's where he had us all, right in the palm of his hand."

Jim Valvano lived the moment. This was his moment. He could throw out the 3x5 card now. Rocco Valvano, his beloved father and coach, the man who packed his bags every year to see his son win the NCAA, had been with him, seen him survive and advance every step of the way. And for all the trials and tribulations that would follow Jim Valvano over the years in his roller coaster career, not his critics, not even his cancer... could take this moment away.

$\mathcal{V}$ & $\mathcal{M}e$

Everybody's Favorite Jim Valvano Story

We should do this every day of our lives. Number one is to laugh. You should laugh every day. Number two is think. You should spend time in thought. Number three is, you should have your emotions moved to tears, could be happiness or joy. But think about it. If you laugh, you think, and you cry, that's a full day. That's a heck of a day. You do that seven days a week, you're going to have something special.

Jim Valvano
ESPY speech, March 4, 1993

BOYHOOD MEMORIES

Nick Valvano, the older brother, begins V & Me *by sharing memories of Jimmy before he became a capital V.*

For some reason, since he's gone, when I think of Jimmy I reflect on our childhood. I was the older brother by three and a half years. The sad thing is that we were talking about me coming down to Raleigh and being together and being friends again when we were adults—and we would have played golf together, been kids again, just like we were in New York.

From the time of my first marriage and his marriage we didn't spend a lot of time together. We were going in so many directions, kids and careers. I'd come down to see him but now I think back on growing up and how much fun he was, back when we had each other. Because of the way we were raised we were very close.

One of the things that Jimmy used to say, and oh, he loved to do this one, he used to say that he never got anything new. He'd say, "I was like twenty-one when I got my first new thing; everything before that was a hand-me-down from Nick. Nothing new." So my recollections are the growing-up things . . . you could see him as an adult and go right back to what he was like as a child.

The Mouth

No difference, just older and bigger, more expensive clothes. The same quick remarks. I remember one time when he was really little and my father was working trying to put a train set together for Christmas. And Jimmy had to be like six. My dad's having a hard time and he goes, "These goddamned trains!" And Jimmy's just standing there watching and he says, "Hey, don't come crying on my shoulder!" Six years old!

Life's a Game

For him life was always a game. There was never an activity that we did that he wouldn't somehow try to make more fun. We shared the same room. I remember we got new beds and I came home from school one day and he'd gotten the beds pulled away from the wall . . . he's got a beach ball and he's turned it into a basketball court. He's shooting between the headboards of our new beds and the wall. Who thinks that way?

No matter what it was, he had to turn it into a game or competition. We'd go to McDonald's and it was always, always, "Okay, who has the biggest french fry?" Now, we'd have to dump out our little pouch of fries and measure each one against each other to see who had the biggest fry. Everything was competition. We did that when we were kids and then we did it with our kids—I still play biggest fry with my kids, that was one of his games. Why, who cares? Then if you had the biggest fry he'd say, "Can I see that?" And he'd grab it, bite it in half, and then say, "Oops, you're disqualified!"

Theater of the Absurd

I don't know where all the theatrics came from unless it was my grandmother; she always acted in the church plays and did all the community theater back in the '40s. A couple of my dad's sisters were singers, so if it's a side of the family that had an inclination to perform in public, [it was] my father's sisters and my grandmother.

People who got to know Jim after he was an adult don't realize that the things he was doing as an adult were just the same things that he'd done as a kid, he was just older. He would hold court, as he did at the Nike coaches' clinics or in his office, when we were kids. Every week after we had a big Sunday dinner our cousins would come over and Jim would entertain. Sometimes joking, singing, or just telling funny stories. He had the greatest ability to take what happened in everyday life, then use the Valvano inclination for coloring a story and embellishing it and making it funny. He did Seinfeld—a show about nothing—in our living room before there was a Seinfeld.

Taking the Act on the Road

Again, there's three and a half years between us, and when I was in grammar school the nuns would bring Jim around from class to class and have him entertain. He'd do his imitation of Jimmy Durante. Very embarrassing, to me—"Hey, Nick here comes your little brother to do the Durante thing!" He did the "Ha cha cha cha. Goodnight Mrs. Calabash wherever you are!" He had no problems that his nose was big, and that was from the time he was little.

Babysitting

And if I went somewhere I had Jimmy. My dad would tell me that I had to take him everywhere with me.

"Nick, where you going?"

"I'm going over there!"

"Take you little brother with you!"

Of course Jimmy always thought he was my age, just a little shorter. All his friends were my friends. And like I said, Jimmy had a mouth on him from the time he was really little.

Every Christmas we used to get a new basketball, every Christmas. So Jim was about 8 and I was about 11 this Christmas. So we each got our new basketballs. He got a small one. So he's in the schoolyard with his new ball, which is small, and he's playing. And the older kids come in there–like maybe fifteen or sixteen years old–big kids. They take Jimmy's ball and they're throwing it around.

He's right in their faces, "You guys wait until my big brother gets here. You're gonna be sorry when my big brother gets here–he's gonna kick your ass!"

Now, I'm only 11 years old, and I show up. I still have the scar from that day, it's right here over my eye. I just walked in and heard somebody say, "Is that your brother?"

Jimmy says, "Yeah, that's him!" Then Jimmy grabs his ball and runs home. They just worked me over. The next thing I know I'm on the ground and these guys are kicking me and punching me. I still have the scar. He got his ball.

He always got his ball.

If the Suit Fits

Speaking of getting his way, there's a picture with both of us in our baseball uniforms, me and Jimmy. Here's the story on that.

I got that uniform for my birthday from my grandfather, my father's dad, whom I'm named for. Jimmy cried and whined for weeks. Finally my mom called my granddad and said, "Pop, will you go buy him a baseball uniform? I can't shut him up!"

Then we get our pictures taken and all you have to see is that picture, he's so happy.

He got what he wanted.

Flushing Out V

When I got to be about thirteen and Jimmy's about nine or ten... well, you just wanted to get rid of him. And we had a friend Anthony, and Anthony was heavy, so his nickname was "Fat." So to get rid of Jimmy I'd say, "Hey, Fat, what would you rather have, a million dollars or Jimmy's nose full of pennies?" And Fat would look at Jimmy's nose and say, "Hey, Jimmy's nose full of pennies!" And Jimmy would cry, run home, and then I'd get a beating.

The Creative Kid

One of the things that I think made him special was that there are so few people who when they are young, and I mean even before they are teenagers, know what they want to do, okay, then have the incredible confidence and determination to go and do it. That's rare! That's rare! And with it comes selfishness; he had that at a very young age.

As a little kid he always talked about coaching. Our dad was a coach so you gravitate to what you know, but he was always able to say what he was going to do and then do it. By seventeen, he wrote it on the cards, but he talked about it when he was in junior high school. When he was a little kid he used to write all these little fiction stories. He was always in them—Jimmy Valvano—and was always the coach. He'd write these fictitious characters and they were hilarious. I remember one time he's writing this story about this All America football player.

I said to him, "What's the name of the school?"

And he goes, "It's New York Polytechnical" or some crazy institute.

I said, "I've never heard of that!"

And he says, "It's a new school!"

Then he had a star quarterback and I said, "What's the quarterback's name?"

And he said, "Helen Mary!"

And I said, "The quarterback's a girl?"

And he said, "No, Helen Mary! Mary's his last name!"

So I said to him, "Well, why Helen?"

He says, "I think you'd have to ask the parents!"

Ten years old and over the years it never changed, Jimmy was still Jimmy.

NOBODY LIKES A SMART-ASS

In the spirit of "What would V do next?" since I'm the writer, hey, I get the next story (and I'll drop in like this from time to time; if no one else is identified in these little introductions, it's me talking).

I was a regular listener to V's radio show. It was a can't-miss in my house. He was funny and informative, and the entertainment level was something that we just hadn't heard in this market. But it was my habit not to ever call in. I looked at those "long-time listener, first-time callers" as self-serving losers who just wanted to hear their voices on the radio—until the night V got on the topic of baseball and made his "first-ever" error.

V was telling the story about the '57 World Series and how Johnny Logan, the Braves shortstop, had been hit by a pitch on the shoe but was denied first base. Logan then proved his point by showing the shoe polish on the ball to the home plate umpire, who gave him first base.

I couldn't resist. So I picked up the phone and called in the correction, knowing that V didn't care to be corrected. I didn't identify myself. I just said, "Coach, on the shoe-black story, that wasn't Johnny Logan, it was Nippy Jones!" A flurry of debate followed, with Garry Dornberg, the show's host, sucking up and agreeing with the coach. So I hung up on the short end of a 2-1 vote. The next morning Frank Weedon, NC State's senior associate athletic director, who had been listening to the show, ratted me out to V. "Hey, that was Cairns who called!" Another brief Logan versus Jones debate ensued, with Frank airing out my credentials as a baseball writer.

Two weeks later I received a note, which is now framed and hanging in my office. Accompanying this missive was a letter from an East Carolina University professor. The ECU professor had presented V with a box score and newspaper article, all the facts. Jones, not Logan, had been involved in the shoe-black incident in the '57 Series. The note on V's stationery—which I treasure—carried a message that says everything one would want to know about *V & Me.*

"Bob... nobody likes a smart-ass... Jim!"

WHISTLE STOP

Referees racing off the court for the safety of their locker room with a coach in hot pursuit wasn't exactly news in the ACC. FRED BARAKAT, who supervised ACC officials during V's tenure, remembers this classic.

I believe this one was the State-Duke game in Reynolds Coliseum. We always had the coaches evaluate the officials after every game. Ten was the highest mark, and then all the way down to zero. So Jimmy gets beat in a close game and there's a big call at the end that went Duke's way. In Reynolds the officials always ran off the court the same way Jimmy's team left the court, right past his bench. So now they've made a big call at the end and State's lost the game and the refs are trying to get their fannies out of there and quick. But Jimmy's hot and he's trying to get to them and he's hollering at [referee Lennie] Wirtz, "Hey, Lennie, Lennie!" So Lennie's shuddering. He's trying to escape and get into the refs' locker room. But Lennie stops and says, "Yeah, Coach?" Jimmy shouts, "Just wanted you to know I'm giving you guys a 10!"

Lennie can't believe it. State has just lost the game on one of his calls. He shouts back, "Thanks a lot, Coach!" And Jimmy says, "And... you three f*&#ing guys can take that 10 and divide it up anyway you want!"

AN OFFER V COULD REFUSE

JOHN SAUNDERS, with whom V worked the Big Monday show at ESPN, recalls his first meeting with his new partner, which turned out to be a "sign" of things to come!

This goes back to Jim's first day at ESPN. There was an old restaurant called the White Birch... a little hole-in-the-wall where all the ESPN people went after they got off work. We didn't know each other well; we'd met on a few occasions, him coaching, me covering sports. So after we got off the air, I asked him if he'd like to go out and get a beer.

Naturally there were a lot of people who worked on the show who were totally excited. So there were about ten others, we went to the White Birch, and we're all at a table, and of course, Jim is telling stories. But he was a little more conservative than the Jim that I'd come to know, a little quieter, more reserved, and he was letting others talk, just feeling himself out, and I was still really wondering what he'd be like.

So there's a couple at the bar and they're within earshot and the guy's a typical biker, dressed in all leather, [with] the hair hanging down, and his girlfriend looks like someone who would ride on the back of a bike, hair tossed up and tattoos showing, low-cut blouse, and her belly's hanging out. Now I can see them because I'm facing the bar, but Jim has his back to them and he can't see them.

The biker is talking to his girlfriend and is pointing to Jim and he's saying, "That is somebody."

So after a few minutes she walks over and she says, "Coach, I know you. My boyfriend knows you're a coach but he can't place who you are or what school."

Jim says, "Oh, no, I don't coach, I work in television."

So now she goes back and I'm watching them and I see the guy's eyes light up. Now he knows who it is.

So here she comes again, and she says, "Hey, you're Coach Valvano, you won the national championship in 1983 with NC State."

So Jim says, "Yeah, your boyfriend's right!"

Then she says, "I really don't follow basketball but my boyfriend is really impressed."

Jim says, "Well, tell him to come over, I'll say hello."

And she goes back to the bar and for whatever reason the guy doesn't want to come over. But now she comes back again and she says, "My boyfriend thinks so highly of you that he doesn't mind if you take me home tonight."

Now everybody at the table is just sitting there with their jaws hitting the floor. Nobody knows Jim well. So how do you handle this one, and we're all waiting to see.

Jim says, "Thank you very much, tell your boyfriend that I really appreciate the offer but I'm married, and so I think I'm going to pass on that one."

So now she goes back to the bar and comes back again, one last time and says, "Will you please just give me an autograph?"

Jim says, "Sure, do you have a piece of paper?"

She says, "No, sign it here!" and puts her thumbs inside of her jeans and pulls them down to panty height and says again, "Just sign it here!"

So Jim, without missing a beat, takes the Sharpie pen and signs, "Dick Vitale!"

BED CHECK

There were many lines that had the press rolling in the aisles in Albuquerque. THURL BAILEY from the '83 championship team recalls one of the first that endeared V to the national media.

As we were playing our way through that tournament there was so much media coverage, and at one of the press conferences a reporter asked Coach Valvano about a rumor that his players were hanging out late and not getting their rest. He wondered if Coach V had bed checks.

And Coach Valvano said, "You know, I was very concerned about that so last night I had a bed check. And I'm pleased to report to all of you that all of our beds were there!"

ALWAYS THE BRIDESMAID

GARY BRYANT, V's first manager at NC State, had been through it all with his coach—from all-night sessions after horrendous losses to those last-minute wins on the road to Albuquerque. Gary was convinced that nothing Jim Valvano would ever do again would surprise him—until the day he stood at the altar waiting for his bride to walk down the aisle.

In 1987 I got married and the wedding was in Atlanta. We invited V and hadn't heard from him so we weren't sure whether he was going to make it or not. Now this was in a small church in Atlanta and I was in the front by the altar waiting for Stephanie and the wedding procession to come in. The church didn't have hallways to the front so the bride's party had to walk from the rooms behind the pulpit outside and then come in the front doors.

As I was standing there at the altar I saw the procession go by through the stained glass windows. So I knew they were on their way. My nerves were jumping, the music starts, everybody stands up to see the bride, the doors to the sanctuary swing open and in comes V. He comes flying down the aisle carrying a plastic Food Lion bag [from a grocery chain] and finally finds a seat near the front. Of course, the whole church just falls down laughing. We're expecting the bride and we get the Italian Stallion.

So once again he's the show. And after the wedding we had this wonderful reception at the Atlanta Athletic Club and V came and of course was the last one to leave. But when he came through the receiving line he handed me that Food Lion bag that he'd walked down the aisle. He says, "Here, take this on your honeymoon, this is payback for all the times you brought me a bag like this!" And in the sack was a bag of Doritos, a cheap bottle of wine, and cigars. This is what the managers got him for his post-game sessions with the other coaches.

That was V. The kind of guy who would fly to Atlanta to go to a manager's wedding and stop his cab at a Food Lion to buy the best gift he could have ever given me.

BLUE-CHIP RECRUIT

Frances Lewis [Lynch] was V's administrative secretary from his first day at NC State until her retirement. She found herself in the swim with her new boss—almost—from the very first day.

When Jim was hired as coach he came in with so much energy. My office was first when you came in the door and his was behind it and he would come by me—swwwttt! He was through there, coattails sticking back, and kept going back and forth through my office, and he never said a word about whether he wanted me to stay or what. So I finally told him, "Jim, I don't want to be inherited, I want to be hired." So the next morning we sat down and we talked about loyalty and about the coaches I'd worked for, which went all the way back to [former basketball coach] Everett Case and [former football coach] Earle Edwards. I told him, "Jim, I thought those coaches walked on water!"

The next morning I opened my door and the whole top of my desk was covered with flowers. He never did anything halfway. There was this note that said, "Dear Frances, I can't walk on water yet but I'm treading like hell. Will you be my secretary?"

And I thought, this young man will do just fine. And that was the beginning of a really special relationship.

LITTLE BIG MAN

Recruiting can be a numbers game. And after the '83 season, when NC State's first choices for point guard slipped through the net, the pressure was on to bring in somebody who could run the offense. TOMMY ABATEMARCO, V's assistant coach and top recruiter, remembers the hunt.

We were on our way to go to the Final Four in '83 and there had been several guards early in the year that we were really recruiting–Kenny Hutchinson, Kenny Smith, Keith Gatlin, and Pearl Washington. I favored Pearl because he was bigger, stronger, and here was a guy who could shoot the ball. Washington's iffy but then he calls up and he wants a visit.

So we bring Pearl in and we have a great visit. To make a long story short, Pearl goes to Syracuse, we lose the others–all great players–and now we're making our run for the national championship and win. But [Sidney] Lowe's gone at the point [after that season] and we've lost all of these great guards we were recruiting for the next year.

So now V comes to me and says, "Hey, what about next year? Terry Gannon's a hell of a player and a good little shooter, but he isn't a point guard. We gotta have a point guard."

So we went back and forth and I said, "I told you we should have gone harder for Pearl."

But anyway we don't have a point guard. So we're scrambling around, and then I remember this kid I'd seen in *Sports Illustrated* named Spud Webb, a little guy who was a real jumper and a big scorer in Texas. So I hunt up this article and I call his coach and the kid was still available. I'd never seen him but he was being recruited a little bit by

Missouri and a few others and he might listen, but he was a real quiet kid. So I get on the phone with his coach and I'm begging for a visit. That's like a Monday so finally like on Thursday I convince Spud to come in for a visit. So I show V the article in *Sports Illustrated* about this little 5'6" kid who can jump and score and I'm telling him, "Jimmy, we've gotta take a shot!"

And so now Spud's coming in for a look at NC State and we're in V's little sports car, headed to the airport in Raleigh to pick the kid up, and we're late. And we get there, we can't find parking, and finally we go into the luggage area and we see this little, really young, guy, I mean he looks like about an eighth grader sitting on his duffle bag, he has this little hat on.

And V looks at me and says, "T, if that's Spud Webb you're fired!"

And the kid waves and V says, "You are fired!"

Now we all have to get into this little sports car, and Spud will not say a word. I'm like way scrimped in the back and V's talking to the kid the whole way back, but he's got one hand behind the seat pinching me and hitting my leg. This goes on all the way back to campus. Not good!

Now V puts the kid in the film room and he's all over me. "That kid can't play here!"

I say, "I don't know, we'll find out."

So we go though the whole visit and now Jimmy's caught because he needs a guard, so now he makes me fly to Midland, Texas, right away to look at Spud in a game. We have to see if he can play. I flew out there, saw him, loved him, a tough little player that could jump through the roof.

Now I bring back a highlights tape for V and he's like, "Okay, let's give him a shot!"

That's the story of Spud Webb, who had a great run at NC State, helped take us to the final eight, and then played in the NBA and won the dunking contest at the NBA All-Star game. Funny now, but not then— I really thought V was going to unload me over that one.

CASE OF MISTAKEN IDENTITY

There has been much conjecture regarding V and his basketball program at NC State University. Was it clean or dirty? Was NC State cheating? During what has become known as "The Personal Fouls Era" at NC

State, the media led many to believe that this was a bad program run by a cheater. DAVE DIDION, now a chief investigator for the NCAA and the man who spent over a year looking through a microscope at V's much-maligned program, offers some first-hand insights.

I was assigned to investigate NC State and what I did back then was do just that, investigate. If I discovered that there were violations I'd draft a document to send to the school... a letter of inquiry [which] includes the violations that were uncovered. The process then moves to a hearing of the case before the NCAA Committee on Infractions.

At NC State there was such a big deal made about the book *Personal Fouls* that I think Jim Valvano actually contacted David Berst, who was the NCAA executive director for enforcement back then. Jim requested that an investigator be assigned to the case. He wanted to find out what was really going on.

The first time I met him was at NC State in the chancellor's conference room in Holladay Hall. Becky French, the NC State attorney, introduced us. I just told him what my role would be and that I needed his cooperation and that I expected it. Then he talked for a few minutes about NC State and the book and the trouble that it was bringing and said that he wanted a thorough investigation done and that the chips could fall where they may. All I knew of him was what I'd seen on TV. It wasn't favorable. I thought I was going to be in for a long case because I thought he was probably some smart-ass know-it-all who would try to interfere in the investigation and try to manipulate the evidence. I was just really wary of him. And I'm sure he felt the same about me.

All he knew was what people had told him about the NCAA. So Jim in his mind is thinking this NCAA guy is probably a real asshole. He has a preconceived idea of what I'm like and I've got my idea of what he's like. So we're both thinking we're in for a long investigation.

I just started out by trying to interview the kids who transferred away from NC State, kids he recruited that he didn't get, talking about their recruitment. I talked to a lot of people and pretty soon I had a fairly good idea of what happened. I think the investigation took about a year and I talked to everyone I could get my hands on. In the end what I came away with was a letter of inquiry with about ten or eleven allegations.

Here's what I was expecting: that the kids would rip Jim and that they'd tell me things that they were offered to come to NC State. There just wasn't any of that at all. What we found was that some of the players had been selling the shoes and tickets that they got free. There was no attempt by Jim or NC State to cover up any of that. We just discovered that kids who got comp tickets and shoes sold them for spending money. Those kids who were involved in the extra benefits told me how they sold the shoes and tickets.

During the hearing I think Jim gained some respect for me and the NCAA's process because he realized that the Committee on Infractions didn't play favorites. The enforcement staff was sitting across the table from the university and both were fair game for the committee. A group of very, very intelligent individuals read the material put before them and then ask a lot of questions about when and how this happened and who said what, and sometimes they ask us [the investigators], "Why didn't you say this or that?"

I remember after the hearing that we were all relieved that it was over. Jim and I shook hands, and he said, "Boy, I didn't know that they would come after you guys too."

And I said, "Sure, the NCAA is fair game, just like the institution!"

It became pretty apparent to me after conducting this investigation that Jim's detractors were people just determined to dislike him. I'm sure that some of them had the same ideas that I had—all they knew was what they saw on TV and they figured that was him. But what I saw on TV wasn't anything like his real personality, it just wasn't the real Jim that I got to know.

There was a moment when I really knew that he wasn't the guy I [had] thought he was. It was toward the end of the investigation and we were just sitting around talking about a lot of the kids that I'd talked to and what they were doing and how they'd gone on with their lives. He really cared about them. It was really funny because I never expected that we would like each other and I can't explain why. Maybe it was because we were honest with each other or there was a mutual respect. In the end the only findings against NC State were the players' sale of shoes and tickets and a lack of institutional control by the institution. There was one recruiting violation. An assistant NC State coach had taken a prospect to the TV station that produced Jim's TV show because the kid wanted to be a communications major. While they were there they ran into the manager of the station and the coach introduced the kid to the manager of the station. That was a violation. And that was it, the only recruiting violation in the case, and that wasn't a serious thing.

So when the case came out and the findings were announced everyone thinks that Jim Valvano is the worst cheat that ever came down the pike. But the truth is he was never even named in a violation because there weren't any that he could be charged with. The worst thing you could say about him was that he was the director of athletics and that he was supposed to exercise oversight over the program and he didn't do it.

Here's how strongly I felt about Jim Valvano and this case. I sent him a letter after the investigation was over. He was taking so much heat in the press and I'd gotten to know him so well. So I just told him what I thought about him and it was really positive. I told him how sorry I was that he was going through [this trouble] because I didn't think it was fair, and I thanked him for all the help I'd gotten from him in the investigation. I didn't mince words, I told him that when I first got the case that I had these prejudices about what I thought he was. Then that when it was over that I thought he was one of the best guys I'd ever met. I closed by saying that if I had a son, I'd love for my son to be able to play for him.

WRONG JORDAN

TERRY GANNON, a Wolfpack freshman at the time, recalls an incident that brings to mind the old advice to boot camp soldiers: never volunteer!

Michael Jordan was just killing us, scoring at will, and V had basically pulled every rabbit out of the hat—straight zone, box with a chaser on Jordan, triangle and two with man on Jordan, match-up zone, three-two zone. Nothing worked. I think Jordan had about twenty-four at half-time. Finally, late in the game V looks down the bench and says, "Okay, who wants to take a shot at Jordan?"

I guess if I was known for anything it would have been the three-point shot and, at least by V's standards, my general lack of defensive speed. So I stand up and take off my warm-up and say, "Coach, let me guard him!" V doesn't miss a beat. He says, "Gannon, this isn't Vernon Jordan I'm talking about. It's Michael!"

LOCATION, LOCATION, LOCATION

MIKE FINN, assistant commissioner of the Atlantic Coast Conference, was the assistant sports information director at NC State when V and the Cardiac Pack won it all in the NCAA tournament in 1983. Finn saw his old friend on one of his last tours with ESPN. Although V had changed in some ways, he hadn't changed in others. The scene was Tallahassee, a deserted Leon County Civic Center, and V showed the players and coaches at the pre-game shoot-around the old Valvano sense of humor.

Cancer had already robbed V of his always youthful vitality. He walked haltingly from the pain, slightly slumped, and he had lost considerable weight. But pretty soon you heard the voice and right behind it came that incredible sense of humor.

He told us, "When Dick Vitale found out I was sick, he called and asked me to move to Florida and buy the house that was on the market next to him in Sarasota. I said, 'Dick, you've got it mixed up. I don't have Alzheimer's Disease. I've got cancer. I don't want to live next to you!'"

SAY IT WITH FLOWERS

NORA LYNN FINCH, NC State's senior associate director of athletics, remembers a rare incident when V opened mouth and inserted his Nike-shod foot.

Dave Didion, the NCAA investigator, was on campus carrying out the investigation of allegations about our players selling tickets and shoes. This was, needless to say, a really stressful time for Jim. And to his credit he was excellent with Didion, showing him that NC State was going to be totally cooperative, helpful, and strictly putting the best face he could on the situation.

So on one of the first days they spent together they came back to V's office. I remember I was in the outer office, just outside the door, when they walked in and Jim discovered a bouquet of flowers on his desk. Well, this was a great opportunity for him to show Didion just another example of how appreciative his fans were of his work. So he goes over, with the NCAA right at his elbow, and makes a grand opening of the envelope on the flowers. He then reads the card out loud. It said (expletives deleted), "I hope you have better luck than I did! Tark."

The letter was from Jerry Tarkanian, his friend and the coach of Nevada Las Vegas, who had not only been put on a major probation [but] was currently suing the NCAA. V didn't miss a beat. He picked up the flowers and handed them to Dave Didion.

"Here, Dave, I think these must be for you!"

NO ONE'S BIGGER THAN THE GAME

Roy Firestone recalls V's thoughts from an ESPN Up Close interview as to one's place as it relates to coaching big time basketball.

I talked to Jim about the game, just the game, and about the fact that so many of these kids who had come along were now—because of their celebrity—known on a first name basis, Sir Charles, Shack, Michael.

Jim said, "No one is bigger than the game. The game is what it's all about. And I'm in awe of it. We won a championship, right? But there's still not a gym that I walk into that I don't want to walk over and take a shot. Gotta take a J. And I have a pretty good J, by the way. I love the game. The biggest thrill is at North Carolina State before the first game of the year, down in the locker room where I give my Knute Rockne speech, which I call number 52. I tell the kids it's for me. People say be calm. But I tell them I work 365 days a year for thirty years for this and people say be calm. How could I be calm? This is it for me, babe. I'm down there and I give a hell of a talk, I dive on the floor, the kids go up, and I hear the band play the fight song and then just before tip off, I go out there and I look at 12,000 people, the cheerleaders are doing back flips, the kids are swinging, and I'm in heaven and that's what it's all about. The moment, the atmosphere surrounding the game. Nobody's bigger than that. I could leave tomorrow and someone else stand in that locker room. But I still would feel privileged to be a part of the sport and that moment."

HUDDLE HEROICS

During the '80s there were some incredible last-basket wins, and **VINNY DEL NEGRO** *remembers the confidence in V's huddles and how it not only affected the players but won games.*

The last regular season game of my junior year we were playing at Wake Forest and I hit a big shot at the end—now when I see Bob Staak, who was the Wake coach at the time, he says, "You cost me my job hitting that shot!" That win started the momentum that didn't end until we had snowballed it into winning the ACC tournament.

So I happened to hit the shot, but this game was probably won in the huddle. Of course, it all started with Coach Valvano. I remember vividly the play that he set up. Mike Giomi was taking the ball out and we had to go the length of the court. I started on the left-hand side full court toward the basket and I got a down pick to come up to the free throw line. Then someone else set a flare pick to come to the right side and Mike just threw a perfect line drive pass to me. I caught it on the right-hand side of the court and I don't remember who was guarding me, I think it may have been Cal Boyd. He went for a steal and he missed it. I took one or two dribbles and just pulled up behind the line and hit the three.

That put us in overtime.

Now here's the way Coach Valvano reacted to that with his players, myself included. We were excited that it put us in overtime but he never showed us that in the huddle. He had confidence in us and we'd just done our job. The pass, the shot, that's what we were supposed to do. That's what he expected and I expected. He might look at me and wink or say something like nice shot, but because he didn't get all excited it was a real positive, made me all the more confident. And when you're a kid that takes pressure off of you.

We won that game in overtime 80–76.

Now, I remember vividly, we didn't lose again after that Wake win, and [in the ACC tournament] we're playing Carolina for the ACC championship, and I had to hit a couple of free throws with fourteen seconds left to put us up. Carolina called a time-out, probably to ice me. We came into the huddle and Coach Valvano made a great substitution. He put Kelsey Weems in because he was very athletic. Kelsey's job was to deny Kenny Smith the ball. It was Kenny's job to push the ball down court and to try to create. We're down by one, like 67–66. So I've got two foul shots to win the ACC tournament. What Coach Valvano said was so typical of the way he coached.

He said, "Okay, after Vinny makes these two free throws, we're going to deny Kenny the ball, everybody get on their man, and that's it!"

It wasn't, Well, let's see what happens at the line with Vinny. It was, After Vinny makes these free throws. It was always like that, a confidence thing! And it didn't matter who was shooting the free throws. We're down by one and even though it isn't easy to make them with the game on the line, we are supposed to make them and that's the way he looked at it. That's how we approached any pressure—because that's the way he did it.

I hit them both, Kelsey denied Kenny the ball, and we won the ACC tournament, 68–67. You remember things like that. I had a lot of confidence anyway but that verbal pat on the back, that was his personality and it carried over with me—in big game situations—during my days in the NBA.

WAR STORIES

Bob Lloyd, Rutgers All-America guard, remembers V as a great teammate and as the kind of guy who you'd want to go to war with—if you're looking for laughs.

Jimmy and I weren't just teammates and college roommates, we served in the Delaware National Guard together. Following Martin Luther King's assassination our unit got called up. Now, Jimmy and I were accountants, but they gave us live ammunition and loaded us up in trucks. We had to guard a power station in a really rough section of

Wilmington, Delaware. We were to report any strange activities. Again, this was a real bad section of town and down under a train trestle there was this gas station. We were supposed to be watching it because this pump might be where [someone might] get the gas to make Molotov cocktails. There were all these burned-out factories, and we had to make sure there was no one down there. Well, the word was that someone in a white Oldsmobile had shot at some guardsmen.

So I look down and see a white Oldsmobile and I tell Jimmy, "Look, there's the Oldsmobile!" And of course he then flips to *Combat* mode, because when we were in college we watched *Combat* on TV.

So he says, "That's how we'll do it, like *Combat.* I'll go on one side of the street and advance ten yards and hold my rifle up, and you'll go ten on the other side and signal me. We'll go all the way down there like that."

So here we go and when we get down there, and we did it just like that—Jimmy whispers, "Now, what do we do?"

So I say, "Let's just yell!" And that's exactly what we did. We yelled and pointed our rifles into the car. And there was some poor guy sleeping in there. It just scared the hell out of him.

Later, in the middle of the night we hear this incredible noise. Now we had live ammunition and so we turn our rifles on this guy. This time it's the milkman, delivering the morning milk.

That's the extent of Jim Valvano's war stories. The only action he ever saw was a milkman and a guy sleeping one off in an old Oldsmobile.

MEALS ON WHEELS

Kay Yow, NC State's Hall of Fame women's basketball coach, remembers an unforgettable Italian catering service—V Inc.

I was diagnosed with breast cancer in August of 1987. On August the 18th I had to have a mastectomy and was in the hospital for a while. My first week at home I was by myself and it was hard to move around. I had to sit most of the time and just to move my arm was so painful.

So I was still working on recovery... just beginning my exercises and trying to get ready to be on the practice court on October the 15th, that was my goal. So here it is, my first week home from the hospital, and at about 10:00 o'clock in the morning the phone rings.

It's Jim, and he said, "Coach Yow, how are you doing?"

I said, "Well, under the circumstances, okay."

So then he says. "We are going to brighten your day—my staff and I are going to come over to have lunch with you."

I wasn't ready to see anybody my first week out of the hospital. I could barely move and here comes Coach V and the men's basketball staff, the whole crowd. I'm thinking, "A group of guys? What am I going to do with eight guys for lunch?"

But he said, "Oh, don't worry, we're going to stop by Amedeo's and buy lunch. What do you like?"

"Well," I said, "anything!"

"Oh, don't worry, we'll do everything."

So along about noon I hear the doorbell ring and it's Jim and his entire staff. They have enough food to feed a small army, they have a little of everything—pasta, linguine, salads, it's a smorgasbord of Italian food. They just blow in the door full force.

Now they've never even been to my house before but in they come and Jim says, "Okay, where are the dishes? You just sit down, we're going to do everything!"

I'm just thinking this is going to be something else! So finally I said, "Jim, what about paper plates?"

Of course, Jim just thought that was a great idea, paper plates, like I'd invented them or something. So now they're putting out the plates and the food, drinks. I wanted to help but I couldn't because I still had a lot of pain. I didn't know pain until we started to eat because it really hurt me to laugh and the only bad part of that lunch, which lasted for a couple of hours, was the pain! Because Jim Valvano had me laughing from the time we sat down to eat until they finally left—at least two hours later.

I don't think I'll ever have as mixed emotions as I had that day—I was laughing so hard that I wanted them to stay but it hurt so much to laugh that I wanted them to go. But you know how important laughter is in the healing process, and that was a day that I can look back on as one that got me on the road to recovery.

Of course, it really said a lot about Jim. He reached out at an important time in my life and lifted my spirits. He was very special to me. A lot of people would have wanted to do something like that but never followed through.

HE WHO HESITATES

Bob Guzzo, NC State's wrestling coach, recalls listening to V's radio show on his way home from a wrestling match and hearing a call that had to be a V classic.

I'll never forget the night a guy called into his radio show who had a really bad stutter. And so I'm driving home and listening on the car radio and the conversation goes like this. First of all the guy says that he stutters a bit and hopes that V will bear with him.

"Caaacoach, I'm aaa real fffan and I jjjust waaant you to know haahow much I appreciate the jooob you're daa doing."

V is very good with the guy and they're laughing about this situation, with V telling the guy to just take his time and relax, that he's only talking to the most famous coach in America. Pretty soon they're having fun together.

So anyway this conversation goes on and on and finally V is trying to wind it up and the guy says, "Wa-won more thaaing, Coach. I faa-forgot to ta-ta-tell you I'm a ba-ba-basketball coach ta-ta-too."

And V says, "I bet you've lost a hell of lot of games in overtime!"

JUST PLAIN DAD

Jamie Valvano, V's middle daughter, remembers her dad as just that.

There were a lot of funny moments. When we first moved here my older sister, Nicole, flipped over the handlebars on her bike and Dad had to take her to the doctor. That's when we knew we were really in

ACC country because the doctor said, "Sorry, Coach, the only thread I have is Carolina blue!"

And Dad said, "That's okay, you should see my driveway, she bled NC State red!"

Although we just thought of him as our dad, everyone else was totally aware that he was Jimmy V. I can remember going to school after State lost and the Carolina fans toilet-papering our car. But looking back on it now, it was such a gift having him as your dad because he shared himself with so many people and was so public. Now this really makes him still so alive for me and my sons.

But we kept him in line. Nicole was a big basketball fan, but LeeAnn and I were the girlie girls, and I remember saying to Dad the year after State had won the national championship, "Dad, what was that big tournament we won last year?"

PENETRATING QUESTION

Rick Brewer, UNC-Chapel Hill's long time sports information director, remembers the worst question he ever heard asked by the media being handled—with great aplomb—by V.

I was in charge of the NCAA press conference following NC State's championship win in Albuquerque, and needless to say it was an electric moment. State had just upset Houston, V was fired up, and the press was wired because they were all facing incredibly tight deadlines. So the questions are coming thick and fast, "When did you decide to run with them?" "At what point did you know that you were going to foul?" "Were you surprised when Guy Lewis slowed it down?"

I'm moving through the room of waving hands, V's being V, firing off entertaining and informative quotes. But I've got eye-contact with half the room because everybody wants to ask their riveting question, and get to their computers or telephones and file their stories. One guy, a local TV reporter, is waving away so I give him the next question and he says, "Coach, I just want to know what you think of our fair city, how did the people of Albuquerque treat you and your players while you were here? Did you find the accommodations up to par?"

The room goes silent. V deadpans an answer that seemed to go on for, well, past a lot of deadlines!

"That's really a good question. First of all, my family and I have really enjoyed the great mountain air, we love the altitude. The people are so typical of the West, everyone just couldn't have been nicer! The restaurants were reasonable, the beer cold, and of course we as a team are extremely appreciative of the transportation system and the hotel accommodations!"

Now, the national press is in this room, *Sports Illustrated, The Washington Post*, CBS, you name it, and just as I'm ready to break in, V ends it.

"Oh, I don't know whether you noticed or not but there was one other thing. NC State just won a national basketball championship!"

SOCKING NEWS

I was fortunate to have many moments with V, and this one, which I collected in the late '80s, was certainly one that—among others—led to the writing of this book.

My son, Matt, was a ball boy for State during three of the V years. Matt would ask me if I knew Coach Valvano.

I'd always say, "Well sure, we know each other, but since you're the ball boy and sitting right under the basket in front of his bench, why don't you just go over during the shoot around and say, 'I'm Matt Cairns, Bob's son!'"

Too shy.

It never happened. Cut to the Peach Bowl, New Year's Eve 1987. NC State has just thumped Iowa in a rain game, and Matt and his little buddies are celebrating the win and evening by playing football in the hallways of the Atlanta hotel. They are sock-less, dirty, but hey, it's their New Year's Eve. So about ten minutes before midnight Matt, no socks or shoes, still muddy from playing at the game, comes sweating into the room.

"Hey, Dad," he says, "guess who I just rode down to the big New Year's Eve party with on the elevator—he was in a tux and everything!"

"Who?" I said.

"Coach Valvano! I told him I was Bob Cairns's son!"

"Great, what did he say?"

"He looked down and saw I didn't have any socks or shoes on and said, 'I'm not surprised!'"

𝒱

REF LESSON

FRED BARAKAT recalls an invaluable lesson, one that he learned early in his tenure from Professor V.

This was my very first year as supervisor of ACC officials and I thought that I probably had an in with Jimmy and [Duke coach] Mike Krzyzewski because we had a background. We'd coached against each other up north. I'd been at Fairfield, Mike at Army, and Jimmy at Iona. They had both recommended me to Bob James for the ACC's supervisor's job.

Well, NC State plays Carolina in Chapel Hill and Jimmy gets whacked. Carolina had that great team, Worthy and Perkins and Jordan. I was there watching the officials work, and after the game I went home to Greensboro. Now this was a televised game and I always taped them. Anyway, about 1:30 in the morning my phone rings.

My wife answers the phone and I hear her say, "Jimmy, how are you doing? Oh yes, he's here."

So, I'm thinking, "Oh shit." Well I get on the phone and I say, "Jim, how's it going?"

He says, "Not good!" And he proceeds to tell me about how he and his coaches have been up all night back in Raleigh breaking down the video watching the officiating. Then he stops and says, "By the way, did you see the game?"

I tell him certainly, I was there in Chapel Hill and saw it.

Now he asks me another question. Jimmy never asked a question when he didn't have the answer. He says, "By the way, what did you think of the officials?"

I'm still trying to wake up but I manage to say, "Well, I thought they did pretty good!" Now, truthfully I didn't know much about officiating then. I was an ex-basketball coach so I was in the learning process.

Now he says, "Oh you do? Well, we broke down the game tape and we've got them making about seventy-five mistakes!"

I said, "What?"

"Yeah, seventy-five mistakes, I think you should see this tape. There's a real crucial call with about two minutes left to go, a charge-block situation that went against us that kind of turned the whole game around."

I say, "Jeeze, Jimmy, you were down 22 points with two minutes left, how did that turn the whole game around?"

"Well, maybe it didn't turn the whole game around, but it was a terrible call!" he says.

Now he wants to know what I can do about it. I find out that he's practicing the next morning, Sunday morning. I'm still about half asleep but I agree to drive to Raleigh to take a look at this game tape. Now he's happy. I get up early Sunday morning and drive to Reynolds Coliseum and at about 9:15 I walk in. They're already shooting around. He sees me and he's fuming. I can see the look. But what he didn't know was that the night before–since I was wide awake at that point–I'd put the tape on at home and taken a look at that one play, that block-charge.

I walk up to him and I say, "Look, before we go see the tape let's do the charge block play right now!"

So he goes, "Yeah, okay!"

I got Lowe and Whittenburg and I get them to recreate the play. Lowe drives the base line and Whitt steps in and boom! It was a perfect recreation of exactly what had happed the night before.

Now, I say to Jimmy, "There, what do you think?"

And he looks at me and gives me the best lesson I ever learned about coaching and officiating. He says, "Who has on the red uniform, Whitt or Sidney?"

That was it, that gave me the insight to do this job. It didn't matter if the ref was right or wrong, whether it was block or charge. Jimmy wanted to know which guy was State and which one was Carolina! And that's the way it is, for coaches and fans. On the close ones, officiating is all in the eye of the beholder. Not what is right, but who is right.

Since then, when I've dealt with coaches, I've always remembered that lesson Jimmy taught me. It's helped me handle the job and keep these calls in perspective.

V

SEVEN TOUCHDOWNS

*Jim Boeheim, coach of Syracuse University, the 2003 NCAA basket-
ball champions, remembers a day when Syracuse was known as a football school.*

When Jimmy was at Bucknell, I was an assistant coach at Syracuse
under Roy Danforth. We played Bucknell up here and it was one of
those games that they couldn't do anything right. We got up by 20 before they scored, led by 50 at the half and just killed them, then won
something like 110–53.

Of course, Jimmy never forgot that shellacking, us running the
score up. From that time on, every time he'd see me he'd go, "Syracuse. Big football school, right? I think you beat Bucknell by what,
seven touchdowns?"

WRESTLE-MANIA

*Sam Esposito, NC State's baseball coach at the time, remembers the
time V refereed a fight that may have cost Sam a blue-chip baseball
recruit.*

V and Tommy Abatemarco, V's recruiter, used to wrestle at lunch-
time in my office in Case Athletic Center. We'd push the furniture back
and they'd go at it. I'd referee—sort of a Wrestle-Mania. V would kick
Tommy's ass and they'd be okay for about a day or two and then they'd
be back at it again.

After a loss Tommy got into this deal where he'd start dancing around
me, wanting to know if I wanted some of him. Tommy was an instiga-
tor, that's just the way he was, hyperactive.

I kept telling him, "I may be an old man but one of these days
you're going to find your ass looking at the ceiling."

Well, the day came. V pins Tommy, I count him out, we walk out in
the hallway. We're standing right in the doorway of my office and Tommy
starts screwing around, dancing around me, making little slap moves at
my face. I grab him, throw him on the floor, V dives down and does the

ref deal, sliding his hand under his shoulders and slapping the floor, counting him out.

I let Tom up. He goes for me and we repeat the act. Now V's really getting into it, slapping the floor counting "One, two..." and about the time he screams, "three!" I'm still sitting on Tommy and I look up and here's a pair of wing-tip shoes, a pair of women's shoes, and two Nike sneakers. It's the shortstop and his family, the kid I've been trying to recruit for about a year there for his appointment with me.

I hear the most famous basketball coach in America say, "Welcome to NC State, we'll be with you in a minute!"

By the way, I won the fight but lost the recruit.

MEN OF SICILY

*There were many nights on stage in Jim Valvano's life. The night he spoke in Springfield, Massachusetts, to a predominantly Italian-American audience was, as **MARK BOCKELMAN**, V's sports information director, recalls, a Classic.*

We came into Springfield to play Houston again, this was the fall of '83 at the Tip-Off Classic, and it was a rematch of the '83 championship game. The flight was delayed and we had to rush through practice and there was a lot of stress from the travel. We had just been running behind all day. So we finally got back to the hotel and got the kids into their rooms.

I learned then that we were invited to dinner by the, I think it was the Springfield Sons of Italy. This was an invite to V and his coaches, a special evening that this organization had planned for him. So we go into this very Italian restaurant, and we're late. But they are all pumped up wanting to honor Jim as one of their own. Here he was—coach of the national championship Wolfpack—coming into this ethnic area. The place was packed.

When we walked into this room, to me it was like something out of the movie *The Godfather*, like what it must be like when the Men of Sicily get together. It was crowded, a real positive ethnic feel to the event, and we sat at these round tables with checkered tablecloths.

I'll never forget this. V was at the head table, but I had a guy named Guido sitting next to me and Tony was across from me and Father somebody, an Italian Catholic priest, was to my right. As we were sitting there I realized—because we were late—that we'd missed a couple of courses of the meal, which they insisted that I eat. Boy, it was something. They played catch-up ball, brought out the first course for me, minestrone, and as they were trying to catch me up these guys—Guido and Tony—were scooping up food and throwing it on my plate, "Son, you needa soma this."

Now, I don't know, maybe it was the mayor of Springfield, maybe the president of the organization, but he was a really little guy and he introduced Jim. And I mean he was really vertically challenged and he had this cigar and he was so excited about having Jim there he just went on and on about the national championship, about Jim being one of their own, bringing honor to all Italians. We thought the introduction was never going to end and it really didn't. All of a sudden here comes V on stage on his knees with a cigar in his mouth and he's like about the size of the little guy who's introducing him. The place just went nuts. The room was just roaring and later, one of the Italian dignitaries came up on stage to hug Jim. And Jim frisked him—right there on stage. That was another show stopper.

They just hung on his every word, a classic, and again we were all exhausted but the lights came on and there he was again just wowing the crowd. By the end of Jim's talk, which was really stand-up comedy—jokes and comments about the crowd and the city and Italians—he laid in a few off-color jokes. I don't remember the actual comment [that led to what happened]— I think it was about his childhood and going to parochial school and the nuns or something—but it offended the priest at my table. Well, he up and left.

As the father was walking out Jim was apologizing, working the crowd the whole time. But V knew what he could get away with, he always knew his audience. Of course, as the priest is walking on him, everybody else is just howling with laughter. All I could think was of how tired we were when we found out we were going to the Sons of Italy dinner and how if I'd passed on this one, I'd have missed one of V's classic performances.

PERFECT JOB

LINDA BRUNO, commissioner of the Atlantic 10 Conference, remembers a wake-up call from Jim Valvano that led a sleepy ex-English teacher into a rather unlikely career change.

I was an English major and after graduating from college I taught for one year in the Bronx. That was not a good experience. So I decided that I'd like to go back to school and get my masters, and so I was really between teaching and school again. I was out one night with some friends and they told me that Jim Valvano, the basketball coach at Iona, had been named the athletic director and that he might be hiring. So early on, I guess, as a whim I sent in an application.

Days went by and it's about 10:00 in the morning and I'm still asleep when the phone rings. I struggle to get the phone and I'm greeted by this raspy voice on the other end. "Jim Valvano!"

I go, "Mr. Valvano, hello!" But my voice must have given me away.

He informed me that it wasn't Mr. Valvano, that it was Jim, then he wondered what I was doing sleeping at 10:00 in the morning. "Get over here. I want to talk to you about a job," he said.

The interview was, well, different. I'd never been interviewed before when the person doing the interviewing does all the talking. That's how it went. And when he was finished he offered me the job.

When I finally had a chance to say something I asked what I thought was a very good question, "What is the job?"

He informed me that I would be his administrative assistant. I told him I had no secretarial experience and couldn't type. He said not to worry about it, that we'd work it out.

And the working it out…what a wonderful experience. It really changed my life. Between the two of us, we were quite a team. I envisioned a large office with a staff. Which was not the way it worked out. My little office was right outside his door. We had this intercom system that neither of us knew how to use. We could buzz but we didn't know how to talk over it.

Here was Jim's solution: "If you need me, buzz. If I need you, I'll buzz. Then we'll yell back and forth through the door."

Six months later a secretary from another department came over and caught our act.

"Why is he buzzing and yelling through the door and buzzing the intercom at the same time?" she said.

I said, "Well, that's how he gets my attention!"

Our training consisted of her flipping a switch. Now we suddenly had a working intercom.

That said, he was a really great administrator, and one of his strengths was delegation. If I knew then what I know now, I'd have been nervous. But he taught you to take on challenges and be responsible.

With Jim it was, "Hey, you can do this!"

Now as the commissioner of the Atlantic 10 Conference there's rarely a day that goes by—especially when I face tough decisions—that I don't remember that wake-up call from Jim Valvano and say to myself, "Hey, you can do this!"

WEIGHTY SUBJECT

For years CHARLIE BRYANT, head of the Wolfpack Club during the Valvano years, traveled with V visiting Wolfpack clubs across the state. During those trips he had an opportunity to hear a great number of V's many and diverse theories. Charlie recalls that when it came to weight loss V had more thoughts on the subject than Dr. Atkins.

Jim was a self-proclaimed dietitian, always worrying about his weight, then concocting diets. If he wasn't on one of his famous pop-corn diets he was expounding on his theory of weight loss, which was: Weight never left the universe. If you lost weight someone else had gained it.

Garry Dornberg or Wally Ausley, our two hefty radio guys, would walk by and V would say, "Looks like somebody lost some weight!"

So one night we're at a Wolfpack Jamboree and we run into Bryce Holt, a former Wolfpack player. At that time Bryce dressed out at about 300 pounds. So here comes Bryce and one of his buddies.

The guy with Bryce says to Coach Valvano, "Hey, check Bryce out, he's just been to a fat farm in Florida and dropped forty pounds."

V gives Bryce the once-over and says, "Congratulations, Bryce. But I've gotta tell you something. Forty pounds for you is like throwing two deck chairs off the Titanic!"

We walked away laughing and because I knew that Jim was on another one of his popcorn diets—where he'd go for weeks eating nothing but popcorn—I asked him how his latest Orville Redenbacher diet was going.

Jim looks at me and says, "Charlie, I'll have to be honest with you. I've been on this f&*%#ing diet for two weeks and all I've lost is fourteen days!"

One of his favorites was the Lee's Tailor Diet. He'd come into my office, loosen his belt and pull out the waist of his pants to show how roomy they were.

"My Lee's Tailor Diet," he'd say. "Lee's let the pants out again; see how much weight I've lost!"

RUNNING THE NUMBERS

Rich Petriccione, a former Iona manager, is now a VP at Iona College. Petriccione will never forget basketball's answer to Scrooge McDuck.

Here was V. You know the dry eraser boards that you can mark and then wipe clean? He would constantly be adding up his numbers on these boards. He loved to keep score with his money.

He'd say, "Hey, Pet, check this out!"

Then he'd write something like NC State $125,000, Nike $100,000, Washington Speakers Bureau $68,000, local car dealer $12,000, TV and radio whatever… and then he'd draw the double line and then he'd make you do the math with him. Eight and three are eleven, or whatever, carry the one and then he'd announce the grand total of his income.

"It comes to a grand total of ———" And then he would say, "Can you f*#&ing believe it? Can you believe it!"

Then he'd say, "What do you make?"

And I'd say, "Well I'm making $16,400."

Then he'd say, "That's what I'm talking about!"

Now this may sound like he was rubbing it in. But you had to know him. He had the ego, and he was so aggressive, but he also was making a point to me, that I could do better. If he could make this, then others could as well.

And the reason I'm comfortable about telling that story is because it didn't matter what he was making or where he was, he always did that, he always had so much going, coaching, speaking at camps, whatever.

So it didn't matter whether it was at Iona where the numbers were $25,000 plus $2,000 or at NC State where they changed to $125,000 plus $100,000. He loved to write those numbers down. It was important to him because it was a sign to him that if someone was willing to pay that kind of money for him—as a coach, a speaker, an endorsement—that it was his worth, what he could bring to the table.

And it was a reinforcement—that he was different, that he wasn't going to stay in nor did he belong in the box that most coaches stayed in and belonged in. But he loved to write down the totals, add them up… and then share!

TAKE A BREAK

SIDNEY LOWE remembers one of V's least favorite signals.

This was the West Virginia game in the Meadowlands, early in the '82–83 season, a really big road win. We had this signal where we'd give V a closed fist if we were so tired that we had to come out of the game. So anyway I'm out of gas and every time I go by the bench I'm giving Coach V the fist letting him know that I'm tired and that I've gotta come out for a rest.

Well the first time by I think that he doesn't see me. So I come by the bench again and give him the closed fist and he ignores me again.

Finally we get a TV time-out and I'm bent over with my hands on my knees and I say, "Coach, the closed fist. I need a rest!"

And he says, "Sidney, the next time you're coming out of a game is when your eligibility is up!"

V DOME

Bruce Poulton, V's chancellor at NC State University after Joab Thomas, differentiates between dreamers and visionaries, remembering V as both.

There are some people who are visionaries—this is different than being a dreamer. We all have times when we sit around and dream. But a visionary is someone who has the creativity to develop a vision and then begin to implement it.

One day I got a call saying that Jim wanted to come see me. When he came in he had this poster board and this big grin on his face. I looked at it and honestly thought it was the complex in the Meadowlands in New Jersey—where Giant Stadium is located. He'd obviously consulted pretty closely with [football coach] Dick Sheridan and what he'd done was taken Carter-Finley Stadium and put the proposed Centennial Center adjacent to it and with this art he showed me how the football program would benefit from a new basketball facility—using the restrooms and the entertainment and share the parking lot.

Now it's called the RBC, and as it turned out it's almost identical to Jim's vision. He had planned a new baseball facility out there and a soccer facility out there. It was a gorgeous facility complex.

The problem was that Jim Goodmon, the president of Capitol Broadcasting, was also interested in creating a complex. But his complex was designed to serve the entire Triangle and Jim Goodmon's idea was to have one that was out near the RDU Airport.

So I said to Jim [Valvano] that it was gorgeous and to locate what we were calling the Centennial Center there made sense, but I said, "I think we need to go over and see Jim Goodmon at Channel 5."

Well, Jim Goodmon's initial reaction was very, very reserved. He understood right off the bat that this would be in direct competition with his idea—which was a very good idea too. But before we left there Jim Goodmon actually came to the position [that] he could support Jim's concept for NC State. He reserved the right to continue with his process but wished us well with ours and he said, "It certainly is something that North Carolina State could use."

Now, every time I go out to what's now called the RBC I remember that day that Jim Valvano came into my office with the artist's conception of this place. And I always wonder how history will ever make us remember that the guy who had the vision for all this was really Jim Valvano.

To my way of thinking they could have done a lot worse than hanging his name on that facility. I know he didn't have the kind of money the way things have worked out with naming rights, but I hope somewhere out there that there will be a plaque or something stating that the original concept and vision for that building was Jimmy Valvano's!

SEINFELD SAVIOR

ED JANKA ran the Nike coaches' events—everything from teaching clinics to the annual wining and dining of the coaches—called the Nike Trip. A big part of this was the hiring of the entertainment and Janka recalls the time that V, one of his talent scouts, endorsed a little-known comic by the name of Seinfeld.

This year we went to Carmel Valley Ranch in Carmel Valley, California. I decided it would be a great idea to get a comedian, someone who was up-and-coming because if you got a known guy like Dangerfield it was going to cost you a ton.

We saw a tape from Johnny Carson. It was Jerry Seinfeld. He seemed pretty funny to me and we liked him, and it looked like the number was right for the budget. But I thought I should ask Jimmy because he was so funny, and he not only loved comedians he really followed them when he was in New York.

So I tell Jimmy we're going to get Jerry Seinfeld and he goes absolutely nuts.

He was ecstatic. "Ed, this guy is great, one of the best young comedians I've seen. Saw him on Carson. I love this guy. You're going to love this guy."

Jerry's going to come in a night early and the plan is to take him to dinner with our wives. We've got four couples at this nice Italian restaurant and we put Jerry at the head of the table, Jimmy and Pam are on his right, and my wife and I are on his left.

So when I tell Jimmy he's having dinner with Jerry Seinfeld, Jimmy goes nuts again, "We're having dinner with him? Great! Beautiful!"

We have this private room and we all sit down and Seinfeld is barely talking, let alone being funny. Nothing. And I can see how disappointed Jimmy is. And I guess that comedians don't think they should be funny all the time. And this particular time he wasn't. So Jimmy just takes over the table. Pretty soon he's got Jerry laughing like crazy.

So now it's the next night, the night of the mini concert. We had about 220 of us in this ballroom, a pretty large room. We had rounds of ten at the tables, and there was this little jazz combo that played... a nice evening. Now it's time for Jerry's act. And Jimmy's really pumped. We're sitting next to each other and he leans over and says, "Ed, this is going to be great!"

So I introduce Seinfeld and he comes out, dark room spotlight on Seinfeld and... Jerry just bombs. He just wasn't funny or he sure wasn't playing with this audience.

Now Jimmy is distraught, really embarrassed because he'd been hitting me with how good Jerry's supposed to be. And the act, it's just kind of laying there.

So Jimmy starts poking me and says, "Ed, come with me, come with me!"

So we go out this side door and he says, "Man, he's bombing!"

I said, "Yeah I noticed, you told me he was going to be great!"

So Jimmy says, "Well we gotta do something, we gotta do something!" The ballroom was pretty big, a lot of open space. So Jimmy says, "Here's the plan. We slip into the back of the room and every time Jerry hits the punch line we start laughing real loud. We'll get the crowd going!"

So that's what we did and it worked. It turned the crowd around and Jerry did about forty-five minutes and... thanks to Jimmy and his back-of-the-room laughs they warmed to Jerry, a guy that we would all come to know as Seinfeld!

HIDING IN THE CORNER

DERECK WHITTENBURG remembers running afoul of V.

Jimmy was known for fouling to win a game. But he always preached, "Don't foul!" when we had a game in hand, up by eight with just minutes to go, no fouls.

So we're playing Michigan State in Reynolds early in the '82-83 season. Now Gannon and I are both in the game; Michigan State has the ball. We're on the other side at the opposite end of the court from our bench. One of their guys starts to drive the basket, maybe Kevin Willis or Sam Vincent, and I foul him.

The whistle blows and Jimmy's jumping up and down because he can't see who fouled. Man, I look down there and Jimmy's ranting and raving, cussing and carrying on.

Now we make eye-contact and he hollers, "Whittenburg, come over here!"

This was my senior year, so I'm one of his leaders on the court and I've just fouled, so I go running over to him, and he says, "What the hell happened? I told them not to foul. Who the hell fouled on that play?"

I looked Jimmy right in the eye and said, "Terry Gannon fouled!"

Now Jimmy goes off, "Send him over here!"

So I go back out and say, "Terry, Coach wants you!"

Man, I looked over my shoulder and all I could see was V going nuts, he's in Terry's face, cussing. Terry's throwing his arms in the air, like what did I do?

We laughed about that one for years, me, Terry, and Jimmy. Terry Gannon, the little sophomore, taking one for the team, covering for senior leadership.

V AND V MOVERS

Commentator and former coach **DICK VITALE** *recalls* The Cosby Show *and one of V's finest nights.*

I guess my favorite story about Jimmy that involved TV was the time that we were on *The Cosby Show.* We appeared as V&V Movers, two moving men. They shot the show in New York and so we flew in for the taping.

You know Jimmy was so funny, when you were around him you just laughed and laughed. I really think he could have been Seinfeld before Seinfeld. And he loved comedians, so being on *The Cosby Show* was a really big deal.

I came into the rehearsals thinking that we'd just do our bit in about an hour or so, pop in and pop out… and be out of there. So when I get there and told him that I thought it would be just a short segment, he's like, "Dick, this is big time, it takes like four days, rehearsals, live audience, taping, and we're doing a big time show here!"

He was right, and it was a lot of fun.

But the big thing for Jimmy was when Bill asked us if we wanted to go to dinner with him. And I didn't really think anything about it so I said that it sounded good but that I'd have to check my schedule.

Oh, baby, when we got back to the hotel room Jimmy grabbed me and said, "Are you crazy? Telling Bill Cosby that you have to check your schedule! This is our shot, this is the funniest man in the world, we are going to dinner with Bill Cosby!"

I said, "But Jimmy, we gotta sound like we're more important than a quick yes!"

So when we met with Bill again, I told him that we'd checked our schedules and that we could go to dinner. Then we go to dinner and that was the night that we both found out what it was like to be with a real celebrity. People were coming up all evening asking to have their pictures taken with Bill. And I'm looking at Jimmy and we're laughing and saying, "Hey, how about us, what are we, chopped liver over here? Don't you want us in the picture?"

And the people are saying, "No, but we'd really appreciate it if you'd take the picture of us with Mr. Cosby."

That night Jimmy [and I] had the time of our lives. And what I remember most about that evening was Bill Cosby, the man that Jimmy called the funniest man in the world, Bill Cosby rolling on the floor laughing at Jim Valvano.

QUOTABLE

HARRY RHOADS, president of the prestigious Washington Speakers Bureau, represented Jim Valvano as a motivational speaker. Rhoads recalls the memorable first meeting his father—Harry "Dusty" Rhoads—had with the coach.

This is my dad's recollection: Jim and I met courtside at Reynolds Coliseum, where he had just finished putting his NC State Wolfpack through practice for the next day's basketball game with UNLV.

This was during the period when he was going through a tough time. So when he came over to say hello to my son Harry, I blurted out, "If you can trust yourself when all men doubt you…" at which point Jim startled me by finishing the sentence with "But make allowance for their doubting, too."

From there the two of us took turns until we reached "And which is more—you'll be a man, my son!" Which was the end of my favorite poem, Kipling's "IF." Jim had carried the lion's share. I knew the poem well. But to my astonishment, he knew it well. He admitted that he was an English major.

On returning home to Virginia, I sent Jim a copy of *One Hundred and One Famous Poems.* I referred him to line six of "Polonius' Advice to Laertes" from *Hamlet*: "Grapple them to thy soul with hoops of steel."

Jim wrote back and said, "I didn't know that Shakespeare was into hoops!"

PRONUNCIATION

LORENZO CHARLES *remembers this great V one-liner as his all-time favorite.*

He used to tell this one and it never failed to make me laugh. It's the one about his trip to the White House after we won the national championship.

When he first met Ronald Reagan, the president leaned over to V and said, "Is it Val-vain-o or Val-van-o?"

And Coach V said, "Valvano!"

Then V said, "Mind if I ask you a question?"

The president said, "No . . . go ahead."

And V said, "Mr. President, is it Regan or Ragan?"

CAMP REFUND

GARY BRYANT also worked Valvano's basketball camps in addition to being team manager. Bryant remembers one of the real camp classics.

V loved Sam Esposito, State's baseball coach, they were really tight. Sam didn't like much other than coaching baseball and shooting the bull with the other coaches. He'd have all the guys come into his office and he'd hold court. The one other thing he liked was being a counselor in V's basketball camps. Sam didn't like many people, so he would only coach the little kids, the first and second graders. He could sit down there and put his feet up on a table and smoke his cigar and just watch them play.

When I was in school, Sam liked me, so he wanted me to be his assistant with the young kids. I'd officiate the games and Sam would be, "Hey you little shit, block out!"

There was this one day that Sam really got V. He didn't mean to, but that's just the way it turned out. Sam, as usual, is sitting there with his feet up on a table watching the kids play, smoking a cigar, and here comes V with a couple of parents. V's got sort of a funny look, and he says, for the parents' benefit, "Coach Esposito, this is Mr. and Mrs. Blankenship. Their two boys are in your group, Johnny and Joey, and the boys don't think you like them."

Now I guess V thought Sam was going to pop up and kiss up to the parents. But Sam just took another puff on his cigar and said, "Listen, Mr. and Mrs. Blankenship (or whatever their names were), I'm sure that Johnny and Joey are right on this one. I've got two kids at home and I have a hard enough time liking them, much less your kids!"

So now V is just standing there, speechless. He's looking at Sam to see if he's going to laugh or something. Sam just keeps smoking and watching the kids play.

Then V finally says, "Well, okay then folks, how about a refund on Johnny and Joey! Would a refund work?"

HEY, MOM

JOYCE ASCHENBRENNER, now in marketing with the Jimmy V Foundation, is a person who knows the value of national TV attention. She learned it first from V.

I was an assistant athletic director at UNLV when Jim Valvano brought his Wolfpack to play in Las Vegas. It was a nationally televised game at our Thomas & Mack Center, home of the UNLV Runnin' Rebels and Coach Jerry Tarkanian.

My job for this game was to operate the "producer phone." I sat at courtside with a television monitor, wore headphones with a microphone, and talked to the production truck. During the game the producer might ask me a question about something going on in the arena. When he needed the game to stop for a television commercial, I would signal the official and he'd stop the game at the next dead ball and we'd go to a "TV time-out."

Thomas & Mack was a tough place to play. It was Tark's house. The crowd knew it. Opponents knew it. And the opposing coaches always insinuated that the game officials knew it (although there were many times that Coach Tarkanian would beg to differ!).

Jim Valvano was not one to back down from this challenge.

He worked the officials the entire game. He stomped up and down the sideline. He screamed, he yelled, he pleaded. He jumped up from his seat, he plopped down in disgust. Every time a whistle blew, Coach V was up and yelling. Tark would slowly shuffle the sidelines with his hands in his pockets and his head down, as most of the calls pretty much went his way.

A whistle blew and the Runnin' Rebels marched back to the free throw line to attempt more free throws. V was vocal. V was livid. V was all over the place.

Second half. More of the same. Coach V was now running and screaming all the way past half court. The official glared back at him, and then went back to setting up more Rebel free throws. I looked down at my score sheet to record the foul.

Suddenly I looked up. Coach Valvano was sitting on the press table next to my monitor! With all attention focused at the other end of the court, Coach V was now leaning over like we're going to have a casual conversation!

It lasted only about thirty seconds and went something like this:

V: What are you doin' here?

ME: (stunned) Ah... workin'?

V: Who you talking to through that headset, the truck?

ME: (still stunned because now a few people are looking at us) Ah...Yeah?

DIRECTOR: (in the truck; I can hear this through my headset) Camera three... What the hell is Valvano doing?

V: (to me) You talking to the producer through that thing?

ME: Ah, yeah....

PRODUCER: (to me into my earpiece) What's going on out there?

V: They know I'm talkin' to you?

ME: Yeah, I think so....

DIRECTOR: (in background) Somebody tell me what the hell is going on....

V: They want to know what we're talking about?

ME: Kinda....

PRODUCER: (in my headset) What's he saying? What's he saying?

TELEVISION COMMENTATORS: (which I hear faintly through my headset) It appears that Coach Valvano has taken issue with something at the scorer's table....

V: (still talking to me) Your mom watching at home?

ME: Probably....

V: Where's that?

ME: Ah... Pittsburgh?

V: Grow up there?

ME: Uh... yeah....

V: Nice place to grow up?

Now, one of the officials walks over to the table.

OFFICIAL: Coach, what's the problem here?

PRODUCER: (in my ear) What in the hell is going on out there?

V: They going nuts in the truck?

ME: Oh, yeah....

OFFICIAL: (who is now standing in front of us) What do you need here, Coach?

V: (now getting off table) Not a thing... not a thing....

OFFICIAL: Well then, get back to your bench.

V: (bending down to me, like we've got a secret) Just wanted to make sure your mother back in Pittsburgh got to see you on national television.

Rebels won by six. My mother became a big Jimmy V fan.

ℂV

FIGHT TO THE FINISH

There hasn't been an announcer in the history of the ACC who didn't refer to the conference as a hard-fought league. BOBBY CREMINS, then the Georgia Tech coach, recalls a night when the fighting just refused to stop.

There was a roast for me to kick off a camp for disabled kids in Georgia called Camp Twin Lakes. My job was to get the speakers. So I asked Mike Krzyzewski; my college coach, Frank McGuire; John Sally; and Jimmy to be on the dais. The headliners were Mike and Jimmy. This was after he'd left NC State but Jimmy was really gracious and said he'd do it. I think he was doing a TV show at Disney at the time and so he flew in from Orlando, Florida. I should have known that this was going to be one of those nights. I sent this guy out to meet Jimmy at the airport on the MARTA, our subway [in Atlanta]. And the guy gets excited and gets off at the wrong stop and finally finds Jimmy at the C concourse, almost an hour later. On the trip downtown it's really late and he's lost and the guy's embarrassed and doesn't know where to get off to get back to the hotel but he doesn't want to admit that to Jimmy. So the two of them rode the train forever.

Before the roast I had my own suite, so I'd had a long cocktail hour. I was really nervous that my speakers weren't going to get there and the later it got I was especially nervous that Jimmy wasn't going to make it. So we were really getting into the wine. Then he got there and I was so glad. Now we really started getting into the wine and by the time for the charity roast we were just lit.

This was a time in his life when Jimmy was really loose. This was after he'd left NC State and at this roast he did exactly what we wanted him to do–which was what he always did–he just took over, put on an absolute show. He was fabulous, the audience loved him, and the roast went really great.

So afterwards we went up to my suite with about forty people and stayed until the hotel security kicked us out, told us we had to leave. Now I decided that it would be a good idea to take them to a hangout called Johnny's Hideaway in Atlanta. Bobby Carver, one of my former teammates at South Carolina, was with me. And we got someone who was sober to drive and Bobby and Jimmy and I went in my car. On the ride over to the Hideaway I was explaining to Jimmy that Bobby and I had played for Jack Curran at Malloy High School in New York City.

Jimmy, he's lit, and he's saying, "Oh, Curran isn't that great a coach!"

Now Carver and I loved Jack Curran. So Carver gets mad and he starts defending Coach Curran.

Anyone who remembers our team at South Carolina knows that Bobby, a New York kid, has a temper and was a real fighter. Well Bobby comes over the back seat after Jimmy and they start going at it in the car.

I say, "Relax, Bobby, Jimmy's just drunk and he doesn't even know what we're talking about."

Now I think they're calmed down. Then we get to Johnny's Hideaway and they get out of the car and Jimmy mouths off again. Bobby says something and pretty soon they're swinging at each other. I jumped in between them and got them broken up and we start into Johnny's. Just as the door opened Jimmy says something and here they go again, swinging at each other.

Now the bouncer at Johnny's sees this and for all the laughs that Jimmy had gotten earlier, the bouncer at Johnny's Hideaway comes up with the best line of the night.

He said, "You know, I've seen a lot of people fight their way out of this place but this is the first time I ever saw anybody fight their way in."

𝒱

RECRUITING BY GEORGE

In this memory of one of his interviews from ESPN's Up Close, **ROY**
FIRESTONE's *questions led V to discuss the temptations and challenges of*
college recruiting.

V: You know it's hard. Let's say I'm recruiting you and I'm in your
home and I ask what you're interested in. And you say anthropology.
And I say, "Anthropology. We have the best anthropology program in the
country. I just played handball with the chairman of the department."
And that's what it's become, because you're selling all the time.

FIRESTONE: Tell me what you really feel about the game. If you could strip
away the wins and losses. Tell me about what you're selling that makes
you feel proud of your sales.

V: You know, I'm going to tell you a story about Lester George at Iona
College. He was from Brooklyn and he had a freshman year that was
horrible. Should he have come to school? Should he have been playing
basketball?

[Firestone: Now I still get goose bumps when I tell this one, because
I can still hear him saying it; Jimmy was in his red warm-up suit on the
show and his hair was long and he looked like Ratso Ricco with sneakers. His voice was raspy.]

V: Lester was a beautiful kid, Lester wanted an education very badly,
Lester should have had that opportunity, sports helped him get that op-
portunity, and now it's the end of his second year and there's this knock
at my door and it's Lester, and he said, "I just want to tell you, Coach,
Lester George is going to become a junior!"

He not only made it, he now works for IBM in Manhattan [at the
time]. Are you telling me he shouldn't have had that chance? We have to
be honest about the role that sports play in our society—everybody wants
to talk about how it's not important, but do you know what? Maybe it's
not, but at the same time take a look around at the sports pages, this
show, and the NCAA tournament and an awful lot of people pay atten-
tion to it. But let's not be hypocritical. The fact is that colleges around the
country do accept student-athletes who are somewhat below the stan-
dards. [Firestone: And Jimmy had his share.] But the obligation of that

school is to make sure that if accepted they have the opportunity. The sin is when the coaches put basketball before the kids' education. We don't do it and the majority of them don't do it. The challenge is this: we should be looking for all the Lester Georges in the world.

HEART TO HEART

*V was criticized for his lack of attention to academics. Many players, like **THURL BAILEY**, tell another side of that story.*

My most memorable moments were when I was with Coach Valvano in one-on-one situations. I always knew that he was a visionary, and as a coach he made you feel like that he was more than a coach. As a young man in college you go through some tough situations and it was nice to have him there for you, not just as a coach but as a brother figure or father figure. You needed to remember what he told you and to hold on to it and take it seriously because it meant something.

My story along these lines involves a day when I had skipped a class and he found out about it. He called me into his office and he sat me down. Now he didn't start in on me about cutting that class. He asked me how I was doing, how everything was going, about school. Then he asked me, "What do you want your future to be like?"

We started talking about my interests in music, TV, and radio. We talked about the NBA.

Then he said, "The one thing that you don't want to do in this life, regardless of whatever you do, you don't want to be looked at as an idiot."

Then he got into the class thing. He told me that he knew I'd missed class that day. He said that he wasn't going to yell at me and he wasn't going to get into why I'd missed that class or what my reasons were. Then he said, "I just want to tell you that you are a very bright individual and you have a great future ahead of you! Take advantage of it."

That was it and I left there with a positive [feeling] that obviously I've never forgotten.

𝒱

BREATHALYZER EQUALIZER

One of V's all-time favorite players was CHRIS CORCHIANI. *He was talented, tough, and would do anything his coach asked to help the Wolpack win—even go inside on defense and play the big guys.*

Coach Valvano wasn't afraid to try anything. He specialized in the triangle and two and the box and one defenses. A real risk taker. One of his big things was that he didn't want the best player on the other team to beat us. And on the college level, if you think about it, there aren't enough coaches who do that. Because realistically there are only a couple of players on a team that can beat you. There are certain players on the court that don't really want to score—like point guards.

My job was to pass the ball. Some point guards can score, but it's just not what they want to do. He used to joke with Rodney [Monroe], saying, "Rodney, you wouldn't get a shot if I was coaching against you. I'd make Chris shoot because he can't do it."

When you'd get into a game that was when he really turned it on. For forty minutes I don't think there was a better basketball coach— change defenses, take advantages of mismatches, get players in and out of the game at the right time—I think that during a game he could hardly wait to see what he'd come up with, that's how confident he was on the bench.

In '88 we've got Georgia Tech in Reynolds and Tommy Hammonds, who goes about 6'8" or 6'9", is just wearing us out. V calls time-out. When he'd ask a question he was like an attorney in a court of law—he already had the answer. So he starts out, "Is everybody scared of Hammonds? Can anybody guard Hammonds?"

Nobody says anything and then all of a sudden Coach says, "Chris, get your little ass out there on him! Just bother the hell out of him. Hit him, block him, do whatever you have to do, just stop his ass."

So I go out there and I'm all over him, setting up in front of him, trying to draw charges, throwing him down with me. He starts getting really frustrated. We won, like 82–68, and Hammonds had gotten a couple of fouls and it had really thrown off his game.

What I remember best about that was, after the game, V saying, "See it isn't all about size—it's heart and guts."

But over in the other locker room Hammonds had another opinion. When they asked him about me guarding him he said, "The worst part was Corchiani's breath!"

PURELY ACADEMIC

Perception being reality, there was very much a dichotomy at work with V's image as it related to academics. CHARLIE BRYANT *remembers a night in Greenville, NC, when a question from the audience hit a nerve.*

In '83, after we'd won the national championship, we traveled around the state and of course, everyone wanted to hear Jim speak–capacity crowds, standing room only.

One evening we were at the Greenville Country Club and the place was jam-packed. This was a very jovial meeting, and Jim spoke and gave them the usual great speech, had them laughing and rolling in the aisles. When he finished his speech, which lasted about forty-five minutes, one of our Wolfpackers in the back, who was somewhat inebriated, said, "Jim, tell us how many of your kids you're graduating!"

Well, the place got kind of quiet. I guess I was expecting a one-liner from Jim because it was such a wise guy comment. That's when Jim really surprised me and everyone else in that packed room.

He said, very seriously, "Obviously that's very important to you!" And the guy said, "Yeah, it is!"

So for the next fifteen minutes–you could have heard a pin drop–we listened to one of the most intelligent commentaries on college athletics and how it relates to the importance of academics, how the two are woven together, how the two both conflict and mesh. It was a talk that every sports fan and every academician should have heard.

I must have heard that man speak 300 times but never better than in that fifteen minutes–off the cuff and from the heart. He quoted educators, writers, philosophers. He talked about the importance of education in his home and reminded the group that his father, Rocco, was a school teacher, and in his house education was the number one priority. I don't know how the guy in the back felt, but I know how the crowd reacted, because they gave Jim another standing ovation.

As we walked across the parking lot I remember wishing that guy could have been on some of the bus trips I'd been on with Jim's team. Because it was incredible. What other coach, on the way to a game, actually held classes? I'd seen him teach them to diagram sentences, read poetry, quote writers and poets, then give pop quizzes as to who he was quoting and the meaning. He'd form teams and hold debates over political issues. I know that didn't go with the image, but that was the real Jim Valvano.

When we got in the car the first thing I said was, "Where do you think that guy was coming from?"

Jim said, "I don't know, but I get damned tired of people thinking that people associated with athletics are some dumb jocks. I was speaking for a lot of people in athletics back there. My family believed in academics. We may not all be blessed with the same intellect but we all, including athletes, have the same academic opportunities. And there's never been a day when I didn't encourage my players to act on those opportunities."

TIE BREAKER!

Former UNLV coach JERRY TARKANIAN *remembers a V moment involving the Runnin' (fighting) Rebels of Las Vegas.*

Here's one of my favorites. Jimmy came to play us in Vegas. In the game right before we played NC State, my kid Moses Scurry got suspended for punching the other team's coach. It was a free-for-all after the game.

In the locker room when the press asked Moses why he'd hit a coach, he said, and this got into the papers, "Man, I didn't know it was a coach. The guy was wearing a sweater. If he'd a had a tie on, I'd have never swung at him. Coaches are supposed to wear a tie."

So now we're playing NC State the next game in Vegas and Moses is suspended, sitting in street clothes behind our bench. So Jimmy comes up to him before the game and says, "Moses, when the fight breaks out today I want you to know that I'm the coach for NC State. Look, see the tie, I can prove it!"

MINNIE PEARL

PAM VALVANO remembers (almost) getting dressed down for dressing V for Letterman.

Here's one that Jimmy never let me forget. He wasn't into buying clothes, and so I pretty much dressed him, did his hair, got him ready for his public appearances. So when he went into make-up for *The David Letterman Show*, the person who did the make-up on the show said, "Did your wife dress you?"

Jimmy said, "Yeah, why?"

And he said, "Because you still have the tag on your new coat!"

Oh boy, he never let that one go. I sent him to *The David Letterman Show* looking like Minnie Pearl!

THE DAY THE CHEERING STOPPED

DERECK WHITTENBURG remembers living one of V's messages

Jimmy always talked to us about preparing for the day the cheering stopped. The one thing about college basketball, it's always been a crock. They use academics to fire you but never to hire you.

This year at Wagner College my team went to the NCAA tournament but we've been doing great academically ever since I've been here. We've had a 2.7 GPA for the four years, and six guys on the dean's list. Plus we had an academic All-America, and this is the entire country and we're small Wagner College. But they only talked about our academics this year, and that was because we won.

What I've instilled in our program here are the things that Jimmy taught me. He always told me that I had to have my degree because there would be a day when the cheering stopped, that I'd just be another guy out there competing for a job.

Now that always sounded good but then it became a reality. I had that great game in '83 against Virginia where I got 27 points in the first half. Then, in the second half, I broke my foot. Well, I came back to Reynolds Coliseum maybe two or three days later and I'm on crutches. The guy at the back door where the players came in didn't recognize me. He asked me for my ticket. Asked me for my ticket! You talk about an eye-opener.

The next day I went to Jimmy's office and I said, "You were so right. Now I know what you meant about the day the cheering stops!"

That helped drive me to hang in there and get my degree. For that I can thank Jimmy Valvano.

𝒱

WAKE UP CALL

LORENZO CHARLES, the quiet force on the NC State '83 Championship team whose dunk was heard round the world, recalls the play and V's pre- and post-dunk comments.

The funny thing was that I had been playing pretty well throughout the whole post season. I was averaging about thirteen or fourteen points from the ACC tournament right into the NCAAs and into the Final Four. But that last game against Houston I really kind of disappeared. I was a back-to-the-basket inside player, that's where I did my damage. I wasn't having a good game offensively because I was where Olajuwon was, and every time I got the ball, there was Akeem. I remember the last thing that Coach said to me in the huddle before we went out there for that final sequence [was], "Lorenzo, you haven't been yourself tonight, I wish you would wake up."

Everything I tried Olajuwon was there, and he either blocked it or altered my shot. Now on that last play I was busy trying to get away from him; I'd actually gone across the end line and come back in bounds. I really didn't even know that Dereck was at the top of the key. When I wrestled away from Akeem I saw the ball in the air and knew it wasn't going to make it to the basket. The reason Akeem didn't jump was because he wasn't sure whether the ball was going to hit the rim. He was probably thinking don't touch it because of goaltending. I know that Thurl, Olajuwon, and I were the only players in the paint. He left me a little bit, so I went out of bounds and came back in. I think maybe he was afraid that Dereck was going to make a move to the basket and that he wanted to block that. And another thing, I'd been so insignificant in that game that if I was Akeem I'd have left me alone too. I think I was like one for seven. If it had been Thurl Bailey he would have never left him. But maybe because it was me he wasn't too worried. I could see the ball was going to fall short, and my real concern was whether there was enough time left on the clock. It was so loud in there you couldn't hear the buzzer. But after I put the ball through the basket I actually watched two seconds tick off the clock.

Had Houston been on top of it they could have called a time-out and gotten the ball to half-court. That team could have done something with two seconds left—two seconds is a long time with the athletes that they had. So before that play, I really hadn't done much that night.

In that last huddle when V said, "I wish you would wake up!" I said to myself, "Yeah, yeah!" because I'm thinking about Olajuwon, of course. I didn't know what I was about to do.

And [as] V was out there running around that court, when he got to me he took me by the shoulders and said, "Lo, you did it. You woke up!"

WHEELER DEALER

Administrative Assistant FRANCES LEWIS and V had some moments over the years, but none would top the day that V was too big a deal to share the details of his latest mega transaction.

The one time that I really got Jim Valvano was a classic. Jim was the consummate businessman... always ahead of everyone else... you just couldn't get ahead of him. He was very proud of his business acumen. He always left his door open and we'd listen in on each other's conversations.

So one day he was in there at his desk and Frank Weedon was with him, and they were cooking up a big real estate deal. They had this big map and they were talking about this property that Jim wanted to buy. Wheelers and dealers! Jim was going to build on or develop this piece of property in West Cary.

So I wandered in and I said, "Jim, can I look at the map?"

Of course, he just dismissed me. "Frances, you don't know anything about this. This is high finance!"

So I leaned in and looked at the map and I spotted the property that they needed to make the deal work. I said, "Jim, what does that say on that tract of land right there? It says Lewis! How about that tract right there? What does it say? Lewis! And that one over there. I believe it says, Lewis! Now what is your secretary's name? My name is Lewis!"

I owned all the land that he needed to swing the deal! It was about 125 acres.

Well, he jumped up out of his chair and he fell down on the floor and started kicking and carrying on, "My secretary's a millionaire, my secretary's a millionaire!"

And it didn't stop there. From that day on he'd go to the Wolfpack Club and alumni meetings and he'd say, "Oh, I see my secretary Frances is with us tonight. Folks, you know she doesn't have to work, owns half of Cary, the only reason she works is because she likes me! She's a millionaire."

GREEN CARD

GEORGE TARANTINI, NC State's soccer coach and a friend of Valvano, was a citizen of Argentina until the night he got green carded on V's radio show.

I remember going to WPTF, the radio station when Jimmy was doing his show. While he would do his coach's show I would sit in the corner and wait and then we'd go out and eat and have a drink. And oh he loved to eat, to drink, he loved life. Now on his show he would never have anything prepared, he was such a brilliant guy.

One day I'm sitting there while he's on the air and all of a sudden he says, "I would like you to know that we have an illegal immigrant at NC State University coaching soccer. This man has no papers and he's taking a job from an American citizen. I want all NC State fans to know that your soccer coach is not a citizen!"

So I looked at him when they go to a commercial and I say, "You don't say that, how can you do that?"

And he looks at me and says, "How can you be a coach at NC State and not be a citizen? We can't have that."

So here's what happened. When we came into the Athletic Department in the morning a lot of the coaches used to all look forward to meeting with Jimmy. He would always have a topic. It could be economics, politics, poetry. But now the topic is George is not a citizen! So he decides that he will dedicate this time to helping me become a citizen.

So I say, "How are you going to help me become a citizen?" And that's when he started to teach me about America.

He said, "We are going to get a book and then we will learn about the United States of America."

For four or five months every single day—the Constitution, about Congress, the Senate, the judicial system. He took me to his office and to his house and he just put me in school.

Now here was my faculty: Jim Valvano and Sam Esposito. Can you imagine those two teaching me to become a citizen? But they did. I had to learn the Pledge of Allegiance. Then one day I rode to Charlotte and took the test and passed.

Now I'm a citizen of the United States of America thanks to Jim Valvano.

MAN OF LETTERS

ART KAMINSKY, V's agent, thinks like an attorney with good reason. He is. And he cites here three letters that said a lot about Jim Valvano—exhibits A, B, and C.

One of my favorites about Jim is the story of the three letters. This is so telling. Three of the most unique letters I've ever seen. One was from Rick Hartzell, the referee who made the horrible travel call on Corchiani in the Georgetown game—Eastern Regionals in the Meadowlands—that knocked State out of the NCAA tournament [in 1989]. How many referees who make horrible calls ever write coaches letters of apology? Probably one, this one! It was a terrible call, it cost them the game. It is exactly something that a referee should apologize for and this one did.

The second was the letter from John Wooden. After Jim won the national championship, John Wooden wrote saying that it was one of the greatest coaching jobs he'd ever seen in the NCAA tournament. Of course this came from the greatest college coach ever.

And then, after all the NCAA investigations were over, Dave Didion wrote one of the most extraordinary letters I've ever seen. Here was V, a guy who had been libeled and had been dragged from pillar to post. And the facts were that the guy ran one of the cleanest programs in the country. And here comes this amazing letter from the guy who was the NCAA's chief investigator. If anyone should have been out to get Jim, take a pejorative negative view, it was Didion. But instead he wrote to Jim and said what a terrific person Jim was and told him if he had a son he'd love to have him play for Jim.

These were very special letters and they said more than congratulations, they said almost everything anyone needs to know about Jim Valvano.

RUN AROUND SUE

Tony Kornheiser, Washington Post columnist, host of the radio program The Tony Kornheiser Show, *and co-host of ESPN's blockbuster hit* Pardon The Interruption, *recalls treasured moments of "interruption" with his Long Island friend Jimmy V.*

I knew Jimmy all the way back to Iona. He went to Seaford [High School], which was two towns over from me. And when Jimmy was coaching at Iona, I did a story on him for *Street and Smith Magazine.* He is the single funniest stand-around guy I've ever met and that includes all the comedians I've met.

I remember at Iona early one season, I went up to do a story on him for *The New York Times.* This was when he'd recruited Glenn Vickers and Jeff Ruland and players like that who eventually beat Louisville—the number one team—in [Madison Square] Garden. So early that season I went up to do the story and I stayed at the house.

Well, we ended up at a place called Joey Defunzo's Railroad Lounge in Yonkers. And Jimmy and I were there until about 4:00 in the morning, and the vision I have of the end of that night says it all about Jimmy. He organized a conga line of about sixteen people all with our hands on each other's shoulders and he had us dancing around the Railroad Lounge singing *Run Around Sue*.

I don't remember the rest, but I assume that Defunzo threw us out! I ended up sleeping at Jimmy's house and waking up wondering, "What on earth happened last night!" But also I remember thinking at that point that if I had been good enough to play at that level that I'd have loved to have played basketball for Jimmy Valvano. Fortunately for him I wasn't good enough so he never had to make the choice not to recruit me.

When I worked at the *Times* in the mid-70s Jimmy was at Iona, [and] Mike Krzyzewski was at Army, and they used to come in once a week for these basketball luncheons at Momma Leone's. And [former coach] Louie Carnesecca at St. John's was the big dog in town. Momma Leone's is now out of business, but at the time it was a highly reputed Italian restaurant. Now Louie used to always come in and order scrambled eggs. And Jimmy would look at me and say, "Tony, if an Italian is not ordering Italian food at Momma Leone's do not eat this food!"

But again, the single funniest stand-around guy I ever met. But also unbelievably underrated as a basketball coach because a lot of people just thought he was funny. There were many occasions where we would talk about upcoming games and he would tell me how the game was going to go and how it was going to come down to a particular play. And it always did. He didn't always win but he knew the game and how it would play out.

Like everyone else, I liked him very much and I was proud that he was a Long Island boy. I wrote a column the day he died and you know, we knew he was going to die. But with death, it may not be a surprise but it's always a shock. And of course, with the loss of a life like his it was... well [after writing that column] I was weeping in the car all the way home.

A MATTER OF INTERPRETATION

No one could outtalk V, even in a country like Italy where he didn't speak the language. Former Villanova coach ROLLIE MASSAMINO remembers.

We went together to Italy and we spoke at this conference. I think [Lou] Carnesecca arranged it, and he brought St. John's to play on one of those tours, and the three of us–Louie, me, and Jimmy–stayed at the same villa in Florence and then we went to Rome for three or four days.

Anyway, CBS was following us, and the clinic was in Florence, and there were a thousand people there from all over the world. And between the three of us we were debating as to who would speak Italian, for directions, just to communicate. Of course, Jimmy voted for himself but I said, "No, let me speak Italian and here's why: because I know how to speak Italian!"

So we're laughing about this and of course, because I was our interpreter, he tells everybody, "I'll tell you how good Rollie's Italian is. He asked for a taxi and they brought us two umbrellas!"

SMART START

It didn't take someone as cagey as former Maryland coach LEFTY DRIESELL long to figure out that the new coach at NC State was in the right line when they handed out the smarts.

I realized at that first ACC meeting just how smart Jimmy was. The rest of us would team up on [former UNC coach] Dean [Smith], try to vote him down. But Jimmy wasn't joining in.

I remember him saying, "Hey, I'm Dean's neighbor. I'm going to be Dean's friend."

I thought it was a smart thing for him to say because we couldn't beat Dean anyway.

Another thing he said, which was meant to be funny, [was], "I may not be able to beat Dean but I'll just outlive him." He said it in jest, of course, and he may have only lived to be forty-seven, but it was like he lived 107 years. He was just that kind of a guy, always upbeat, having fun, and just a super guy to be around.

One of the things that made him such a good coach is that he would always come up with little trick defenses to beat you. One year he had Spud Webb–what, 5'6"?–jumping center. He was always doing wild things like that–he had Corchiani guarding the big man Hammonds from Georgia Tech–just to frustrate them. Always unorthodox. That's one of the things that I liked about him; he wasn't just old school, wasn't going to play you just man to man or straight up zone. He was going to look at a situation and adapt and might just throw anything at you—very tough to prepare for.

I remember the one time we played Jim a diamond and two. Most people just didn't know how to attack that, some would run a zone offense and some play it like they were up against a man to man. But not Jimmy. He just took two of his guys and stuck them out in the corner and played us three on three the whole game.

I thought, man, this guy is different. I had to take two of my guys and put them out there in the corners with his guys. So here we were playing three on three. And I don't remember for sure but I think his three beat my three guys that game. If I'm not mistaken that was '83, the year that he came up with a lot of other great moves and won the national championship.

WHO THE HELL IS JIM VALVANO!

FRANK WEEDON, NC State's senior associate athletic director, remembers V's incredible celebrity.

This was after a holiday tournament and we were checking our luggage, leaving Honolulu, Hawaii.

A guy spotted Jim and said to me, "Do you think he'd sign an autograph?"

I said, "Sure." So I watched him go up to Jim who, affable as usual, was making conversation while he signed. When the guy got the autograph he walked back by me and was looking at it, shaking his head.

"Who the hell is Jim Valvano?" he said.

I said, "Why, he's the coach of the NC State Wolfpack; they won the national basketball championship."

"Hell, I thought it was Al Pacino," he said.

Boy, I could hardly wait to get on the plane and share that with Jim.

STREET FIGHT

Bob Lloyd recalls a "Rocky" night on a Philadelphia street for the "other guard."

Right after Jimmy and I had come home from basic training in the Air Force, Jimmy was staying with me. One of my best friends was getting married and I was best man in the wedding. So Jimmy goes into Philadelphia with me to the bachelor party.

Now, before we left basic they had just shaved our heads, so we were interesting looking to say the least. We go to the bachelor party in Philly and afterwards we're pretty loaded, walking down the street in the middle of the night. Jimmy walks into this guy by mistake.

Well, the guy pulls a knife on Jimmy. And he has the knife about six inches from Jimmy's throat and I'm really scared. I'm like circling around behind the guy trying to decide what to do.

And Jimmy looks at the guy and puts his finger up and says, "You see this hair? I just got back from Vietnam. I killed people with my bare hands over there. You have exactly five seconds to put that knife away or I'il kill you."

The guy puts the knife away and backs away, and when he turns his back, just as I'm heaving a sigh of relief, Jimmy shouts, "Hey, I just saved your life, buddy!"

NATION BUILDER

LeeAnn, V's youngest daughter, remembers her dad's all out enthusiasm for learning and... building a better country.

He would come to my school and read and when he did he was like a celebrity, even to me. But I just loved him like my dad. But after he left NC State, when he was between jobs, he would take me to school every morning. That was so special because he hadn't been around much because he'd been coaching. I was in the fourth grade and we'd listen and sing along with Frank Sinatra on the way to school. Then there was this project, a gifted class project. The assignment was to create a country. Maybe most parents would have kind of helped, maybe take pictures or go get clay. But not Daddy. He made everything an adventure and did everything a hundred and ten percent. Boy, he really got into this project.

We named our country after my grandpa, Rocco, and we called it ROCCOCO! This was my favorite project ever; I still have it. We made it an island off Italy. We wrote a national anthem, had a president, set up a whole government. We created the national food of ROCCOCO, which was the ROCCO noodle. We made the money, and the lire were called Angelinas, after my grandma. We would count the money, "One Angelina, two Angelina!"

He just was into things like that so much, made it so fun and was so creative. One of our big jokes was–this was something that we all learned–whenever you wanted to ask a question for your homework, if you went to Mom, you'd get the answer. But if you went to Dad, you'd be sitting in there for an hour because he'd not only tell you what the answer was, he'd give you all the facts about it, the history. He'd interpret what it meant, he'd get a poem out and read it to you and show you how it related to the question, or how the poem or a famous quote could help you put your point across. He was just so committed to everything, every moment. To him even a fourth grade project was huge.

HANGING ON TO V'S COATTAILS

JIM REHBOCK, the Wolfpack trainer, was a man with a unique and challenging job–keeping Jim Valvano in his place. A new NCAA rule required coaches to stay in a prescribed area of the bench, called the coach's box. Rehbock remembers trying to keep V from "crossing the line" and tells the story behind one of the most historic photos in NC State history.

The coach's box came in the mid-1980s, maybe '85 or '86. Every year they'd come and explain the rule changes–maybe Fred Barakat, the head of ACC officials, would explain the new rules to the players. One year it was hand checking and then in this particular year it was the coach's box.

What the refs were trying to do was have the bench have a little bit more decorum. And limit the celebrations. One of the big problems that they'd been having was that these coaches could run out all the way to mid-court, chasing down a referee, and so they were running into problems with coaches slamming their fists down on scoring tables, and they wanted to stop that behavior.

There was a hash mark for the five-second rule, and if you went across that hash mark they started the five-second count on the offense. So they had a line that you couldn't cross, and the players and coaches had to stay in that area or box or [they'd] pick up a technical. The way that bench was set up for us, my seat was right next to that hash mark. Of course Jimmy put a funny spin on this and called this the Italian Coach Rule; he said, "They put this rule in just for Italian coaches. We are a very active race."

Jim very rarely got technicals, which amazes people. But now I had a new job. He told me, "I don't care how you do it but your job—other than being our trainer and keeping up with time-outs and TV time-outs—is to keep me in the box." He said, "I don't want any techs this year. So you keep me in that coach's box."

Of course he would get really mad when I did it because I'd stick my arm out to keep him back. So we're playing Maryland at Reynolds Coliseum. V is trying to get Vinny Del Negro to get out of the lane and come back. He wanted him on the defensive end. Vinny couldn't hear him and V's screaming at Vinny. Then he turns to scream something at our bench and when he did I thought he was going to finally sit down. But all of a sudden he turns and just bolts past me. And all I could do was grab his shirt and coattail. Simon Griffiths was the photographer, and he got this great shot of me—all you see is my back and Jimmy coaching, with me holding on to his coattail. He was on me about that one forever, but it saved him a technical.

FRIENDLY WAR

Former Wake Forest coach **BOB STAAK** *recalls V and the series of NC State–Wake Forest games that ended for Staak in what might be best described as a "wake."*

This was my last regular season game coaching at Wake Forest. It was Senior Day and we were playing in Greensboro. It was a four-overtime game! We had so many games like that with NC State. I think the year before we lost in double-overtime in the ACC tournament to Jimmy. Then there was the one where Del Negro beat us at the buzzer. Another one when we held the ball and lost by one at Greensboro, bizarre crap like that.

But this is the last game of the season my last year there and we have the game won. Muggsy [Bogues] makes two free throws and we're up like three. Then we foul and Kelsey Weems goes to the line and he can't shoot fouls worth a crap. He miraculously makes the first one.

So I put in Sam Ivy and so now we've got all big guys in there and I tell them, "The guy next to you, just keep him away from the basket, that's all you have to do!"

And Rodney Monroe was right next to Sam Ivy. So Weems missed the shot so bad that when Ivy stepped into the lane to block, Rodney Monroe is on the right side and he goes around the back, catches the ball on the baseline, and throws it in to tie the score. We go four overtimes and Dick Stewart, who coached me my junior year at UConn before Jim got there, well Dick's sitting on the NC State bench as one of Jimmy's assistants. Now, I didn't have a whole lot of players and we're in the third overtime.

And Jim would look at Stew and say, "Did Bob substitute?"

Dick, "No!"

Then Jim would say, "Well then I'm not substituting!"

Next time-out, "Did Bob substitute?"

Dick "No!"

Jim, "Then I'm not substituting!"

Jimmy wasn't going to make a move unless I made a move, that's the way he was. Well hell, it ended like 110–103 in four overtimes.

They told me later Jimmy kept asking Stew every time about me substituting. I don't even know what he was up to, there was no telling. But after it was over, and again that was my last game at Wake Forest, I went out to their bus and he was sitting there drenched in sweat. I was drenched. I remember he was there with his elbows on his knees and I sat next to him and both of us were physically and emotionally spent.

Then at the same time—two great friends—we just looked at each other and said, "What a game that was!"

LAST SHOT AT DEAN!

JAY JENNINGS, a WRAL-TV cameraman, recalls the insider's tip from V that led to capturing one the most memorable moments in the history of the University of North Carolina's Carmichael Auditorium.

On a Wednesday at a practice in Reynolds Coliseum before NC State played Carolina–in what would be the last game at historic Carmichael Auditorium in Chapel Hill–V came up to me and in that V rasp of his, he said, "Hey, Saturday at Carmichael when the game's over, no matter who wins, follow me!"

I tried to get him to tell me what he had in mind but he said, "Just be there. You'll get the shot of the day!"

Now fast-forward to Saturday at Carmichael and an NC State loss. Not really a close game, so Carolina closed Carmichael in style. When the horn blows and the fans are storming the court all the other cameras run to the Carolina celebration. But I'm looking right at V. And I still didn't know what he was doing.

Suddenly he grabs a basketball and heads to the other end of the court. Now I'm right behind him. All of a sudden, just as he gets to the basket he takes this little dribble and hop and makes a lay up.

He turns right into the camera and says, "Last basket scored in Carmichael Auditorium... Jim Valvano!"

SCREAMINGLY FUNNY

BILL FOSTER (not V's college coach), who coached Clemson when V first came to the ACC, recalls his screamingly funny introduction.

I met first met Jimmy in the spring of 1980 at ACC meetings. I really liked him, he was such a breath of fresh air, so smart, funny, and great for the league.

The first time he came down to Clemson to play us was the following season and I dropped by his shoot-around and just made a casual remark, inviting him to come by our house that evening. I lived way out at the lake so I just gave him my phone number, saying that there wasn't much to do in Clemson and that when he got to his room after dinner, I'd come pick him up. I didn't hear anything, so I just thought, "Well, maybe he doesn't think it's a good idea to get together the night before a game." And I understood.

Well, that evening I was sitting in the living room reading the newspaper [and] watching TV and my wife was standing at the kitchen window doing the dishes. I heard her scream and ran in. Here was this face pressed up against the glass. That unmistakable Valvano nose just mashed up against the window. It scared the hell out of both of us. I still don't know how he got there or how he found our house. But that was a night to remember.

I called over some neighbors, and at about 2:00 in the morning we were still screaming, but now with laughter.

KIDS' GAMES

Roy Firestone, host of ESPN's Up Close, *got some rare insights into the little (New York) boy in V.*

He talked about his growing up in Queens…in the big metropolis, and he said, "It's a shame that everybody couldn't grow up in an area where you gotta make up games. You have to play Johnny on a pony, kick the can, stickball. We have kids today that unless you drive them somewhere and they have Joe's Drug Store on their backs, they don't play. I used to get up in the morning and go to the park and play and when I'd come home my dad would say, 'Did you have fun?'

"You go to games today, the moms and dads sit in folding chairs and yell at the ump. I'm not knocking Little League but when the game is over you're supposed to be happy with the effort."

And then I asked Jim, "Would you have been the same guy if you'd have grown up in Missouri?"

He said, "Well, we're all a product of our environment, and I grew up in Queens with relatives all around, uncles, cousins. And we ate at 2:00 on Sunday and we all went in and had a little pasta. And everybody had a mustache. Then I move from Queens out to Long Island and I meet this kid called Rusty. I thought rusty was a condition, and I said, 'What's your name?' and he said, 'Rusty' and I said, 'That's a condition. Your name has to be Anthony.'

"When I got to Raleigh they were shocked to learn that I'd never been fishing. I said, 'How do you fly cast into a fire hydrant!'"

That was Jim's childhood, which, of course, he never gave up. He treasured his childhood and remained a New York kid his entire life.

SMOKY AND DOC

Golfing buddy FRANK MCCANN remembers a monumental "Good Walk Spoiled," the weekend V ran into two of the toughest competitors he'd ever faced–Smoky and Doc.

Jim and I and our wives went to the beach over the Fourth of July. We went down on Thursday night and decided to play golf at this little course in Pine Knoll Shores, NC, called Bogue Banks. It's very short but can drive you up the wall. Jim was in good health then and we were playing a lot, and so we get on the first tee and there are these two old guys standing there with their little pull carts. Because we just walked on, the pro had said that we might have to hook up with another twosome.

So there they are and Jim says, "This is going to be a long day."

Little did we know.

We make the introductions and learn that we'll be playing with Smoky and Doc. Doc is seventy-six years old and Smoky is seventy-eight. Pretty soon Jim and I realize that Doc can't hear and Smoky can't see.

Jim immediately suggests a bet. The young guys against the old guys, he says. They have no problem with that, and then Jim says, "What do you want to play for?"

And Smoky looks him right in the eye and says, "Doesn't matter to me, I'm rich!"

Jim and I look at each other and say, "Uh oh!" So fortunately we played them for a nominal fee. They shot the reverse of their ages. Doc shot 78 and Smoky shot 76! And they beat the living crap out of us, about $24 worth.

Well now Jim's going, "This isn't right!"

He could not stand to lose. So we ask for a rematch the next day. Smoky says, "Hey, whatever you want, it's all right with me!"

So we will meet them on Saturday. Well, with Jim this is serious business—we've just been horsewhipped by two old men and so all Friday night it's a strategy session for the next day's game. So we play them on Saturday and now we're playing handicaps. I was about a ten, Jim was a fifteen. We learned that Smoky was an eight and Doc was a six.

They kick our asses again.

Now Jim is absolutely ripped. And to add insult to injury Smoky and Doc were anything but dumb... but they were deaf and blind. Smoky would hit, and he couldn't see you, the ball, or the green. And Doc, he'd be out in the fairway and he couldn't hear so balls were flying by him all the time. It was like something out of *Caddy Shack*. We line up another game for Sunday.

So now it's Saturday night, we've been pounded again by a couple of guys in their late 70s, and over dinner that's all Jim can talk about—Smoky and Doc and how tomorrow's our last chance to get even.

So we tee it up on Sunday. Now they are so pleasant, wonderful guys, but Jim and I are here for blood. I wanted to beat them but Jim is wild. "I'm not losing to these guys again!"

So it all comes down to the 18th tee. We were one down going into 17, won the hole, and now it's all even, and all Jim can see is bragging rights. We may never ever get Smoky and Doc again, and we're running out of golf holes. Jim is acutely aware of all of this.

I tee it up and put the tee shot out of bounds. So it's up to Jim.

He looks at me and says, "Nice job, what a fine time to do that. You leave me alone!"

But now I'm his coach and so we get to the green, they're down in five, and Jim needs to make a five-foot putt to tie them. To tie these two old men! Well he makes the putt. Nothing, not since the NCAA championship win over Houston, has made Jim Valvano so happy. He sinks a five-foot $20 putt to tie two guys in their 70s and you would have thought he'd won the Masters—jumping around, screaming, going wild.

If he were alive today and you asked him to give you his Top Ten Thrills Of Victory, the five-foot putt to tie Smoky and Doc would have been right up there!

V

HOT SHOT QB

BOB STAAK, who played for UConn and then served as an assistant coach, remembers that V's search for talent wasn't limited to the hardwoods. He once tried to point the UConn football coaches in the direction of a talented quarterback, a kid from Long Island's Seaford High.

When he was an assistant at Connecticut he was doing a lot of recruiting. And you know he was a pretty good high school quarterback on Long Island, at Seaford High, all-county. Well, he gets an old game film of himself playing quarterback at Seaford where he threw like five or six touchdown passes. So he takes it to the football recruiters and head coach at Connecticut and says, "Hey, I was down on Long Island recruiting a kid and there's this quarterback that they kept talking about, this kid who can really play. I thought you might want to take a look at some film, thought you might be interested!"

So he gives the staff the film of himself in his big game. Now he waits and doesn't hear anything. So he checks in with them, wondering what they thought of this kid from Long Island. This goes on for a while, still no response. Finally the head coach just says, "Thanks, Jimmy, we looked at the film. He's really not good enough to play at this level!"

Oh pissed, V was not happy!

THICK MAN

Pound-for-pound the most diet-conscious coach in the history of NCAA basketball, V was always on some bizarre diet. No one escaped his "Atkins" eye, including RAY TANNER, NC State's assistant baseball coach at the time (now head coach at South Carolina).

V always called me Thick Man.

Pam would defend me and say, "Jim, Ray's not that thick!"

Then V would say, "Oh yes, he is! Ray is extremely thick."

I remember one time I was dating this girl in Raleigh and V and Pam saw us out at a restaurant, T. K. Tripps. She was a cute girl, maybe a little short for her weight, but very cute. So anyway V sees us, comes over to our table, and was very pleasant, of course. But the next morning when I got into the office I had a message on my phone, "Call V!"

So I called him and I said, "What's up?"

And he said, "I saw you with your date last night and I just wanted you to know that if you two ever have children... they will be thick!"

𝒱

LATE NIGHT WITH JIM VALVANO

V, a legendary insomniac, loved company when he couldn't sleep. GEORGE NIXON, a Wolfpack manager, recalls the night that V not only kept the entire team up with him, he made them burn the midnight oil.

In '86 we had a really good team but got beat in the first round of the ACC tournament by Virginia; it was a squeaker, like 64–62. So we went into the locker room (this was the Friday game in Greensboro) and so Coach V said, "Okay, we're going home and I want you to be in Reynolds at midnight for practice." And the managers kind of looked at each other. It was spring break and we were young and we wanted to party. So we had to be there at 11:00 and get the Gatorade poured, set up the court.

So when they got there at midnight, he told them to sit on the court. Well, this was better than any party we could have gone to, because he proceeded to give a two and a half hour talk. Not about basketball but about life. We were just spellbound. If anyone else had heard that one they'd know why the companies would spend $25,000 for one of his speeches. He was just incredible.

He said, "One of these days you guys are going to have families and 8-to-5 jobs. You don't realize how special it is to play college basketball for a university like NC State, to play in a conference like the ACC." He just talked on and on about life after basketball and families and how important it is to live every day for what it's worth. We were mesmerized, and then the team went out and had this great practice from like 2:30 until 4:30 in the morning.

And it worked. Because that was the year we went to the NCAA's and beat Iowa, Arkansas, and Iowa State and just about got by Kansas, which would have put us in the Final Four. But we went all the way to the final eight before finally losing to Kansas. He knew that first-round ACC loss to Virginia could have been devastating. And there's no way that we would have gotten to the final eight of the NCAA's if it hadn't been for his speech in Reynolds that night.

NEED TWO!

My father died in 1984. He was in the hospital in Maryland and so I was making a lot of trips north from Raleigh to see him. He was a huge Jim Valvano fan, so when V's book Too Soon to Quit, *chronicling the '83 championship season, came out I took a copy in and V signed it for my dad. I have many great memories of my father but the one that has lasted over the years is his laughter. The credit for one of those great laughs goes to V.*

I took my dad to the NC State Faculty Club for the weekly Tip Off Club luncheon—a place where I always suspected that V tested his new material. We were there for the debut of one of the great V one-liners of all time.

In the middle of his talk he just stopped and said, "Oh, there's this new NCAA ruling that limits our recruiting, so I told my wife, 'Pammy, it looks like I'm going to be home for the whole month of August for the first time since we've been married.' So Pam said, 'Great, I want sex at least four times!' And I said, 'Okay, put me down for two!'"

HOME AWAY FROM HOME

NICOLE, V's oldest daughter and the family jock, remembers her dad and the best home away from home that a kid could have.

My relationship with Dad was different than my sisters. I think he enjoyed having someone in the family who played. We'd talk about offenses and defenses and things that happened in games. And he would come to my high school games in Apex. Basketball was a real common ground for us.

One of the funny things is that people always ask me about playing one-on-one with my dad in our driveway. But we never had a basketball hoop at our house in Cary, NC. I don't know whether that was because Mom didn't think that it went with the decor or what. But we didn't have a basket at home. I'm sure she would laugh and say that's what it was, not going to tacky up the house. But I had something much better than that because I played basketball with my dad in his office, Reynolds Coliseum.

We moved to Raleigh when I was about twelve and until I was about fourteen or fifteen I would go to his camps and practices at NC State. Those were great days with my dad, just spending time with him in Reynolds Coliseum. He was extremely focused and competitive during practice but as soon as he'd see me coming it was, "Hey, come on out!" and a big hug. We'd shoot hoops. I felt like a part of the team and family.

The national championship is a great a memory, but one of my favorites with my dad is this really cool thing we did at one of the half-times of an exhibition game in Reynolds. This was when I was about fourteen. There were three of us: Linda Page, who played for Kay Yow's team, a great three-point shooter, myself, and Dad. We played H-O-R-S-E at half-time to entertain the crowd. I lost to Linda but I beat my dad.

I think that I would have lived in Reynolds Coliseum if I could have; I just loved the place. Later, when I went to school at NC State, Dad was still there and it was really special to be able to stop by his office.

I loved basketball and I loved my dad and so it was really the best of both worlds . . . being Jim Valvano's daughter at NC State.

CAR QUEST

*Former Wolfpack player **WALT DENSMORE**'s story of V coming into Alabama is reminiscent of the movie* My Cousin Vinny. *V, not unlike the Joe Pesci character, was looking for a "yute" (to play for NC State) and could have very easily had a run-in with the law.*

I went to high school in Alabama and my dad, Walt Densmore, Jr., was a really good player for the University of Virginia. So I came from a basketball family, and when Jim Valvano came to sign me to a scholarship to play for NC State, it was really a big day for us down in Alabama. Our house was packed, friends, relatives, neighbors. We knew what time his plane was supposed to land and what time he was going to arrive, and frankly, we were all really excited.

Well, the time came and passed and still no Jim Valvano. I mean we started to worry. At first we thought maybe he isn't coming at all. Then maybe something happened to his plane. Well finally about an hour after he was due to arrive the phone rings and it's Coach V. This was the only time I ever saw him embarrassed. He asked to speak to my dad. Dad gets on the phone and is nodding and then finally says, "We'll be right there!"

V had stopped about fifteen minutes from our house to get a Coke or something and had locked his keys in the rental car. He had spent about a half an hour trying to break into the car and couldn't. So here go my dad and uncle. They get over there and pop the window and then bring him back to the house. Well, he walks in and says, "How embarrassing is this? A guy from New York has to get two guys from Alabama to teach him how to break into a car!"

HONEST ASSESSMENT

Former Iona player JEFF RULAND recalls one of V's attributes that moved him to sign with Iona College—honesty.

When V was recruiting me, my high school team hadn't played in about two weeks and he came out to see me play. I just played horribly. There was a ton of coaches in the stands and one after another they came up to me afterwards and said, "Great game!" "Nice game!"

And I was pretty much my own worst critic and I knew that I'd played like crap.

Then here comes Jim and he says, "Boy, you really sucked!"

And I respected him for that, knew he was my kind of guy. I was recruited by Kentucky, Indiana, and the University of North Carolina, but I ended up at Iona. There's no question that he was the reason. He could have sold real estate in Florida and been a billionaire.

BIG NAME COACH

Tom Penders, a basketball coach whose career includes head coaching stints at Tufts, Columbia, Fordham, Rhode Island, Texas and George Washington, remembers V as a guy who was impossible to beat–as a player and a coach.

I was a guard for UConn and we were playing Rutgers; this was our last home game, and we had a guy named Wes Bialosuknia–the leading scorer in the country. Bob Lloyd, Jimmy's teammate at Rutgers, was second in the country. These two guys are guarding each other that game. Anyway, Wes and Bobby had really been lighting it up that night. So now I'm getting ready to shoot a free throw and Jimmy comes up to me and says, "You know, Penders, if you guarded me and I guarded you like those two guys we could score 30 tonight!"

I was a good free throw shooter and I don't even think I hit the rim after that line. That may have been my only career air ball from the line.

Our paths crossed so many times; he was at Johns Hopkins and I was at Tufts, and then we're both ready to move up, and we end up being finalists for the Columbia head coaching job. Well, I got the job, but I found out later that he was so funny in his final interview that he scared the hell out of the faculty and so they gave me the job by default. Then he got the Iona job right after that and conned me into scheduling Columbia to play him. I don't think we ever beat him. So he always said that if he had gotten that Columbia job instead of me he would have never lasted in coaching.

Jimmy could talk you into anything; we really had a great team at Columbia. and in those years the Ivy League was pretty darned strong. But I coached against him at least three or four times and Iona was always a team on our schedule that we should beat–but we never beat them.

He was the best at working referees and the best big game coach I ever saw. Out in Albuquerque in '83 at the NCAA finals I was the one who told Mike Lupica that Jimmy was the best big game coach in the country and I expected him to win the national championship. This was before NC State played Houston for the national championship when everybody was picking Houston. Mike based his whole column on what I'd told him. Then Jimmy went out and did it. A big game coach and he coached the game of his life!

𝒱

ARTFUL DODGER

BOB GUZZO, NC State's wrestling coach, recalls the night V got "a hold" on him and thousands of other fans in Atlanta's Fulton County Stadium.

I was running a wrestling camp one summer in Atlanta and the guy who asked me to run the camp was Dale Murphy's brother-in-law. Murphy was the star center fielder for the Atlanta Braves at the time.

So one night I'm invited to go to the Braves game. They gave me seats right behind the Atlanta dugout. I'm sitting there and in about the third inning I happen to look over and see an older guy in front of the Los Angeles Dodgers dugout in a Dodger uniform straightening bats. I do a major double take. The freakin' bat boy for the Dodgers is Jim Valvano, my friend, my athletic director, and one of the most famous basketball coaches in the country!

V was the Dodgers' bat boy!

Now I've gotta get over there. So I start working my way through the box seats until I get right behind the on-deck circle and I start hollering, "Jim, Jim!"

He's in his Dodger uniform down on one knee behind the bats and when he finally hears me he turns around and shouts, "Guz. What in the f%#* are you doing here?"

I tell him I'm in town for a wrestling camp. Now the real question is what in the hell he's doing here. It's a long story, V and Tommy [Lasorda, the Dodgers manager] are friends, etc.

He insists that I hang around after the game and have a few pops with him and Tommy. Now all this time the game is going on. Pretty soon he starts shouting into the dugout to his friend Lasorda, "Tommy,

Tommy!" Lasorda pops his head out and V says, "Hey, I want you to meet our wrestling coach. This is my friend Bob Guzzo!"

So, with thousands of fans looking on, now I meet Tommy.

Then V says, "Hey, don't forget, come by the locker room after the game. But I gotta go back to work now."

And off he goes straightening the bats again.

CONTINUED CONFIDENCE

LORENZO CHARLES remembers that V's confidence in him never waned. It started when he was a recruit and not only remained but helped Lo help win some crucial games.

Ray Martin, one of V's assistant coaches, made the initial contact with me. Ray followed me throughout the season until I made the final commitment. A lot of people ask me why I chose NC State. I really didn't choose NC State. I chose Coach V.

What happened was Ray came and saw a lot of my games at Brooklyn Technical High School. Eventually Coach V came to see me play and the two times V saw me play I stunk up the gym. The first time he just looked, didn't speak to me. The second time I stunk it up again and after the game he waited to talk to me. And I'm thinking there's no way this is going to work out with them. I was being recruited by Syracuse, St. John's, some pretty big schools in the Big East but I'm thinking there's no way that NC State is going to be interested, not now.

He just said, "Lorenzo, I want you to come to NC State!"

I was thinking, what?

He told me that single games didn't mean anything, that he saw something in me, and that was a tremendous boost to my confidence.

That's why I chose Coach V, not NC State. He was always there with that kind of support. Everybody remembers the dunk that won the national championship but the game that got us to the Final Four, the two foul shots that I hit to win that one was really bigger, it put us up on Virginia 63–62 and some of the credit goes to V again because he just gave me so much confidence.

This was exactly the way he was in the huddle, as far as building your confidence. He'd say, "After Lo knocks down these two free throws we're going to fall back in a zone," or whatever defense he was calling. Sidney [Lowe] and I laugh about this now because then he would pull Sidney aside and maybe say, "If Lo misses, here's what I want you to do."

Here's what happened in the Virginia game in Utah, the one that took us to the Final Four.

We were down one, 61 to 62, and Sidney made a move to the basket, beat his man off the dribble. [Ralph] Sampson, who was guarding me, went to help defend and Sidney dumped the ball off to me. I went up and Ralph fouled me. Then they called time-out to freeze me, to let me think about that moment and the two foul shots. That's when—in the huddle—Coach V talked about what we were going to do after I made the two free throws. Actually that was all he talked about, this sagging zone that we were going to play to keep Sampson from beating us. Everyone in the building knew that if I made both free throws that they'd be down one and they'd go inside to Ralph, that he was going to go to the basket for the two points or the foul.

Most conversations with Coach V in the huddles were about defense. His philosophy was, you don't let the star beat you. If we were going to get beat, we were going to get beat by a jump shot from one of the lesser players. You make the other players take the big shot at the end of a game; if they beat you, then so be it. But he was never ever going to let the big gun get you. He would tell us he could accept a loss if the role players beat us. If we played Carolina and Buzz Peterson knocked down a jump shot to beat us, he was okay with that, but not Michael [Jordan]. He wasn't going to let the big guy beat you. We practiced that: someone would play the part of the star player and we'd work on that, what we were going to do to stop him.

So end of story, I hit the two shots, we chased Othell Wilson, sagged on Sampson, and [Tim] Mullen had to take the shot from the corner. Mullen missed, we won, and we were on our way to the Final Four.

X-RAY VISION

DR. DON REIBEL, the team's orthopedic doctor, remembers V, Dr. Manley, and a classic.

During the national championship game, V was sick as a dog. He had the flu, and the night of the game he was really sick, so when he finally got back to Raleigh he really needed some time to recuperate. On top of that he had a hernia.

Jim Manley, our other team doctor, finally convinced him to get into Rex Hospital to get the hernia repaired. He'd been putting it off for a long time. Of course there was a lot of talk about how lucky NC State had been to pull off all those upsets to win the national championship. So when Doc Manley got Jim in the hospital he took the X-ray of the hernia and taped a horseshoe over the X-Ray and then reproduced it.

Then he brought Jim in to look at his interior, to get a better idea of what was going on with the hernia. He put it up on the light board and pointing at the horseshoe said, "Jim, I found the secret to the championship; you really did have a horseshoe up your tail when you won all those games."

ROAD KILL

Assistant coach ED MCLEAN remembers V's thoughts on runners and the day he shared this philosophy with Tommy Abatemarco.

Jim wasn't always fun and games. When it came to his assistants he was fair and great to work for but he could also be tough, he expected us to work hard and be there when he needed us.

Tommy Abatemarco, our recruiter, had been with Jim since Iona. They were old friends. Tommy was an obsessive runner. He'd run like at least five miles, twice a day. Sometimes before he came to work and again at lunch time. This drove Jim crazy. He wanted Tommy to be there when he needed him.

There were days when Jim would come to me and say, "Where's Tommy?"

I'd just say he had somewhere to go. I wouldn't tell Jim because I knew he'd go off if he knew Tommy was running again.

One day Jim's driving back from lunch and sees Tommy running along Western Boulevard. He pulls up next to him in the car and shouts out the window. "Tommy, I've got two things to tell you!"

"What?" Tommy says.

"Successful people don't run, they don't have time. Look at me. Do I run? The second thing is... if I see you running along here again success won't be an issue!"

Tommy shouts back, "Why?"

"Because I'm going to run over your ass!"

FE FE FI FI FO FO FUM

Manager GEORGE NIXON recalls the time he found out that where there's smoke ... there is fire!

One of the few times that I ever saw V surprised, no actually he was shocked, was an incident that involved Panagiotis Fasoulas. He came over from Greece–about seven feet four inches, long hair, a shot blocker. I think he was only here for a year. Panagiotis was a big man, played inside, and he had played, I believe, on some national teams in Greece.

So anyway the first game he played for us was the Red and White game and before the game the players are all sitting around in the locker room, and V comes in and sees Panagiotis leaning up against his locker and V just stops dead in his tracks, "Panagiotis, what the f*&%# are you doing?"

Panagiotis says, in this real thick accent, "I'm smoking a ceegerette!"

He was having a pre-game smoke. In Greece this is what they all did. They all were big smokers.

V goes nuts, "I don't want to ever see you smoking a f*&#@ing cigarette again, do you realize this is our locker room?"

And, of course, the players are really getting off on this, laughing like crazy, and V's playing it up because with his sense of humor you know he thought it was funny.

But to see V's face when he saw Panagiotis taking a big drag on the cigarette in the locker room... it was hilarious.

୯

CANDOR PERSONIFIED

ALEX WOLFF, Senior Writer, Sports Illustrated remembers V for his candor and as one of his favorite interviews.

It's really rare when a coach, even when he's off the record, will be really honest with a reporter. But that was Jim Valvano.

I can remember him talking about fighting the Carolina double standard. When one of Carolina's players got in trouble no one ever heard about it, but if something happened on State's campus that involved one of his players, it was in *The News & Observer* the next day. I guess one of the most honest and candid off-the-record statements I ever heard from a coach was the one that Valvano made after he'd beaten Houston the second time, this was the year following the '83 championship. He admitted that NC State shouldn't have been able to beat Houston because they didn't have the talent, and then he called Houston, "The dumbest f@&#*ing team in America."

My fondest memory of him is one from the early '80s, before he won the championship. We were in his office in Raleigh at NC State and he just had this free-flowing thought process that was so different from the normal ask-a-question, get-an-answer interview. It was more like a monologue or stand-up than an interview.

He went off into this lengthy, how-Valvano-reads-*Sports-Illustrated* speech: "The first thing I do is turn to the thing in the back—For the Record—to see if I died or got fired. Then I turn to the front and read Scorecard, or whatever, the place where you guys write about the little fish in Wyoming, about the dams, and how we should be concerned about these little gilled animals becoming extinct and what we should do to save them."

Of course he was describing the early '80s *Sports Illustrated* and this was during a time when we did a lot of impassioned environmental pieces. I don't tape when I do interviews, but he was so entertaining that now, as I look back and remember the times that I was with him, I'm sorry that I didn't get any of this on tape. He would just gallop off at warp speed with that incredible mind churning out so many refreshing thoughts and as he went down these side roads, you didn't want to miss being along for the ride

FOOTBALL RECRUIT

The former high school quarterback eventually would be a football analyst for ESPN—V covered European Football, interviewing players on a couch at mid-field at half-time. CHRIS CORCHIANI saw V's talent in the booth at State's Carter-Finley Stadium during a recruiting visit to the NC State campus.

This was in 1986 and NC State was playing South Carolina—the famous Erik Kramer-to-Danny Peebles Hail Mary Pass Play—at Carter-Finley. I was in the press box with V, and he called every play in that last drive as the Pack moved the ball down the field.

So for the last few minutes he's up there quarterbacking, "Kramer down over the middle, we've got plenty of time." And amazingly getting every play right. I'm watching this and he's saying, "Plenty of time, got them right where we want them."

I'm thinking, "You are in trouble, Coach, there's no way."

And he's still, "We're fine, we're going to go deep and win this thing."

Then on the last play [after time had apparently expired] South Carolina jumps off-sides and State gets one more play. Kramer hits Danny Peebles in the end zone on that famous Hail Mary pass and I'm jumping up and down and screaming at Coach V, "We won, we won!"

That's when I knew I was coming to NC State. He had me. I was screaming, "We won!"

NIGHT RIDER

Player **MIKE WARREN** *remembers V making sure that his players always got their rest.*

My freshman year, this was the 1981–82 season, we played Notre Dame away. So we were in South Bend on the bus coming back from practice and Quentin Leonard fell asleep. Now he is the greatest guy in the world, but Quentin was "Country Come To Town."

So now Quentin's dozing and V sees this and when we get back to the hotel V starts whispering to us, real quiet, "Now, everybody, just be real, real quiet, just get off the bus, we're going to send Quentin for a ride!"

So we all ease off the bus and V tells the bus driver to just take off and drive Quentin around South Bend until he wakes up!

V says, "When he wakes up, tell him that it's Saturday night and that Notre Dame beat us by five!"

TALE OF THE TAPE

V was never more V-ish than when he was recruiting athletes. He'd walk into the living rooms of total strangers and say, "Give me your son!" in a most atypical way. **VINNY DEL NEGRO** *remembers.*

When I think of Coach V, I think of the first time I met him. He came to where I played prep school basketball, and we had a meeting at my prep school coach's house. The week before the University of Kentucky was in to talk to me, [Coach] Joe B. Hall and [Assistant Coach] Leonard Hamilton. They came in their Kentucky blue blazers and ties and talked to my parents and coach and they were very formal, just sat around and talked.

Then a week later here comes Coach Valvano and Tom Abatemarco in their Nike sweat suits. Right off they started kidding around and pretty soon they broke out this little portable tape player and played me a game [audio] tape. Well, the announcer had me in it, winning the ACC tournament, you know, "Seconds left, Del Negro with the ball, he shoots, scores, and the Wolfpack wins the ACC tournament!"

Now after I hit this shot on the tape player coach Valvano and Abatemarco tackle me, they're high fiving, and then they wrestle me on the couch. This was a lot different than the Kentucky blue blazers. And it worked because this was much more my style and my family's style. The conversation was so open and relaxed and it was just a natural fit. Then we went over to an Italian restaurant where my cousin was a chef and had a big Italian meal. I signed with NC State. Right there. We were all just so comfortable with Coach V.

The funny thing about that tape that they played: In 1987 we ended up winning the ACC tournament. I hit two big free throws with fourteen seconds left. So it was funny, the tape wasn't as hokey as it may have sounded.

With Coach V everything and anything was possible, and you never knew what might happen.

CANTEEN BOY

V's practices were both organized and strenuous. GEORGE NIXON recalls the day that excessive water breaks by the players inspired V to come up with what to him was a very logical solution.

The thing about V was if you played for him you had to play hard and you had to practice hard. If you didn't, you weren't going to play. I can remember plenty of times when he'd come into practice with a tie on—maybe he'd been to some event or something—and he'd see a loose ball get away without effort. To make his point about hustle he'd dive on the floor with a suit and tie on to get a ball... just to let them know how he played and how he expected them to play.

"Hey, damn it, if I'm thirty-nine years old and I can dive on the floor with a suit and tie on, why the hell can't kids in short pants?"

Then he'd do it again. He'd take the ball and roll it down the court and say, "Hey, watch me dive!" and he'd be on it again.

Another one of his pet peeves was that he hated it when players would be stopping in practice and drinking Gatorade. I was the manager so that was my job, to get the Gatorade and keep them supplied. One day they had been drinking a lot, and he said, "Damn it! I'm so sick and tired of stopping practice for these Gatorade breaks. I'm going to get some canteens. Hey, if an army can fight a war sipping out of canteens, you guys can practice basketball drinking out of them! I'm going to put the f*&%ing things around your necks!"

The other managers and I are laughing so hard that we have to turn our heads. But after practice V comes up to me and Dan White and says, "George, I was serious about those canteens. I want you all to go and find some canteens!"

So here we go out that night to some Army Surplus store and we buy canteens for all the players. And the next day Coach V starts practice by saying, "Guys, I've come up with a way to solve our massive drinking problem!" And he hangs a canteen on a little rope around each of the players' necks. Well, needless to say, there was a lot of laughter. But he made his point. That's just the way he did things. There was often a message hidden behind the laughs!

LADIES' MAN

KAY YOW remembers her friend V as a men's coach who knew and loved all sports, including women's basketball.

We were both English majors and we both had a great love for reading so we had that in common. And I really miss this part of our friendship so much because he was always reading a lot of motivational things, and I like that kind of writing too, and we talked about those books and shared them.

It also amazed me how much he knew about women's sports. In women's basketball he knew the teams that were ranked. He would always talk to me about our team, come to me and ask me questions about women's sports. Maybe he'd be going on a talk show and he wanted to be up on everything. He'd ask me just to be sure he was on the right track.

He read stories, sports anthologies, and he'd tell me about a story he'd read and its point. Then we'd discuss it. This was really important to me. We both gave motivational speeches and he was a tremendous help there. We'd go over the points–motivation plus belief makes one successful! He was a very optimistic person, most incredible.

It was Jim who always reminded me, "Hey, win a championship? Why not me!"

$$\mathcal{V}$$

DRIVE TIME

WRAL's JAY JENNINGS can't–try as he might–forget what it was like playing golf with V.

Everybody should have golfed with Jim Valvano–at least once! Long before the Jimmy V Charity Classic he had a tournament at MacGregor Downs for the media and some of his sponsors. I played in it a couple of times–a beer cart running around and a lot of carrying on.

I'll never forget the first time I played. Bob Holiday, a WRAL-TV sports reporter, and I were getting ready to tee off on 18. It's an elevated tee over water, toughest hole on the course, a real beast. What I didn't realize was that V had a cart and he and Don Shea, his assistant, who also has a voice like a foghorn, were riding from foursome to foursome, playing a hole with each group. Just as we're getting ready to get on the tee box on the toughest hole on the course we hear this incredible racket coming from over the hill, a combination of voices at the top of their lungs, golf clubs banging in the back of a golf cart.

Of course, it's our host.

V comes flying over the top of the hill and screeches to a stop. V and Shea are the last thing I needed. I'm already pretty puckered standing over my ball and of course, etiquette went right in the water with our drives. We're trying to hit, V's holding forth. We're hitting balls in the water. He's busting our balls and critiquing our swings while we're flailing away. We're just splashing ball after ball, bringing up white caps on the lake.

The next thing you know he says, "Let me show you guys how it's done."

Now I was about a fifteen and he wasn't close to being that good at the time. But he reaches in his bag and pulls out his driver. This is a picture I'll never forget, it's an old persimmon-headed golf club that screams "yard sale," probably something that was Rocco's that he'd stolen right out of his dad's attic. The thread that tied the persimmon head to the shaft had come loose and was hanging down. This thing looked more like a fishing rod than a golf club.

He holds it up by the string and says, "Hey, I use this to gauge the wind!" Then teeing up his ball he begins to announce—in a "V" whisper—his own shot, "Valvano's on the tee. He checks the wind. He's exceptional off the tee, very long, leads the tour this year in fairways hit!"

We're all praying for the sound of a splashing MaxFli. But no! With that antique club and yapping away, he proceeds to stroke about a 250-yard drive right in the middle of the fairway. Oh man! Now he goes into this English accent, "Valvano has to be happy with that one!"

It was just one of those V moments. And of course it didn't end there. For the rest of the hole he's dogging us about the drive. He'd hit that shot in front of a bunch of nobodies. But it really didn't matter because he just loved being the guy. He wouldn't have taken a hundred bucks for that drive and the reason I know that is because he was still talking about it years later.

"Hey, Jennings, remember 'The Drive!'"

RAINCOATS IN THE MOVIES

MIKE WARREN, back-up on the '83 championship team, remembers some rainy days in V's film room.

Nobody wanted to sit in the front row in the film room. Practice the day before a game would end at like 6:00.

V would say, "Be in the film room by 7:00."

So we'd catch a shower and eat at the training table in Case Athletic Center and then come wandering in about 7:00. We learned that the worst seat in the house for one of these film break-downs was the front row.

Coach McLean would do this incredible job of breaking down the team we were going to play on video—offense, defense—he would run everything that they were going to do. Hollywood couldn't have done a better editing job. Every play that a team would run. But poor Coach McLean would work his ass off on this editing and then only get about two plays run for us.

V would jump up there in the front and say, "Ah, that's enough of that shit. You all know that on the first play they're going to pick and roll and then they're going to start trying to go back door on you. And if any of you get back-doored your ass is coming out of the game."

Then he'd get really going, forget the game plan, the video, he'd be all pumped up and start giving one of his V speeches, ranting and raving. When he did this—which was just about every film session—he spit all over the place.

So man, we learned pretty quickly that in V's movie house you needed a raincoat if you were going to sit up front by the screen. The very best seats were in the back of the house and the back row was always full.

SERIOUS ABOUT FUNNY

Roy Firestone remembers an interview on ESPN's Up Close *where V discussed the double-edged sword that comes with being perceived as a clown.*

I asked Jimmy, "Is it true that you don't get the credit you deserve because you are such a showman?"

He said, "That's very interesting because it's something that I'm very sensitive to. The funny thing is that in this business people label you: you're studious, you wear the suit, you wear the glasses, then you're the X and O guy. Or you're the recruiter; you can be a personality or you can be a character, but you're not allowed to be funny and also serious. I'm definitely serious but I don't take myself seriously. The kids that play for me, I want them to understand that someday the cheering will stop. You don't get introduced every day, 'Starting at left desk... let's give him a hand.' Because once this thing is over with it's the real world."

V

ILLEGAL PICK

SAM ESPOSITO remembers a Saturday morning when V got caught setting an illegal pick.

We used to love to meet on Saturday mornings in the office at Case Athletic Center, just have coffee and shoot the bull. Of course V didn't like to have our ritual interrupted in any way.

So one morning he comes rolling in and I'm behind my desk talking to a mom and a dad and a pitcher I was trying to recruit for our baseball team. The pitcher and his parents have their backs to V and can't see him.

V's pissed, so he shoots me the bird. Then he looks to the right and there's the recruit's little brother sitting on the couch looking right at him. He'd nailed V, just seen the most famous basketball coach in the country walk in and shoot me the bird.

So do you know what V did? He takes his middle finger and starts picking his nose, like he wasn't shooting the bird at all. Now, everyone knows he's there and I introduce him. When everyone is impressed to meet the great V, he excuses himself. I wait about five minutes and then tell the parents and kid that I need a minute.

I walked into V's office and said, "You are the sorriest bastard in the world!"

V says "Why?"

I said, "Who else would get caught by a little kid giving someone the finger, and then cover it up by picking his nose!"

HOT TO TROT

CHRIS CORCHIANI remembers a conversation over pizza with V that was loaded with anchovies, so to speak.

Some of the best conversations that I had with Coach V were after the *Personal Fouls* book came out. V was on the hot seat, and they were trying to get him to step down as our coach. I thought that he might be asked to leave, and I was running my mouth about transferring. I said that if he left that I was leaving NC State. So one day he calls me up and wants to go to lunch. I thought this will be fun, good for some laughs.

So we sat down at the Pizza Hut and I said, "Coach, I don't care if John Wooden replaces you, I'm leaving if you're not here."

Man, he really blasted me, really lit into me. He said, "Who the hell do you think you are? You're not going anywhere. John Wooden's not coming here. Your ass is staying right here!"

I remember getting on the phone that night and calling my dad. My dad just loved V. I told him what V had said, "You're not going to win this battle for me and lose the war for you. I've lost this battle and you're going to do what's best for you. Don't sacrifice yourself. You need to stay here. This is where you belong!"

I was so pissed off at the university and how they handled the situation. All V would have had to do was agree with me, or not even comment when I threatened to leave and I'd have been gone. But he took the high road. He wasn't thinking of what was good for him. He was doing what was right for me! And you just can't forget things like that.

RED-LETTER DAY

SARAH SUE INGRAM, the assistant sports information director at NC State when V's Cardiac Pack won the national championship, recalls what might best be described as a red-letter day.

After the championship Jim Valvano's office looked like a Toys 'R Us—toys, cards, presents of all kinds came rolling in daily. Ed Seamon, our sports information director, suggested that I go up to V's office, go through the loot, and write a press release. It was incredible. There were four Santa Claus sized bags of mail that he hadn't even opened yet. You couldn't even walk through the room, there was stuff everywhere. And right in the middle was this huge red leather executive-like chair with white letters that said something like "NC State Wolfpack–1983 NCAA Champions."

As I made notes for the story I asked Jim to share some of his favorites. And that's when he surprised me. I saw him weekly and those visits were like being with Robin Williams, V up carrying on, entertaining me, making me laugh. But this time he was quiet. He simply pulled two letters from his office desk and we read them together. The first said, and I'm paraphrasing because it was a long time ago, "The two best coaching jobs in an NCAA tournament that I've ever seen were Don Haskins, Texas Western, in 1966 and your 1983 win over Houston." The letter was signed by Jim's hero, John Wooden, the famous UCLA coach.

Jim was beside himself... so very proud of that letter.

But the second letter moved him more. This was from two grandparents, and they wrote to Jim about a little girl, their grandchild, who had just died of cancer. I'm not sure of the exact words of the letter but the gist of the message was: "Our granddaughter was terminally ill with only days to live when you and your Wolfpack team began to win games that resulted in the national championship. For weeks she had no hope and no interest until your team started to win. She attached herself to your team, lived with each win, and made it to see you beat Houston. We want to thank you and your players for making her final days so very special."

V was choked up and of course so was I. Obviously, no one knew that ten years later Jim Valvano would apply the "Never Give Up" philosophy to his own life as he fought cancer. But this was a very poignant moment. When he read that letter you could see how much he cared. This wasn't the laugh-a-minute Jim Valvano that so many people thought they knew.

GIVING CREDIT WHERE CREDIT'S DUE

FRANCES LEWIS loved her boss but when it came to "credit," Frances defended her friend Pam.

Jim really did know how to watch a dollar. Not too much slipped by him when it came to money. And that Pam, who is one of my very best friends by the way, is a shopper. She went just about every day and I'll tell you she kept herself and those girls looking good. I mean that woman has terrific taste and she can shop.

Jim used to say that she was All-Mall, that three words Pam has never heard were, "Welcome to K-Mart!" He'd be speaking at Wolfpack meetings and tell people he hoped that the next time she was shopping at Crabtree Mall someone would snatch her purse.

He'd say, "Hey, whoever gets those credit cards could never spend the way she does!"

But seriously, I remember days when he'd come in to the office and he'd be all excited. And I'd say Jim, "What are you so happy about?"

He'd say, "I just cut up Pam's credit cards again."

I'd say, "Jim, why did you do that? You know you're just going to go and get her other ones."

Then he'd shake his head and say, "'I know, but it slows her down!'"

WALL BALL

GEORGE NIXON recalls that the only thing that V loved more than playing games was winning those games.

He loved all kinds of games, darts, golf, anything that ended with a win or loss. I remember that Bobby, his younger brother, came by to visit at NC State one time and we were up in the office.

Now V was the athletic director at this time and Bobby walks in and Coach V gets all excited and they're hugging and talking and it's just like they're kids again. Well, pretty soon they start talking about wall ball, this game they played when they were kids. They're going back and forth about who did what and so Bobby says, "Go get the ball!"

V goes in his office and grabs a ball and they go out in front of Case Athletic Center and the game is on, wall ball, this game that you play like handball with a basketball. You could hear them screaming probably halfway to the Bell Tower. They were like ten or twelve years old again and really going at it. V was so competitive, and I went out there and just sat and watched, I couldn't believe it. I mean this was serious stuff, playing their brains out.

I thought, "Man, these Valvanos are crazy."

UNCLE CHUCK

TERRY GANNON remembers the one when Chuck Nevitt, V's 7' 4" center, announced that he was going to be an uncle... or at least that's what Chuck thought!

One of my favorite V stories is the one Chuck Nevitt used to tell. V was getting the team pumped up for a Big Four game with Wake Forest.

Chuck wasn't starting at the time so V goes over to him before the game and says, "Look at Chuck. Chuck here isn't even starting but he's like me, he's nervous about the game. Right, Chuck?"

Nevitt says, "Not really, not about the game!"

V says, "But you're nervous, right? You're pumped, tell us what you're pumped about."

Chuck tells V and the team that his sister is about to have her first baby.

So V says, "That makes you nervous, why?"

"Because I don't know whether it's going to be a girl or a boy. I'm kinda waiting to find out if I'll be an aunt or an uncle!"

Now, there's a line that can get a team focused, bring a pre-game locker room up for a big game.

FISHING FOR A TRANSLATOR

JIM GRAHAM, North Carolina's commissioner of agriculture for thirty-six years, spent a lifetime supporting his alma mater's basketball program. Graham, a close friend of every coach from Everett Case to Norm Sloan, recalls that there was only one coach that he just couldn't communicate with.

The only problem that Jim Valvano and I had was that we couldn't understand what the other one was saying.

The first time we had breakfast together we talked for about an hour and laughed and carried on and when we were getting ready to pay the check Coach Valvano said, "You know, Commish, I don't know whether it's that cigar you have in your mouth or the Southern accent. But other than an occasional you-all, I didn't understand a word you said!"

I laughed like hell and looked him right in the eye and said, "Well at least we got that settled this morning. We're going to need an interpreter because to tell you the truth I had to fake half of my laughs because I don't understand New York and I can't speak Yankee... never could!"

We became great friends. Oh, he was so funny and from that first meeting on... every time we'd see each other he would say... "Here comes the Commish, get the interpreter!" When I'd give a speech and he'd follow me he'd always get up and say, "The Commish is the best public speaker in America. He does about fifteen minutes, nobody has a clue what he says, and he gets a standing ovation."

Here's one that I'll never forget. I got up first and was talking to a group at the NC State Faculty Club about fish farming. It was something the Department of Agriculture was promoting in North Carolina, a way to give our farmers another market. So Jim Valvano is going to follow me on the same program. When I'd talked about the virtues of fish farming and how it would help the state's economy and could be the new crop for our farmers, Valvano gets up to speak.

He looks down at me in the audience. He always called me Commish. He says, "You know, Commish, when I was in New York I was into fish farming!" Of course everybody laughs and then he says, "I'm serious. I used to harvest my crop in Queens once a week. For like six days I'd open the manhole cover in the street in front of our stoop and drop in a bunch of fish food. Then on like the seventh day I'd just drop a line down the hole and start pullin' them out. We had some great fish farming in Queens! If you do that well here in North Carolina you're really going to be on to something."

That's how fast he was. He had no idea that I was going to talk about fish farming when I spoke. Hell, I didn't even know I was going to talk about fish farming.

V

MEN IN TIGHTS

Chris Corchiani remembers V making him feel like a pair of brown shoes with a tuxedo. It was the day V broke out the Unitards.

Coach Valvano always had something going on and I remember the practice, this was 1988, when he told us that he has something special for us... like it's a special gift.

So we go down in the locker room and he breaks out the Unitards— a uniform that he and the Nike people had come up with. Unbelievable, these little tunics with tight-fitting pants. And so he's passing them around like it's Christmas morning and we're supposed to be excited. Some of the taller, lean guys put theirs on and they looked pretty good. But I tried mine on and I'm short and stocky, and it really wasn't the look I wanted. Actually I looked like hell in mine.

Of course Coach Valvano thought that this was going to be a V original, a line of uniforms that took basketball by storm. We went out and played Temple on national TV wearing those things. And we wore them a number of times that season, but it became obvious that they weren't going to light up the fashion world.

And after that season Coach V is saying that if he hadn't had this little short fat point guard that he'd have made millions on the Unitards.

V

COMEDY COACH

Jeff Gravley, a WRAL-TV sports reporter, remembers V and one of his first assignments, which turned out to be a comedy clinic.

When I was a young pup at Channel 5, I got to go over and interview Coach V. He was so accessible and easy to talk to and I'd just learned this great joke. On the way over I was like boy, I can't wait to tell Coach V this one. So I got through my interview and I said, "Coach V, I've got a joke for you.

"A guy walks into a bar and orders a beer. There's a dog sitting on the bar licking his balls. The guy says, 'I wish I could do that.' The bartender says, 'Go ahead. He won't bite!'"

I went though the whole thing, and I thought I'd really nailed it. After the punch line he just looked at me. Nothing but silence.

Then he put his hand on my shoulder and with that raspy voice of his he said, "Son, the greatest thing about being a comedian is timing. And you don't have it!"

Then he took the joke, word for word, and repeated it as only Jim Valvano could. When he hit "He won't bite" it was so good that he got me. I was laughing at my own joke, like I'd never heard it before. He had just heard it once and repeated it word for word but his pacing and timing and the way he delivered the punch line, it was all perfect.

Then he said, and everybody in the room was howling laughing, "Ya see what I mean, kid? Timing, it's all about timing!"

I learned two lessons that day. One was about comedy and timing and the other was, well, I never tried to tell Coach V a joke again.

AIR SMITH

As to the question of what the relationship between former UNC coach Dean Smith and Jimmy V really was, **DEAN SMITH** **remembers.**

There were so many times that he made me laugh. But the one that was just unforgettable was the time that Jim and I met in the Atlanta airport. We were both on an Eastern flight to Houston, Texas, to see Shaquille O'Neal work out, this would have been the summer of '88.

We ended up sitting together on that flight and from the time we took off from Atlanta I just had tears in my eyes, I was laughing so hard. He had this new high-tech notebook organizer that he was explaining to me, and of course, he could make an organizer funny. I told him that I wasn't very organized and that I didn't know he was.

He went from the organizer to golf and told me about playing at the Country Club of North Carolina, and this one took about half an hour and ended with him saying that a guy he'd played with down there had asked him to move because the shine from Jimmy's new shoes was blinding him when he was trying to putt. Then he told me about all his speeches that he was doing for IBM and all the big corporations.

He said, "You know, I always take a speaking engagement after a loss on the road, right there in that area where we just got beat."

I asked why and he said, "Because they're always going to give me a standing ovation!"

I was laughing so hard and as we de-boarded the plane, I was walking behind Jim and the stewardess grabbed me and said, "Sir, how could have you possibly sat there with that man the whole time without speaking? He never gave you a chance to say a word!"

I said, "You don't know Jimmy Valvano!" Of course, I couldn't have said anything anyway; I was too busy laughing.

NERVOUS TICK

FRANK WEEDON *remembers V's idea of a sympathy note.*

I'd been working at my house at the lake and gotten a tick bite. I had to go to the hospital where they treated me for Lyme's Disease. So I missed one of the baseball tournaments and the guys from the ACC–Clemson and others who were always at these events–sent me a card saying that they had taken a vote on the get-well wish and that it was three in favor and that Ed Seamon, our sports information director, had abstained.

Later, when Jim heard about me being in the hospital he added a note of his own. He said, "Yes, I was sorry to hear about that. I understand the tick died!"

AGE BEFORE BEAUTY

MIKE GRAY, the popular host of WUNC-TV's Almanac Gardner, remembers preparing to tape an interview with V, who had just been named NC State's new athletic director. Gray, recognized by TV fans in North Carolina by his flowing white mane and matching beard, tried to think of just the right line to open with.

We were standing on the sidelines at Carter-Finley Stadium and I was getting ready to interview Coach V and Dick Sheridan, the Wolfpack football coach.

I'd never met V and when he walked up, I opened with an incredibly lame line: "Hi, I'm Mike Gray; did you know that we're the exact same age!"

V looked at my hair and said, "Wow, what happened to you?"

LIGHTS, CAMERAS, NO ACTION!

All V needed was a camera. And TERRY GANNON, his shooting guard, recalls the pre-game speech being taped for a film called Cutting The Nets *when the director didn't shout "cut!" soon enough.*

Here's something that isn't exactly news. When the cameras were on, Coach was on! We're in the locker room before the Virginia game and there are cameras all over the place because they're filming V's motivational film, *Cutting the Nets.* He's wild. It's like TV evangelist meets Knute Rockne. He's just going nuts, getting us pumped up for the game. "Who are we going to beat?" "Virginia!" we scream. Then he did the "Neva', eva' give up!" line. This went on and on... and it's retake after retake and pretty soon one of the assistant coaches comes running in and says, "Coach... the buzzer just went off, they're ready for us up there."

V says, "Hey... we're ready for them... one more take!"

The cameras roll and we do another one. Finally a referee comes in and breaks it up and we literally struggle up the steps and onto the court. We were exhausted by our theatrics... physically and emotionally drained. And so we get blown out by Virginia. If anyone ever gets a chance to see *Cutting the Nets*, take a look at the locker room scene. V was never better. Of course what the film doesn't show is us staggering up and down the court after his speech. No nets were cut that game. We peaked, along with V, right there... left our game with the film on the locker room floor.

GRINCH!

JAMIE VALVANO remembers her dad reading one of the all-time classics.

When LeeAnn was in kindergarten Dad went to her class to read *The Grinch Who Stole Christmas*. When he had finished a little boy in the back of the room raised his hand. My dad thought he was going to ask a question about NC State basketball.

The little boy said, "Mr. Valvano, why do you spit so much when you read?"

Dad said, "Obviously you've never heard an Italian read The Grinch!"

BABY-SITTIN'

ART KAMINSKY, who counseled V on everything from business deals to his NC State coaching contracts, remembers the day his client gave him some "fatherly advice."

There was an incident that I remember which showed an interesting side of Jimmy. This was when NC State played in the Meadowlands and lost to Georgetown in that controversial call with Corchiani. I took my daughter down to that game, which was in the evening. So we were in the hotel with Jim and the team that afternoon. I thought we'd hang around Jim a little bit and chat.

Well, when we got there I had to do something, see some people. So I told my daughter to stay in the hotel room, that I'd be back in a few minutes. Well, one thing led to another and I was gone longer than I should have been. When I got back to my room she wasn't there. Of course I was really concerned. Then I thought maybe she had gone up to Jim's room because I'd introduced her to him earlier. So I called his room. Boy, did he give me a lot of grief.

Then he said, "Come on up here."

When she called up there to see if I was there Jim had come down and brought her up to his room. So when I got there, there they were, he had ordered pizza and had been entertaining her for the last hour.

Now this was before the Georgetown game, a pretty big game that night. But that was the kind of person he was—baby-sitting on the afternoon of one of the really big games of his career. And she still remembers that very fondly, not just V entertaining her—he made sure that she had pizza too.

T FOR V

During the "V" years, trainer JIM REHBOCK was about as close to Jim Valvano as you could get. He sat at the end of State's bench and was often the last man between V and the referees.

One of the classics was back in the '80s and then they only had two officials. Hank Nichols, who is now the head of all NCAA referees, was calling the game—this was at Maryland. Hank makes a call that Jimmy didn't like. Jimmy would talk to officials all the time but he knew better than to show them up.

He'd always say, "You never swear at them and if you talk to them, you talk to them so it looks to the crowd like you are coaching the players."

So Hank had made a call that he didn't like and the ball had come down to our end of the floor. Now this was before the coach's box, and so Jimmy goes up to almost center court and he says, "Hank, can a coach get a technical for what he's thinking about an official?"

And Hank's watching the game and he says, "No, not for thinking something!"

So Jimmy gets up closer to where Hank can really hear him and he says, "Well, I think you stink!"

DRESSED FOR SUCCESS

JOHNNY RHODES, then a Myrtle Beach restaurateur, remembers joining Pam Valvano for a most important shopping spree—suiting up V.

I owned the Gullyfield, a seafood restaurant in Myrtle Beach. During that time we had a lot of celebrities eat with us. Jerry Lewis–and I don't mean Jerry Lee Lewis, we had the Jerry Lewis–Linda Ronstadt, soap opera stars, country and western stars…you name it.

No one got the attention that Jim Valvano got. People just went nuts over him. I got to know him really well because our restaurant hosted the ACC coaches during their spring meetings. We had the annual dinner and cocktail party at the Gullyfield, and this was for years. One night, when he first came into the league, I was standing at the cocktail party talking with V and Pam. He was wearing the damnedest ugly green coat, a lime green, a plaid shirt, and these stiletto shoes. It was the Emmett Kelly look!

I said, "Jimmy, are you planning to audition for a part in *Guys and Dolls* or what? You're in the South now; you need to learn to dress like you have some taste. You make Skeeter Frances look great!"

Pam jumps in and says, "I've tried to tell him!" And then she said, "Jim, look at John, look how nice he dresses."

This is on Monday night and the coaches' meeting was on Tuesday so V just says, "Okay, I want to look like John when I grow up. You two girls like to shop, so John can come by, pick Pam up tomorrow, and buy me some southern clothes."

He gave us his credit card, and we went to the Hub the next day and used that credit card pretty good. We got him a black and gray silk coat, kind of a plaid. I had one that Pam liked so we bought him one just like mine. We got him charcoal slacks and a nice dark blue shirt, some yellow ties. This was a couple of years before he won the national championship.

And after '83 when he'd come in, I'd say, "Hey, you're a big deal now but remember who dressed you for the part—Pam and me!"

Pam and John's coat and slacks appear on the cover of V's biography, Valvano: They Gave Me a Lifetime Contract, and Then They Declared Me Dead.

ᑫ

GURU MCGUIRE

GEORGE TARANTINI remembers the day that V's guru gave him the secret of life.

Jimmy loved [former coach and broadcaster] Al McGuire, and Al McGuire was in Raleigh to cover a game. So Al calls Jimmy from his hotel and asks him to come see him, something he wants to talk to him about. Now, Al is different, very different. Jimmy wants to know if I want to go along with him to see him. Sure, why not!

So Al's downtown in a hotel and so we go to his room and knock on the door.

We hear, "Come in!"

Now we walk in and the room is dark. It's the middle of the day and the room is dark, and here's McGuire sitting cross-legged in the middle of the bed. He's wearing nothing but a flannel shirt or a kimono and the room is black. It was like visiting Howard Hughes, that strange. Dark, mysterious, and the guy's sitting cross-legged in the middle of the bed. You don't meet somebody sitting in the middle of the bed like a Buddha. Jimmy is walking around the room in the dark, talking a mile a minute. I sit down and don't say anything.

All of a sudden McGuire—and I'll never forget this—he just says. "Jimmy, sit down, sit on the bed!"

Now Jimmy has a lot of nervous energy, and nobody tells him to sit down. You don't do that to Jimmy. But Al says sit, and so Jimmy sits down on the bed.

Then Al McGuire looks Jimmy straight in the eyes and he says, "You are going too fast. You are a train going 200 miles an hour. Where are you going? Slow down. You are going to crash!"

And Jimmy is very silent, I'm quiet, the room is quiet, because this is very powerful what he just said.

Al saw it coming. That was a day I'll never ever forget. Al McGuire telling him that he needed to stop and in that unforgettable scene—Al sitting on that bed in the dark in that robe, cross-legged like some kind of Buddha—and that was just about a year before Jimmy got sick. Everybody wanted a piece of him, everybody wanted him somewhere, and he was running so hard, and that's what Al McGuire saw.

BORN COACH

Retired UCLA coach JOHN WOODEN, V's ultimate basketball idol, recalls the kid from New York who was born to be a coach.

My first memory of Jim goes back to a basketball camp in the Poconos run by Harry Litwack and Bill Foster. Bill Foster was the coach at Rutgers at the time, and I think that Bill was recruiting Jimmy Valvano and another player named Collins. I got well acquainted with Jimmy then. He was rare in that he was just a sponge for basketball. He would talk to Harry and me and all the older coaches who were there, always asking, so inquisitive about the game. And I just knew right then that he was born to coach. He was one of two, I had one other player who in all my years, that I said that he was born to coach. I was very fond of Jimmy, impressed by his eagerness and vitality and just enjoyed him so much.

Over the years I had a little contact with him. But, of course, it was hard because we were across the country from each other. I was so very, very happy for him when he won the Championship in 1983. It did not surprise me. I do remember writing him a letter to congratulate him on the outstanding job that he did. I don't remember the details of that letter, but I know that I was so happy for him. I think I may have mentioned Don Haskins from the University of Texas at El Paso, because those two—his and Jimmy's—were two of the most outstanding coaching jobs in an NCAA tournament.

But I wasn't surprised to see him win. He was so upbeat, always. And I saw that just when he was in college, that incredible vitality was amazing, very catching, very catching. He was so entertaining and such an enthusiastic person.

Over the years I developed a [leadership] program, and in it I talk about the Pyramids of Success. The cornerstones of the Pyramids of Success are industriousness and enthusiasm. They are the cornerstones for success in anything. And if anybody ever had them, it was Jimmy Valvano.

BEST SEAT IN THE HOUSE

V's moment, that run for a hug after Lorenzo Charles dunked home the national championship, was seen by 50 million people on network TV. But the man who sat in the catbird seat for that piece of history was none other than V's center, COZELL MCQUEEN.

There are so many stories about Coach Valvano. Like the one about him recruiting me. I was from South Carolina, and there was always this thing about North and South Carolina. I've heard this one a million times: supposedly when I signed with NC State I told Coach V that I wanted to come to NC State because I wanted to play in the North.

I never was sure whether I actually said that or that was one he made up for laughs.

But there's one I'll never forget. I tell this one all the time.

I know where I was when Jimmy V made his famous run around that court after we won the national championship. As soon as Lorenzo slammed the dunk home, I headed for the other basket because I knew we were going to be cutting those nets down. If you look at the video you'll see them lowering the basket, and I got down there and pulled myself up and got up on the rim. Then I pulled myself up again to the top of the backboard.

So V's down there running all around the court, the place is going crazy–we've just won a national championship-and I'm up there looking down on all of it… from the best seat in the house.

THE GREAT PRE-GAME DEBATE

JIM REHBOCK, the Wolfpack's trainer, recalls pre-game stretching rituals as being both physical and intellectual.

He really was very intellectual and really well read, and not just on sports. I can remember taking a trip in the early years back when Chuck Nevitt and Max Perry were on the team and we got into this philosophical discussion on the bus going to Winston-Salem to play Wake Forest.

It was a Saturday game and we went up that morning. All the way over Jimmy led this discussion, and the topic—now this was on our way to play a nationally televised game—was suicide. Whether it was an act of bravery or desperation. And V turned it into a formal debate. He was the moderator and one guy, maybe Scotty Parzych, would say it was an act of bravery because it held the death penalty. Others were saying an act of desperation or stupidity because you only have one life. We talked about that all the way to Winston-Salem with Jimmy commenting on their points, adding his thoughts, commenting on their reasoning.

When the bus pulled into War Memorial Coliseum, V said, "Okay, we have a basketball game to play. But we'll continue this discussion on the way home."

Story Time at the V House. Here (left to right) Nicole, LeeAnn, Pam, Jamie, and Muffin listen.

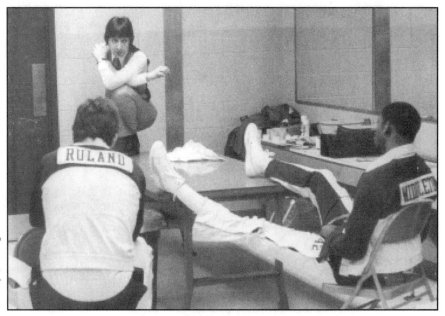

V and his *first prize* recruit Jeff Ruland.

V & Rutgers All-America guard Bob Lloyd, the great player
who made fans refer to his friend Valvano as "the other guard."

V with Bruce Poulton. The NC State Chancellor remembers V as audacious,
a brilliant coach, and one of those rare creative types who was also a great visionary.

Jim Rehbock, the Wolfpack trainer responsible for making the coach *think inside the coach's box*, grabs a tale for V&Me. (See "Hanging on to V's Coattails.")

Kay Yow enjoying one of the thousands of laughs she got from her friend V.

V & Me

Simon Griffiths Photography

This wasn't the first nor would it be the last hug V gave Dereck Whittenburg and Sidney Lowe, the stars of his '83 Championship team. (See "Coming Home to Roost.")

Reprinted with permission of The News & Observer of Raleigh, North Carolina.

V & Willis Casey, the athletic director who V ended up kissing on the lips during his wild "Thrill of Victory" run after winning the NCAA championship in '83.

Reprinted with permission of The News & Observer of Raleigh, North Carolina.

Dean Smith and Coach K probably *not* collecting their compelling stories for *V&Me*!

Simon Griffiths Photography

Two and two are four! V with (left to right) his fellow coaches Ed McLean, Tommy Abatemarco, and Dick Stewart. (Ray Martin must have been recruiting.)

Terry Gannon telling V his side of the story. (See "Hiding in the Corner.")

Courtesy The V Foundation for Cancer Research.

V and friends Frank McCann and Dick Vitale take this photo op to promote a book or three.

Simon Griffiths Photography

Hope springs eternal. V springs for the microphone!

V created his own off-beat golf tournament and called it the Rossie, in honor of his favorite TV golf analyst, Bob Rosburg. Pictured here (left to right) at the first Rossie are: Bob Lloyd, Harry Rhoads, Nick Valvano, Mo Davenport, John Saunders, Bob Valvano, Tim Brando and V.

V surrounded by love at the 10-year celebration of the 1983 NCAA Championship, his last visit to Reynolds Coliseum.

KNOCKOUT PUNCH

V's half-time speeches were legendary. But as former NCSU guard CHRIS CORCHIANI recalls, it was the one at the Louisville game in Hawaii that really packed the knockout punch.

We were in Honolulu, Hawaii, playing Louisville; this was Christmas of '87. At half-time we were down by about 12 or 13. V was still outside screaming at the referees and we were in the locker room waiting, knowing he was just going to rip our asses. The locker room door was kind of like a swinging door, and Dr. [Jim] Manley, our team doctor and a great guy, maybe about seventy years old, happened to be standing right inside the door. So we're kind of ready for V, knowing that he was going to be wild.

What we didn't know is exactly how wild his entrance would be. All of a sudden–boom! That swinging door flies open and hits Dr. Manley right in the back, and down he goes. I mean he's in pain, really groggy.

Coach V doesn't lose a step. He says to our trainer, [Jim] Rehbock, "Get him out of here, I've gotta few things I have to say here."

So Rehbock drags Dr. Manley over into one of the locker stalls and he's working on him, reviving him. And V's just going nuts, giving us hell about how we'd played. We're listening to him but watching Rehbock work on Dr. Manley, hoping he's getting him straightened out.

So anyway we come back and at the end, pull it out and win, like 80–75.Now, we're getting on the bus after the game and Dr. Manley's sitting up there having a few drinks, starting to feel better.

V comes on, he's happy now, and he starts up and down the aisle of the bus, he's screaming, "Dr. Manley, the next time we're down by 13 at half-time, I want you to get in position right behind that door. Because if I have to knock the hell out of you again to get these guys' attention, that's what I'll do."

SPEECHLESS

PAT KENNEDY remembers the "unknown" speaker who walked into the Kennedys' basketball camp in the Pocono Mountains of Pennsylvania and didn't leave until he had become a legendary speaker.

My dad owned this great basketball camp and we had the best speakers in the country. That's what we thought until this unknown coach from Bucknell filled in one day. What he did was this great shtick about living the dream, and the kids just absolutely loved it. The premise was Norman Vincent Peale's *Power of Positive Thinking* and the belief that someday they would all cut the nets down in Madison Square Garden. At the time he hasn't coached in the Garden because he's at Bucknell, but he's on his way. So he was fabulous, and we hired him for the next five weeks. He came every Monday–Monday was V Day.

Gymie the Rat

So Jimmy came in every Monday for that first summer and the kids were always going to learn and laugh. Then he comes back the second year and he's really mastered his lecture. Now he has this thing he did where he'd tell the kids that there were two kinds of players–big timers who think they're a big deal, and the rats that come from the gutter and work their tails off, take charges, and dive for balls. He'd tell them that Jim Valvano was a rat, and he'd pull his hair back and turn his face around, and with that nose he looked exactly like a rat. So this rat philosophy became a huge thing in our camp. He had T-shirts that said, "I'm a rat!" and eventually he had this little stuffed rat on a skateboard that he dragged around with him.

Now here's the story about the rat on the skateboard. A bunch of high school coaches from Ohio, headed up by a coach named John Daley, loved Jimmy. They'd been here the summer before as counselors. They drove their trailers in and stayed in the cabins and were great guys, and they were all there at Jimmy's first lecture where he did the rat thing. So at the end of the second summer they killed a rat, stuffed it, and mounted it on a skateboard. Then they had it standing up on the board like the rat was taking a charge. So the last week that Jimmy lectured, the coaches from Ohio present Jimmy the rat on the skateboard.

Crash Landing

We get into the third summer and now Jimmy's lecturing every-where, and the word has gotten out: he's the best lecturer in all the camp circuits in the country. So he's everywhere, with Sonny Hill, at the 76ers camp, the Foster camp. He could come in here and in two days speak in four camps. For him, he's making a lot of money. So the third year he came to our camp he's got the whole ritual; we introduce him—the kids go nuts, chanting V! He does the lectures about the big timers and the rats and hands out the T shirts, and now he has the new prop, so he pulls a sheet off the rat on the skateboard and holds up the rat.

They're actually mesmerized; they think they're going to hear some boring basketball stuff, and we got a dead rat on a skateboard. But that was just the tip of the iceberg with Jimmy. He always had to top himself, do something special, something really bizarre. So now it's the last week of his third summer, and the night before his speech we're out drinking beer and eating pizza. He's coaching at Iona now and he's getting fired up and shooting pool and throwing darts; a lot of famous coaches are there, so he's really in his element.

I've gotta go back to the camp but before I leave he grabs me and says, "Listen, introduce me at 10:30 tomorrow morning. But I won't actually, physically be there. So you take the kids out on the court and introduce me!"

So I say, "Okay."

Now I go back and tell my brother Bobby, and we just shake our heads. At this time nothing that Jim did shocked us—we thought!

So at 10:30 the next morning after we'd done our station drills, I get the whole camp on the main court. We had about 400 girls in camp that week. I walk out and Jim's not there. But I go out and introduce him anyway, and I start stretching it out because there's still no Jimmy V and now I'm get-ting nervous. I do the introduction like three times, adding things, stringing it out. And just as I start to run it by them again I hear this whump, whump, whump. Here comes this old helicopter over the mountain. And it's one of these all glass-enclosed choppers. The night before in the bar he'd met this old Vietnam chopper pilot who owned a helicopter somewhere outside of the Pocono Mountains. V had talked the guy into dropping him into his speech, landing right there on the court with all these kids waiting. This chopper was old and all of a sudden I say to myself, "Oh, shit. It's him!" Now the girls have heard about Jim Valvano all summer so now they are going absolutely nuts, cheering, jumping up trying to grab the helicopter.

So what does V do? He makes a pass at them, lets the crowd build, down he comes and up he goes. And I'm going, "Oh man, where is our insurance policy?" Back he comes again, another pass. The second swoop he's holding the rat up, and then he pulls his hair back so he looks exactly like the rat, and he presses that big nose to the glass on the chopper. Now the kids are wild. And for the big finish back he comes for a third pass.

This time he totally tops himself. He threw up!

He got sick as a dog and threw up all over the rat, the glass windshield, the pilot. The pilot looked like a typical Viet vet, he'd probably smoked two joints before he took the plane up. But he brings it in and finally lands there on the main court. And Jimmy jumps out of the chopper, and he and his rat are covered with vomit. But the girls are still going crazy. They pick him up on their shoulders and carry him and his rat to what we called the Outhouse, where these big outdoor showers were. They throw the rat and Jimmy, with all his clothes on, in the shower.

He gets cleaned up, jogs down to the court, and gives one of the best two-hour lectures on basketball and winning and attitude that you've ever heard in your life!

TP TIME FOR V

*Player **MIKE WARREN** remembers one of V's most observant moments as a coach.*

This was a beaut. We're playing ECU, and there's this guy who was a freshman that had to be about twenty-eight years old, and he just lights it up against us in the first half, maybe 16, 18 points. V's got a half-time plan to stop this guy, of course. So the second half starts, and the guy isn't on the court, in fact we didn't ever see him come out of the locker room. So this is the topic of conversation at my end of the bench, probably me and Dinky Proctor. And then all of a sudden we see him coming out of the locker room and they put him in the game like immediately.

And the first time he goes down the court, V kind of sidles down the bench and he says, "Hey, guys, check the shooter out!" And we look and he has toilet paper hanging out of the back of his shorts!

DEALS ON WHEELS

LARRY GROSS, former NC State soccer coach, remembers the day that he finally outdealt Mr. Wheeler Dealer.

Jimmy used to tell everybody that I was the only dumb Jew he'd ever met. And he was just so quick you couldn't get back at him verbally, he was really so funny. Never mean spirited, and I never had a problem with the political incorrectness of his jabs. I grew up just several miles from where he did on Long Island, and that's just the way it was where we came from. Jimmy was a Wop, I was a Jew, and so we used to go at each other with that kind of back-and-forth here at NC State. Now, Jimmy had this Mazda B-2000 truck that he really didn't need. He wanted to sell it, and so he literally coerced me into buying this truck.

He just kept saying, "Hey, Gross, you like to buy cars, I've got a deal for you."

Well, he never really came up with a price, and finally he caved and asked, "Okay, you know cars, how much will you give me for the truck?"

The fact is that I really didn't need it. So I low-balled the hell out of him and offered $3,500. I'm thinking he's going to tell me to take a hike. Jimmy was tight as a tick with a buck and you just couldn't outdeal him.

"Sold!" he says.

I couldn't believe it. So I was the new owner of the Jimmy V B-2000 Mazda, a really nice little truck. I don't know how long it took him but I remember the day that he discovered the blue book value. It was about $7,500. Oh man, he went absolutely nuts.

I just said, "Hey Jimmy, how's this for history? 'World's dumbest Jew and driving a pickup truck!'"

HUDDLING WITH V

As NC State's point guard, SIDNEY LOWE was V's floor coach. Sidney recalls the messages that he took into the game and how they were delivered.

In the huddle, even with V's enthusiasm, when it was time to be calm he always spoke very positively. Whether it was about a guy we needed to stop or if we were going to shoot a free throw, he always said positive things.

Now, what he would do after the other guys broke for the court, he would grab me and say something different. Like if he told Lorenzo or Cozell that they were going to make a foul shot like it had already happened, he'd say to me, "Sidney, if he misses this thing, foul the first f*&%er you can!"

And, of course, I knew what he was doing, and he'd tell me things because he knew that I'd relay it to the guys if they needed to know it.

Here's a situation: one game he told us that we had to take the open shot, and so if it's there, we take it.

"I want Sidney to penetrate and make something happen, find the open man, I don't care who it is, just get it to the open man."

And as we are going out he stops me and says, "Now you know I want it to go to Thurl or Dereck!"

So Lorenzo and Cozell were out of this play, but they were young then and he knew it; he wanted them to stay confident, and that's just the way he did it.

REAL RIP

GEORGE NIXON remembers going on a "tear" with Coach V.

It was the first round of the NCAA tournament and we're playing Iowa in Minnesota. During the first five minutes of the game I split my pants. My underwear was showing so I had to take a jersey and wrap it around my butt. Then during the game, Coach V ripped the hell out of his pants and he had Dr. Manley sew them up. He's going out at half-time and the doctor is behind him still putting the final stitches in his pants.

So at the postgame press conference he described the game, which we won, as being so exciting that it was a two seater: both he and his manager had ripped their pants. I remember that line being in the Minnesota paper the next day and what a good laugh we had.

$\mathcal{V}$

CORCHIANI BY A NOSE

GEORGE TARANTINI remembers V and a comedy of manners.

Jimmy is recruiting Chris Corchiani, and he wants Chris very bad. We had this kid on our soccer team who was a two-time All-ACC player from Chris's high school in Miami. So Jimmy invites me to eat lunch with the Corchiani family when they visit our campus.

Instead of going out somewhere, Jimmy decides that we will have lunch inside Case Athletic Center, that he'll have it catered—upstairs in the lobby outside his office. So he got a table and ordered some food, and he had Chris's mother and father and Chris. Jimmy loved Chris, his toughness, his talent, his desire to win.

Now this is a big lunch because he wants Chris bad. This isn't some little recruit, this is big. So he invited me to be a part of the thing because Henry, my soccer player, was Chris's friend. So we sat at the table. Everything is up and up and very professional and everyone is saying the right things, everything is going great. Then the dessert comes out. And Jimmy and I loved to eat, that was one of the things we had in common.

One of the things with Jimmy was that if you ate with him you had to eat every single ounce of your food. You had to clean you plate. So we had this cheesecake and just as I'm eating my cheesecake, Jimmy makes a joke. I don't remember what he said, but it was funny and I start to laugh, and I tried to control it but I couldn't and I get to laughing so hard, in front of the whole Corchiani family, that a piece of cheesecake came through my nose. I'm embarrassed and trying to hide it.

But all of a sudden Jimmy says, right in front of this prize recruit and his family, "Hey, George, you've got a piece of cheesecake coming out of your nose!" I swear to God, right in front of everybody. Now they're all looking at me.

I said later, "What, are you nuts? You're trying to impress this family and you tell them that the soccer coach has got cheesecake coming out of his nose!"

But that was Jimmy. That was the way he was about recruiting, about people. He knew people and he knew that those people wouldn't be offended. He used to tell me, when we'd talk about recruiting, "It isn't about money or how much you want somebody, just be normal because it's all about people. The people who make decisions are just like you and me!"

V

TROUBLE IN PARADISE

Frances Lewis recalls several days when the marriage of coach and assistant looked like it might be on the rocks.

One of Jim's favorite stories, which he told all the time, was the one about flying to the wrong Greenville. He thought he was going to Greenville, North Carolina, and ended up in Greenville, South Carolina. Here's how that happened.

This was right after he became the head coach here at NC State, and he came rushing in from practice one day and said, "I have to be in Greenville for a Wolfpack Club meeting, see if you can get me a flight." Well, I thought that everybody knew that there's no flight to Greenville, North Carolina. So I naturally assumed that he was talking about Greenville, South Carolina. So I sent him to Greenville, South Carolina.

So when he gets off the plane in South Carolina, he starts looking around for his ride. Dave Hoffman, with the Wolfpack Club, was supposed to pick him up. But Dave was in Greenville, North Carolina, waiting to take him to Tarboro. Well, that became his number one story for his Wolfpack Club meetings. How he's walking around the airport in Greenville, South Carolina, in an NC State red coat, telling people he's the new Wolfpack coach... wondering why no one seems to care!

But he got even with me.

They had a big event honoring the Employees of the Year at the Student Center and I was nominated. Well, he gets up and tells that story and blames the nominee for the Employee of the Year for sending him to the wrong city. I was mad as I could be. I went stomping out of there and here came Jim, he was right behind me. Now the chancellor and all these VIPs were there, and they came chasing after Jim wondering why he's leaving.

And he said, "I can't talk now, I have to go get Frances." He was running and shouting "Frances, Frances!"

When he caught me he put his arm around me and said, "I'm so sorry I embarrassed you. If you'll forgive me, I'll never do it again!"

We had our moments. Here's another one.

We each had these little buzzers under our desks, and one of the things that I did was, when I thought someone was in there too long and that he needed to go, I'd buzz him. It would give him an excuse to end a conversation. So one day he had a reporter in there. But this was a day that he was supposed to speak at the Faculty Club and we were going together. The truth was that the person who was speaking before him was someone that I wanted to hear. But Jim's still there in his office with this reporter and he was wound up.

So I buzzed him. He paid no attention.

I buzzed him again. Still nothing.

So I just got up and I told the secretary, "When he comes out, just tell him that I went ahead without him."

Well, I got my seat, and the other speaker was going on, dragging out his speech trying to stall for Jim. And here comes Jim flying in the door, and he gets up and says, "Frances, where are you?"

He's looking all around. Then he spots me and says, "There she is! She ran off and left me. That's why I'm late!"

I got a napkin and put it over my face and just slid down in my seat. We had a little talk about that one when he got back.

HOORAY FOR HOLLYWOOD

JEFF MANN, the associate vice chancellor for business at NC State during the V years, remembers when Warner Brothers came to campus to film The Jimmy V Story *for a CBS TV movie. The first scene wasn't in the movie. It took place in Holladay Hall in the chancellor's conference room at what would become the project's bargaining table.*

There were a lot of things about that project that made us uneasy. Coach Valvano had passed away just two years before, and so on one hand we wanted to cooperate, but on the other there were flags that kept popping up that made us think that they might not get permission to shoot the movie on our campus. Frankly, we were afraid of the end product. We knew that the University of South Carolina was their fallback [location for shooting the movie] and that [the USC administration] probably wouldn't have the same concerns that we had—so the movie was going to be made.

First, the script was inaccurate and had been written by someone who clearly didn't know basketball, Jim Valvano or NC State, or the characters. There were real people portrayed in the script in very inaccurate ways.

Once we had penciled in our suggested corrections, notations on things that had to be made accurate, we invited the producer, director, and site location guy in for a meeting. They came into the chancellor's conference room in Holladay Hall, full of greetings from Governor Hunt. They said that the governor wanted to let us know that he wished us well in this project. Now, these guys had just gotten off a plane from California the day before and our impression was that they thought we'd just fallen off a turnip truck.

Jim Hunt is an alum of the university, someone that we had weekly contacts with—in fact we all knew him personally. So this kind of chutzpah didn't sit too well with our vice chancellor for finance. He was the man who would ultimately decide if they'd be allowed to shoot on our campus—and what the location fees would be.

There were many times that we've all wished V were still with us. This scene was one of them. They opened with the Governor Hunt is very supportive of this project line and then left themselves open to one of our resident wise guys.

As they searched for the appropriate seating around the big table, the movie's director said, "Where do you want us?"

And our guy from the PR office said, "How about South Carolina!"

The dance began. They told the story of a made-for-TV movie and how limited budgets were—and how important this would be to our university, all the positive publicity, etc. (bad tack).

We had set prices for shooting and our rate card matched other universities—Carolina, Duke, etc. When they finished poor mouthing, the vice chancellor read them our rates. With each pricing the Hollywoods shook their heads and uttered (under their breaths) "deal breaker."

When he was finished the producer gave an impassioned speech as to why they couldn't afford our exorbitant rates.

Then the vice chancellor countered. "I'm not finished," he said. "We intend to give all of the proceeds from this project to the Jimmy V Foundation for Cancer Research. So we'll stick to our rates, and then we'd like you to match this with a like amount as a charitable gift."

Never in the 100-plus year history of Holladay Hall had so many Gucci bags left one room so fast. We had agreed to take the beleaguered visitors on a courtesy tour of the campus to see where their movie would be shot. As I passed the vice chancellor in the hallway he called me over.

"If this movie is going to be made—and it will, I think—we have a better chance of it being accurate here. I was just getting their attention in there. We'll work a deal with them!"

The deal was finally struck. And I remember the night they shot the final scene in Reynolds Coliseum with the actor [Anthony] LaPaglia, who played V, giving the Coach's farewell speech at the ten-year celebration of the '83 championship. We'd all seen it in person on that same floor just a few short years earlier. So it was very moving. The script, if not perfect, had been improved greatly, and I was very proud to be able to give Pam Valvano and the head of the Jimmy V Foundation a check that night for over $11,000, our fee for the use of the campus.

FUN COACH

JEFF RULAND, one of the most heavily recruited players in the country, had a good opportunity to compare the various styles of coaches from all the big schools—Kentucky, Indiana, Notre Dame, and oh yes . . . little Iona College.

Long Island is flat but where I grew up there are hills. At Iona, V had this old shitty brown Maverick, and when he was recruiting me, we went to eat at places like Beef Steak Charley's and then rode around in that little car. I remember just watching V and his assistants and thinking these guys are great. The beer was flowing and he and the assistant coaches are jumping in that old brown Maverick and screaming off like felons—flying over the hills at eighty miles an hour like Steve McQueen in *Bullitt.*

This was a coach who led the NCAA in fun.

When we were with him, he was much younger, of course, and I'd talk to him like a friend. He'd lead the fast-break drills in practice. And we'd go to his office, and he'd break out the marker and tell me what a great X's and O's coach he was. I'd tell him he was full of shit, that my high school coach was better—and at that time he really was. But boy, he could motivate and he could have fun.

This is how loose he was then: We came into Raleigh to play in the NCAA's, and after practice he took us to a Gentlemen's Club. Now we're all wearing our yellow Iona Gaels T-shirts, sitting in this place with our coach.

I remember sitting in a team meeting and he, of course, had one of the first really small portable tape recorders. So he'd taped the famous rah, rah speech from the Knute Rockne movie. We only had a few white guys on the team, so almost nobody knew who Knute Rockne was. The brothers were sitting back there going, "What the f*&%# is this?"

That was one V motivational speech that put them right to sleep.

SNO-BIRDS

Jim Rehbock remembers the day that V and the Wolfpack, much to Bobby Cremins's chagrin, weathered the storm.

One of the times I'll never forget was the snow game against Georgia Tech. We were supposed to play on a Sunday, fly out on Saturday. But this snowstorm hits. We get to the RDU airport and it's so bad that they put us up there in a hotel, which is only about fifteen minutes from campus. So half the night we're up planning who to put on any Sunday morning flights that might get out.

Now, the reason V wants to make sure we play this game is: (A) it's on national TV, and (B) Georgia Tech's big guy, Hammonds, is out. If we play it, Cremins won't have Hammonds.

So finally V makes up his mind. It will be the five starters, two subs, two coaches, and me, the trainer. When we finally get to Atlanta, it's really late on Sunday morning. Now this is a 1 P.M. national TV game. The bus meets us at the terminal. We'd dressed the kids in the hotel in

Raleigh, put them in their warm-ups, and we don't even have time to pick up our luggage. So here we come running through Atlanta's airport in our warm-ups. Of course that caused a big hoopla.

We get to the bus and off we go—straight to the Alexander Mack Coliseum. But on the way we get behind this funeral procession. We're already late, it's like noon, and we are behind this funeral procession and Jimmy wants us to pass the funeral. Of course you can't do that because they've got a police escort. Then we hit this road construction, now he's really fuming. Finally we get to the Coliseum and here's Bobby Cremins waiting in the parking lot. Bobby says, "I know this is a national TV game but don't hurry, take as much time as you want to relax, I could care less about the TV." The refs give V an option.

V wants the TV.

So, we agree to play, do a few layups, and then let them toss it up for the 1:00 TV time.

Oh, there was another obstacle that almost made us miss the tip-off. That was the season that we wore the Unitards, the little body suits that V and Nike had created. So these guys are looking really funny anyway, they've just flown though the aftermath of a snowstorm, held up by a funeral. Now, they're suited up in those tunics and have to hit the bathroom. So the locker room at the Coliseum had two urinals and two toilets, and we've got these eight guys trying to get out of their warm-ups and their unitards to pee, and it was hilarious. But V's happy, he got a big kick out of that, and he knows that they're going to make the TV game, and Bobby won't have Hammonds.

We actually beat them by a basket and it was a great finish. We were up by two with the ball with seconds left to play. At the end we had to get the ball in with like a couple of seconds left, and Jimmy designed this last-second play to make sure it got to Brian Howard. He didn't want anyone else to touch it because Brian was so dependable—he wouldn't dribble it out of bounds or screw up. So V has the play, we'll get it to Howard. And we knew that they were going to try to make a steal. So the ball's under their basket, we get it in to Brian, and now there's just seconds left, but instead of holding the ball, Brian throws it up in the air. Alexander Mack is a dome and the floor was sunken. So he just heaved it up into that dome, and V's up screaming, "No, Brian, no!"

But by the time the ball came down the horn went off. A happy ending to one of the more memorable trips and games that V ever coached. He'd beaten Tech's whole team with seven guys, two coaches, and a trainer... and done it on national TV.

BATTLEFIELD PROMOTION

ED MCLEAN recalls a moment that V thought could be McLean's big break in college coaching.

I remember we were playing in Hawaii in a holiday tournament; we're playing Chaminade, the team that beat [number 1 ranked Virginia and star center] Ralph Sampson, a real good program. During the game Jim gets really dizzy and actually passes out. They had to take him down into the locker room. I think it was just a blood-pressure thing, but anyway after that game, which we won, he just turned it into an opportunity to entertain the press.

He said, "I started to get whiter and weaker and pretty soon I'm staggering and now I see Ed McLean watching me out of the corner of his eye. Now Ed's thinking this is his shot. And as soon as I went down Ed jumps up and starts changing defenses, running substitutes into the game. I'm going out and I hear him say, 'Hey, let's put Fasoulis in!'

You have to give the guy credit. If the guy goes down in front of you, grab his gun and keep going!"

CONTINUING EDUCATION

DERECK WHITTENBURG, who won four letters at NC State, remembers one lesson that he'll never forget.

I was probably one of the only players who stopped by his office almost daily. We talked about everything from world affairs to U.S. politics. I'll never forget the time... my junior year, he showed me a letter from one of the fans. This was the year before we won the championship. This fan was complaining about V playing an all-black lineup.

So we started talking about this, and V was saying, "Even though this is ridiculous, I'm glad he wrote this, because it's a reminder for you: this is what a great number of people really think."

When he showed me that letter, he said that it was the very reason why I had to get my degree, because "they" think that black players are just basketball players, that we can't do anything but play basketball. He turned a negative into a positive. And said, "Okay if one person actually wrote that, how many more were thinking that?" And that the only way we, as black athletes, could change that perception was to get our degrees.

It was an education: he never failed to take the opportunity to remind you of the importance of your degree.

TWO FOR THE ROAD

MIKE LUPICA, one of America's premier sports writers, knows and appreciates a good line. V rarely let him down.

Jim was a New York guy and we had covered him at Iona, the son of Rocco Valvano, who coached locally here on Long Island. So when Jim went to the Final Four, he was our New York story. There were so many moments with him, but the one that I'll never forget was in Albuquerque on Sunday afternoon after the press conference. Jim and NC State were going to play Houston for the national championship on Monday night and the whole tone of the press conference had been whether he was surprised to be there with this NC State team and ... that he didn't have a chance to beat Houston.

And so we're walking along, and he starts off, "Does UCLA have a chance? I don't think so! Does Kentucky have a chance? I don't think so!" He rattled off the six biggest basketball powers in the country that had been eliminated.

Then he said, "I kind of came here thinking I had a chance. That's why I brought two suits!"

$\mathcal{V}$

JOLTIN' JOE

John Saunders remembers the story about the time V met Joe DiMaggio and literally jolted "Joltin' Joe."

We were out playing golf and a guy came up to us and said one of the dumbest things that I'd ever heard.

The guy had hit his ball into our fairway and he sees us and he shouts, "Hey, Jim Valvano and John Saunders... wow, you look a lot fatter on TV!"

And so I say to Jim, "What makes people say something that stupid?"

And Jim says, "John, I would agree except I really know what it's like to say something that dumb."

So I go, "What?"

And he says, "Well, my dad's favorite baseball player of all time was Joe DiMaggio, he absolutely loved Joe. And Rocco saw him at an airport, went up to him, shook Joe D's hand and this was the greatest thing that ever happened to my dad... he got to meet Joe DiMaggio. Now, my dad died that same night of a heart attack.

"So a couple of years later, I'm at a golf tournament, and I look over at the buffet line and there's Joe DiMaggio. So I tell Pam I've gotta go meet Joe and tell him how much it meant to Rocco that he'd shaken his hand.

"So I go up to Joe D, and he's got his arms full of plates of pasta and rolls and I say, 'Mr. DiMaggio, I'm Jim Valvano, the head coach at NC State, and I just want to tell you I'm a huge fan of yours. But I'm only one tenth of the fan that my father was. And he always wanted to meet you and one day he finally did; he saw you in an airport and you shook his hand. And then he died.'"

Now Jim says that Joe DiMaggio turned as white as a ghost, drops his head, and walks away. So now Jim slinks back to his table and says, "Pam, I think I just told Joe DiMaggio that he killed my father!"

THE ROSSIE

Most people associate V with the Jimmy V Classic, a nationally known celebrity golf tournament, which has raised millions of dollars for cancer research. But long before the Jimmy V there was a classic by another name. FRANK McCANN remembers the early days of a rather loose event called The Rossie.

The Rossie was played after Jim left NC State. He was well then and I remember that he came to me and a fellow by the name of Danny Sullivan and asked us to help put it together for him.

We were always organizing things and he said, "I want to have a golf tournament and I want it to be for my friends. But I don't want it to be a normal golf tournament, golf is so uptight."

He laid out the ground rules. We'd have a black tie dinner prior to the golf, but it would be at an Italian restaurant with checkered tablecloths, not at some posh hotel. The tournament gift bag wouldn't be one of those expensive leather satchels. Jim chose a Harris Teeter [grocery chain] paper bag, which would be stuffed with gifts that made no sense.

He wanted all of his friends there and wanted The Rossie to be the "toughest ticket in town." Oh, and the rule was, once invited you were always invited. But if you declined you were out for life. No excuses, no matter what your reason.

So we created this tournament and of course, he worked on a name and finally decided. One day he said, "You know I like this guy Bob Rosburg, the ABC announcer, he's always right. A guy will hit it into the woods, and they ask Rossie what the guy is going to do next and invariably Rossie will say, 'Well he's going to hit a low fade over the water and run it up the right side of the fairway.'" Then Jim said, "That's what happens, the guy will do exactly what Rossie says he will. Rossie's my idol," he said.

So we named the tournament The Rossie. But we would not invite Rosburg. That would be too normal, run-of-the-mill. Jim decided to invite Rosburg's son. He didn't invite Michael Jordan, he invited Michael Jordan's chauffeur. Rosburg's son… came and played.

So it was a reverse from a normal tournament.

The first Rossie black tie was held at Amedeo's, a great little Italian restaurant in Raleigh. We were in the banquet room, had to be black tie on a Saturday night. We called this the pairings party, and this was about forty players. The only thing traditional was the head table on a riser with each member of The Rossie Committee speaking, explaining everything from the gift bag, which contained packages like coffee and condoms which Jim labeled The Brew and Screw, that kind of thing. Jim introduced me as Father Frank [most present had never met McCann] and I came out in a priest's collar and gave an irreverent speech.

Then Jim came on. It was like being at a $100 a seat Vegas show, he was that good, that funny. Of course the golf was great; everyone had to wear white socks, white shoes, and shorts. Jim bought the players Rossie golf shirts. This was about as much fun as a golf tournament could be—people from all walks of life, some famous, some not famous.

The Rossie went on for a number of years, at least three until his sickness. We tried to maintain it after he died; it just didn't work, we couldn't do it. Then the Jimmy V Celebrity Golf Tournament took over my time, and now millions of people know about the Jimmy V Celebrity Classic. But the forerunner was The Rossie, which was just so very much Jim and in its own unique way just as special.

THE CLINIC

KAY YOW remembers the best game coach she ever saw—V.

The best game coach? I can't think of a better one than Jim.

I remember when they were going to go play UNLV, and Las Vegas's defense was just incredible. I went into Jim's practice before that game to watch, and he was working on like a five-out offense with just cutting: he'd spread the court.

I knew that this wasn't his offense, so I asked him what he was up to, and he said, "Hey, against that team we'll never make an entry pass, we can't run our offense against that defense. If we try to, it won't work, we won't have a chance. So we're going to spread the floor and cut and cut and pass and cut. This is what we're going to do."

And it worked. He was the best on junk defenses—triangle and two, box and chaser. He would do something that would look just crazy, like put Chris Corchiani on a huge guy like Tom Hammonds at Georgia Tech—a little guy on a big guy, to deny him the ball. And it would work. He had a great mind for the game, a risk taker who would go outside the box.

𝒱

WHAT ARE THE ODDS?

ART KAMINSKY recalls an educational bus ride, one that revealed V's incredible aptitude for the game.

NC State beat South Carolina in the first round of the '89 regionals in Providence, Rhode Island. I remember that we were driving over in the bus to see Georgetown-Princeton, another first round game. As it turned out, V's team would play the winner the next week in the Meadowlands. I was sitting next to him talking about the upcoming game.

I went to Cornell, and we'd played Arizona the year before in a similar match-up—something like a one seed, playing a sixteen seed—and we'd lost big. Thinking about what happened to Cornell the year before, I said I thought that Princeton would get killed, and asked V how much he thought Princeton would lose by, forty or fifty points?

He said, "No, I think Princeton can win."

I couldn't believe it. Georgetown had Alonzo Mourning.

Then V said, "Let me explain something to you. You have to look at the match-up, John Thompson and Pete Carril at Princeton. John Thompson is exactly the kind of coach that Pete wants to coach against. You have to be patient to take Princeton apart and if you aren't, their system can just kill you. And I think that Princeton can win the game."

He was the only person in America who thought that was going to be a close game. Princeton led the entire time and only lost on a horrendous call when Mourning fouled the Princeton center, just bludgeoned him, and got no call. So this is how smart Jimmy was about basketball and just how well he understood the game. Only Valvano would have made that call about a game that now has gone down as one of the great near-upsets in the history of the NCAA tournament. I think the final score was 50–49, and Jimmy called that one right out of the chute.

BIRTH WATCH

Bob Staak played for V, coached against V, and baby-sat for V.

Nicole was like two at the time, and my wife Jo Ann and I are at another friend's house for dinner when we get the call from Jim. Pam's ready to deliver (Jamie), and he needs a sitter quick.

Jim says, "I'm getting ready to take Pam to the hospital!"

So I'm all nervous because we've got to keep Nicole, and Pam's having a baby. Jim has this big old green Cadillac that he called The Hog and we get them out of the house and on their way to the hospital. I'm afraid that the water is going to break in the house so we get them out. Nicole's already asleep and finally they're gone. But like three minutes later here's Pam at the front door. And I panic because I thought she was back to call 911, but she'd just forgotten something. Now they're gone again and Nicole's asleep. Everything is okay so Jo Ann and I went to bed in Jim and Pam's bed.

Problem.

Nicole came in during the middle of the night to crawl in with her mom and dad, and there are two strangers in their bed. Man, she just went nuts, crying and really scared and no wonder. It was unbelievable. So we had the hardest time putting her down and once we did and finally got back to sleep ourselves, here's another knock on the bedroom door.

Another Valvano.

It's Jim now; he's home from the hospital, and he wakes us up and says, "We had a girl, we named her Jamie. Bob, come on downstairs and we'll crack open a bottle of champagne!"

Now I'm half asleep and he wants me to sit up and drink with him. And this is something he never let me forget. I just rolled over and said, "Congratulations, Jim!" and went back to sleep! I never heard the end of it, Jim has a baby and Bob Staak, his "great friend," won't get out of Jim Valvano's own bed to drink with the new father!

V MEETS MUHAMMAD ALI

Bob Lloyd recalls perhaps the one and only time that V got talked down and backed down.

Rutgers was playing in the Garden and Jimmy found out that Muhammad Ali was training in one of the gyms there. Just by luck he met Angelo Dundee, Ali's trainer, in one of the snack bars. So of course Jimmy's chatting him up, asking Angelo if he can get in the ring with the Champ.

After practice our team is walking by the gym and Dundee sees Jimmy and turns to the Champ and says something like, "There he is, there's the basketball guy who wants to get in the ring with you!"

Well, Ali starts yelling at Jimmy, telling him, "Come on up here, chump!"

Now Jimmy is scrambling but we grab him and put him up there in the ring with Ali. But it didn't happen, Jimmy chickened out. And you know, missing that was one he had to regret. Because it was a natural photo op for the New York newspapers, RUTGERS GUARD KEEPS GUARD UP FOR CHAMP!

CLEAN SWEEP

Woody Webb, the attorney who handled Valvano's "departure" settlement with NC State, recalls V's response when the legal counselors representing the university suggested that if V should stay he might find himself in a janitorial position.

I was retained by Jim personally as his attorney. He wanted somebody his age, somebody that he could interact with who could understand where he was coming from. So one of the first meetings that I had with the legal representatives of NC State included the chief deputy attorney general, a guy named Andy Vanore, for whom I have a great deal of respect. The university had also retained Howard Manning, a special counsel from the private sector, nicknamed the Bear.

So anyway we were meeting and things were getting hot and heavy. There were also numerous exchanges in the media. We met at the law offices of Manning, Fulton & Skinner, at their law firm; we always met there, never anywhere else. And Manning says to me, "If we don't get this resolved soon, what we're going to do is relieve Mr. Valvano of his duties as the head basketball coach and put him in the position of being the janitor at NC State."

This, of course, was completely contrary to his personal services contract and couldn't have been done. Later on when I talked to Andy Vanore, he totally agreed with my analysis. It was an intimidation comment. So I went back to V and I told him, "Manning says he's going to make you the janitor at NC State." And V said, "That's all right, I'll dress up as Art Carney, and I'll go out there at half-time [at Reynolds Coliseum] with my broom and I'll sweep the court. That'll be great. I'll wear a sign on my back that says 'Former Coach!'"

So I called up Andy Vanore and I told him, "You know, V wants to be the janitor. You can't do it legally, but he really wants to be the janitor. He says, 'Tell Howard that I'll be out there on the court dressed up like Art Carney, sweeping the court at half-time with a sign that says "Former Coach" on my back. It will really be good publicity for you guys.'"

BUS . . . TED

MIKE WARREN recalls one of those moments that ball busters like V lived for.

V was such a ball buster. And Ray Martin, our assistant coach, was a real sharp dresser. We called Ray "Dice!" V tried, but he couldn't come close to "Dice" when it came to apparel.

So now we're at Duke and there was an old coach at Duke who ran the facilities over there. Ray had these really slick outfits, and one of them was a blue suit, a blue shirt, and a dark blue tie. So we're standing there on the court before the game and it's V, Ray, and the other coaches. The Duke coach, a kind of a crusty old guy, comes up to Ray and says, "Hey, I need you to move your bus, I've gotta get some other vehicles back there in that lot!"

He saw Ray's blue-on-blue outfit and thought he was the bus driver. Oh, man, poor Ray, right in front of V. Well, V just flipped on that one. He never let Dice forget it, calling him "Bussy." If V got something like that on you... well, Dice knew he was in for a long bus ride back to Raleigh.

ROOM OF DREAMS

CHANCELLOR BRUCE POULTON recalls the day that he knew his head basketball coach had room to dream.

The guy was a dreamer! But the difference with him and many people who dream was that he would put his concept of what a dream could do for you into effect.

He called me up one day and said, "I'd like you to come down to Case Athletic Center and see my new Dream Room."

So I went down and he had taken a room, which he called the Room of Dreams–and installed a multi-media presentation system with wrap-around screens. There was one big comfortable chair in the middle of the room, and he sat me in that chair and put earphones on me. Suddenly I was subjected to half an hour of the most imaginative dream, what it would be like to play basketball at NC State. It jumped from films of great games to him on the screens talking to spotlights flickering on and off, showcasing championship rings and game balls from past victories.

It was incredible, really impressive. He was going to use it for recruiting and... all I could think as I watched this unfold was how impressive it would be to young kids; they would be captivated by that experience. But he believed with every ounce that he could win another national championship and that this room would enable him to get bodies in there to combine with his superior coaching talents.

I believe that if he had lived long enough and had gone back into coaching, he would have won another national championship; he never stopped living his dreams.

LOVE NOTE

V was known for his rather short and to-the-point notes. RICH PETRICCIONE treasured this one.

I was a finalist in 1987 for the Monmouth head coach's job. It came down to me and the coach at Columbia. The president at Monmouth wanted the coach at Columbia. I really thought I was going to get it but I didn't.

Well, I get a letter a couple of days later from V and it says, "Why would you want to work at a school that means 'My Mouth' in French?"

PANTS DOWN

Nothing more clearly defines V's creative sense of humor than his ability to invent games that were inherently fun and funny. BOB STAAK, his friend and fellow coach, can never forget the image of a V game called "Pants Down."

Jim instigated this game when he played with Bill Foster at Rutgers. Bill would leave early to go recruit or something and

Jim and Bobby Lloyd, Dick Stewart, all those guys would play Pants Down.

Then Jimmy would get us playing it in his basketball camps at Bucknell. This was when I was the assistant at Penn, and Jim was the coach at Bucknell. I worked his camp and in the evenings after the kids were back in the dorms, we used to go down to a place called the Bull Run Inn. This was in Lewisburg, Pennsylvania. We'd go down there and drink beer and have pizza ,and then when we got enough beer and pizza in us—about 12 or 1 in the morning—the counselors and coaches would go back to the gym and play.

You had to play Pants Down with your shorts down around your ankles, so you couldn't really run. Your foot would move maybe a foot and a half, and you'd shuffle up and down the court. Now Jimmy would organize these games, and we'd play Pants Down like full court, four on four. Jocks, shorts, whatever you had on under your shorts, but your shorts were down around your ankles.

Now this was hysterical. Try fast-breaking going full court, half shit-faced with your shorts around your ankles. Jim loved that game! And, of course, if you didn't watch him he'd cheat, one leg out. He had to win. We used to catch him all the time! That was one of Jim's creations. Was he something or what?

SUCH A DEAL!

Rollie Massamino remembers an Italian shopping spree ending with V searching madly though his dictionary looking for the Italian word for... refund!

Jimmy featured himself as a great shopper, very hard to beat on a deal. When we went to Italy together on a speaking tour, after we did the clinics we'd go shopping. Now we go into this leather store and we see a briefcase that we both loved.

So now Jimmy wants this briefcase. But I'd seen it first, and I wanted it too and the guy says, "I only have one!" Then he tells us that it's the same-style briefcase that President Kennedy had. Now he's got Jimmy. And it was beautiful and Jimmy has to have it.

I said, "Well, I want it too."

So now Jimmy's trying to get the price down and we think there's only one, and finally the guy sees he's got two fish on the line, and he says, "Well, I might just have two!"

He goes upstairs and comes right down with another briefcase. We're like ecstatic now because we are each going to have the genuine Italian Kennedy briefcase. We buy them and we're both so proud of the new briefcases. And I don't remember how many lira but about $600 dollars a piece for these stinking briefcases because they're the ones that President Kennedy had.

Now, about six months later Jimmy calls me, he's all upset. "Rollie, are you having trouble with your goddamned Kennedy briefcase?"

I said, "Why?"

He said, "Mine never stands up! The leather has gone limp!" He's really hot, "Every time I put it up, it falls down. Every time I try to make it stand up, it just falls down!"

Until the day he died, we were still laughing about the presidential briefcase. What a deal! And of course, he's saying he wished there had only been one and that he'd let me have it.

Here's another one.

When we were over there in Florence, we were with our wives, and now Gucci was the hot name, and Lou Carnesecca says we've gotta send the girls to this store, that there are these new bags over here called Gucci Plus. So obviously they're a knock-off.

So Jimmy says, "Oh Gucci Plus, they've gotta be better than Gucci!"

So now Screwball makes this whole thing up about Gucci Plus and tells the girls that Gucci Plus is their top of the line. So we spend hundreds of dollars on Gucci Plus bags to bring back to everybody, and oh boy, Jimmy just loved that, "We'll tell them nothing but the best for our families and friends, Gucci Plus!" And I'll tell you they broke apart faster than that Kennedy presidential briefcase went limp! But that was another one we laughed about for years, the JFK briefcases and those Gucci Pluses.

GLASS "SLIPPER"

V was a party, through no fault of his own, to what appeared to be the perfect PR opportunity for a basketball university. I was working in the news bureau and uncovered a piece of engineering research on a high-strength basket called the "Gorilla Goal." I was positive it would make national news for a big time basketball school like NC State. Unfortunately it did!

Frank Hart, an NC State engineer, developed a high-strength basketball goal with a name that couldn't miss: the Gorilla Goal. It was built with playgrounds in mind. Made up with a blend of metals that mimicked the response of traditional rims, the Gorilla Goal could withstand 800 pounds of dunkage. Kids could swing from it to their hearts' content and the Gorilla wouldn't bend or break.

With this story came a nice juicy sidekick. Hart had also studied glass backboards and determined, through computer-generated video, some interesting facts. When glass boards shattered (there had been a number of TV highlights in those days), the breakage wasn't due to weakness in the glass. Hart discovered that glass boards that hadn't been leveled were subject to shatter. If the boards were leveled and secured in a way that eliminated the tension, then it would be almost impossible to break them.

So I went to V and told him I wanted to bring in the press for a dunking–Gorilla Goal and backboard demonstration. All I needed was a few players from his (unbeknownst to us) soon-to-be national championship team. The demonstration would take place in Carmichael Gym before one of V's practices.

V agreed to let Thurl Bailey, Harold Thompson, and Mike Warren do the dunking. Sorenson and Christian, the rim manufacturers, and I would be responsible for leveling Carmichael's glass backboards. We agreed to be done and out of there by 4:00 P.M. at the start of V's practice. I set up a video of the backboard research, had Sorenson and Christian display a rim bending machine, served drinks and snacks, and even had Dr. Hart, the researcher, on hand for quotes.

Must have been a slow news day; the press came in droves–all the local stations, *The News & Observer*, Associated Press, even a free-lance crew shooting for ESPN.

Dream day goes nightmare!

I had the three dunkers ready to slam on the Gorilla Goal at the north end of the gym when Don Shea, then a WTVD-TV sports reporter, cruised by and asked if he could get a quick shot of some guys dunking on one of the baskets. He had to get back to Durham to make the 6:00 news.

I said, "Yes, but make it fast because we're getting ready to start the dunking demo."

I turned to say something to Sorenson, the rim manufacturer, when I heard something akin to a stampede—cameramen, photographers, and reporters clattering to the south basket.

I looked and there they were, 200-plus-pounders Harold Thompson, swinging from one side of the basket, and Mike Warren from the other. A group of teammates was lifting State's captain and star point guard Sydney Lowe to a centerpiece position. And then there they were . . . all swinging from the basket. Not what I had in mind. I turned to Sorenson, "Your people leveled those backboards, didn't they?" And just as he was saying, "Not yet!" my PR exploded.

Do you think that kind of moment might make the evening news? A glass explosion. Falling basketball stars. A trainer dabbing blood and glass from Sidney Lowe's forearm.

RESEARCH EXPLODES AT NC STATE, was WRAL-TV's tease on the evening news.

Enter V!

There was a kid on that team named Dinky Procter who, shall we say, had a reputation of having a bad touch as an outside shooter. In basketball terms he threw up bricks. So here's this incredible mess being documented for the nation to see, players sitting in glass, and V takes one look at the destruction and says, "What happened? Did Dinky try a jump shot!"

CUCKOLD

DAN WHITE, one of V's faithful managers, remembers the day that he lost V's trust.

When we'd go on the road, my job was to stock V's room. We'd go to the grocery store and make sure that he had beer, wine, cigars, and snacks for after the game. We got to where we were doing this thing where we'd get him something really outrageous, a random item—can of Vienna sausage, things like pig's feet, just to make him laugh. We got on this one winning streak and we'd bought him Animal Crackers and man, after that it was hell to pay if we didn't get him Animal Crackers.

We were in Kansas City [in the regional finals, where NCSU played Kansas]; if we win there we go to the Final Four. This was '86 and V had some kind of meeting. Pam was with us on that trip and he gave me the key to his room so I could drop off all the stuff. When I came into V's room I heard the shower, and I hollered, "Mrs. V?"

Well, she was just coming out of the shower. Now she had a bathrobe on but her hair was wet. And we sat there and talked and I had a beer. While we're talking the door opens.

It's V and one of his friends. And of course, you can imagine what happened then. Here I am, a kid manager with his wife, and V walks in with an audience. I think it was someone from Nike. Man, he just won't let up.

"What the hell is going on? Danny, I can't believe this! I'm so shocked! I take you under my wing for four years, take you halfway around the world, and here you are trying to nail my wife!"

Of course, the guy with him is laughing like hell and Pam is laughing. But it was classic V. I knew when that door opened and I'm in there drinking a beer with Pam, man, I'm in for it now. I turned about five shades of red.

Of course, it didn't end there; he told everybody, "Did you hear about Danny, my 'trusted' manager? I caught him with Pam!"

TAPS FOR V

DAN WHITE remembers V and the loss he'd never live down.

V had this game he loved to play called "Taps." He'd play it with us at practice all the time. It would be two on two and V's claim to fame was that he'd never been beaten at Taps.

The game was played with one guy outside and one in and if the outside shooter missed the foul line extended jump shot, the inside guy could tap it in and that team got to stay on offense. If you miss you turn it over to the other two guys. Well, one day at practice Gary Bryant, our other manager, and I were playing V and Ray Martin. Playing the un-defeated Team Valvano, he said, who he announced as former star guards from Rutgers University and the University of Notre Dame.

Now if he were alive today, he would tell you that he was still unde-feated, but that wouldn't be true. And by the way, the reason he had the long run of wins was because he cheated, he'd change the rules to win. Cheated like hell.

Now, when you got to 21 you won, but you had to make the last points on the jumper, so after a tap you had to get the ball outside, up and in the hole. And on that last shot, then and only then, the other team could come out and guard you. So whenever Gary and I would get close to winning, he'd make up some new rule to beat us—you're over the line, didn't count! You throw your hand up, and he'd hit it with the ball and say, Penalty!

So this time we're playing Team Valvano in Carmichael Gym. Gary and I weren't great players, but we could shoot the ball and that day we got really hot. We're knocking them down and they were playing pretty well. We hit our last shot, and I ran down under the basket and caught it out of the net and fired it back to Gary outside. If V had gotten the ball he'd have walked out and handed us the ball and been in our face. We wouldn't have had a prayer. Now, Gary nailed it and we beat them. And oh man, you should have heard V.

He tried to come up with all kinds of violations, but we just started jumping up and down screaming "Down goes Team V! Down goes Team V!"

And if he were alive today it wouldn't be the story I just told. I don't know how many wins V had in Taps, but I know what his record was, something like 600 and 1.

V AND CO

SIDNEY LOWE remembers Cozell McQueen as a guy who not only took the coach's confidence and ran with it but who took it and ran over the opposition.

There's no doubt that the players took on the V "I can do anything" philosophy.

During the championship run Cozell McQueen was posting up against Ralph Sampson. And Co just smacked Ralph right in the face by mistake, he was throwing his hands up asking for the ball. Ralph goes down, and I throw the ball to Cozell, and he wheels around and scores. Ralph is on the floor and Virginia has to call a time-out.

And Cozell was so pumped up, I mean he had been told by V that he could do anything and at this point he was really starting to believe it. Because as we go back into the huddle, poor Ralph is staggering off the floor.

So now we're in our huddle and Cozell doesn't even know what he's done, he's jabbering away at me and V telling us that Ralph can't guard him.

I'm thinking, didn't he see what happened there?

But he's saying, "He can't guard me!"

And because V had him thinking that way, that's the way Cozell played against everybody.

That was the V factor.

V

THE TRUTH ABOUT DRUG TESTING

There were accusations in the book Personal Fouls *that related to drugs and drug testing in regard to V's programs. JIM REHBOCK, who was responsible for conducting the voluntary testing of the athletes, recalls what actually happened.*

Here's what happened in the one instance that became really public. We were drug testing our athletes. This was voluntary, not mandatory. But there was a time when nobody showed up. So I had to go to V and tell him. It turned out the coaches forgot to tell the players the time and date. So V had me write this letter, send it to him in writing telling him what had happened. Then he'd fix this problem.

Well, when the inquisition was going on that resulted from *Personal Fouls* they got hold of this letter. And it said that no one showed up for drug testing. So now it was: "Oh my God, V's the AD and no one showed up for drug testing." So I remember the SBI guys coming into my office about this. I explained it in great detail, exactly what happened.

When this happened (the players missed the drug test) I wrote the letter, then V and Kevin O'Connell, an assistant athletic director, met. V asked why they hadn't shown up and the coaches said they forgot about it.

So he said, "Okay, we're going to reschedule it and your people better be there!"

So we rescheduled the test and we did it. Kevin O'Connell and I took care of it, but I never wrote anything to that effect. I just didn't think to write another letter because we had done it right, taken care of it, and everyone knew that we'd taken care of it—coaches, athletes, etc.

So the inquisition—SBI, Poole Commission—gets hold of this letter that said we didn't do it, and they ripped Jimmy about that. He was very upset because here one of his guys—me—while he's trying to fight for his life, has written this letter. The problem had been taken care of but the letter was still out there, so it was, "Why didn't you do something about this!"

I ended up writing a letter and hand delivering it to Dick Spangler, the president of the UNC-System, and to the state commissioner who was in charge of the investigation. I explained that I'd talked to the SBI about this and that we'd done the testing and done it right.

When Spangler went on TV to talk about the inquisition and V, he mentioned that the head of sports medicine said that the testing had happened, and he mentioned my letter. But it was too late to help V.

CADDY SHACK

As a golfing buddy, FRANK McCANN recalls what it was like to play with V. Does anyone remember the Rodney Dangerfield character in Caddy Shack?

He had this unbelievable irreverence for the game itself. He wouldn't be quiet, never, never be quiet. Although he was an incredible competitor, he was just a fifteen handicap, but you wanted him as a partner. He wouldn't shut up.

He'd say to all of us, "Look, if my guys can stand on a foul line with 15,000 people screaming at them, you can make a five-foot putt with me ten feet away talking. So don't give me that crap."

The thing about Jim was that he knew how to use [his handicap] when it came time to negotiate and play. He had this banana slice, and if there was water to the left he'd play it over the water. If you were playing against him it would drive you nuts, because you would watch it and it would come back into the fairway. And once the money was down, then the confidence and the competitor in him would kick in. He'd get up on the first tee, on say a par four, and it would be like drive, approach shot short, chip up, two-putt for his five.

And he'd start looking at the scorecard and go, "Well, I'm one over now. Where am I going to get the birdie?"

I'd say, "Jim, forget about getting even. You're a fifteen, you aren't going to play this course even."

And he'd say, "No, I'm one over. I've gotta find the birdie hole."

Then he'd study the card figuring where he was going to pick up that stroke. He was serious, that big a competitor.

Of course he had all the negotiating skills, and all the way around he'd be adjusting, making side bets, which he usually won. The regulars, the guys who he played with, never let him forget the one he lost. Al Masella, Governor's Club, Chapel Hill. The greens at the Governor's Club are big and full of breaks, and Masella, one of our regular players, is looking at about a hundred-foot putt that breaks about sixteen ways from Sunday. I mean it's a snake.

Damned if he doesn't make the putt and he's jumping around and we're high-fiving and Jim looks at him and says, "You couldn't make that again if your life depended on it. I'll bet you $100 to a dollar!"

Al takes him up on it, puts the ball right back where it was on the green, and runs it home again from about a hundred feet. This cost Jim a hundred dollars. And oh man, it just killed him, he was such a competitor and he hated to lose. Then Al does it to him. Oh, it was so great and we never let him forget it.

Then there was that incredible wit.

Somehow I always managed to maneuver myself to the position where he's going to come at me. I am going to be it! One day we're on the first tee, and we got out of the cart, and he had a green 7-Up sweater on with a logo on the chest. He had green 7-Up pants. He had this humongous green 7-Up golf bag, with green head covers on his clubs.

And just as he got on the tee, I said, "Where did you get that outfit?"
Oh, man, bad mistake, big mistake. From that time on–I probably said
that to him in 1991–he never let up on that one, never let me forget it.

"Where did I get it? I think I got it from Coke. No, or was it Dr.
Pepper, no, that's right, it was Pepsi. Maybe the YooHoo guy dropped it
off. Where the hell do you think I got it?"

And you knew just as soon as you said something you wanted to
grab it and take it back. You were going to get it! He would run with a
good one for two or three years. And I just got nailed constantly.

He had this trick with a cigar that he used to pull on the golf course,
usually on the first tee, just before he hit. He could take a lit cigar, flip it
in his fingers like a little baton, and stick it back in his mouth so quick
that it would look like he had put the lit end in first. He loved to pull that
one on the golf course, especially if he had an audience, someone who
hadn't seen it before. And it was good, I mean he used to make us
cringe, and we'd seen him do it a hundred times.

I'd say, "How do you do it?" and he'd show me.

So I made up my mind that I was going to learn to do the cigar trick.
I practiced and practiced and finally I had it.

So one day we're playing and I go to Jim and say, " Jim, the cigar
trick!"

And I lit it, flipped it, rolled it along my fingers, and stuck it back in
my mouth and... ohhh! I stuck the lit end in first, burned the hell out of
my tongue. He, of course, just laughed his ass off.

"Hey, Frank, show us the cigar trick!"

Never a dull moment on the course with Jim, talking a mile a minute,
the cigars, the 7-Up outfit, that banana ball, the side bets, and the whole
way around–always–doing everything humanly possible to win.

LASTING MESSAGE

Sidney Lowe recalls V's influence as one that was lasting.

It wasn't just in games that V's style influenced me. It impacted me a
great deal later when I was coaching in the NBA, especially in the relationship with the players. The NBA is so different because you are dealing with

a different animal—millionaires. But the confidence that V had in us, that's the way I treated my players when I was coaching in the NBA.

Coach V would allow you to go out and play. Now what you had to do was show him that you were capable. If you couldn't, he'd tell you. I did some of that in the NBA. And I certainly used his huddle strategy, meaning anytime I was in the huddle if someone was on the free throw line.

I'd say, "Hey, after we make these two shots this is what we're going to do."

Never "if," always "after the shots have gone down, here's the plan..." and that was V.

1-900-V

Nick Valvano remembers V's late night obsession, the infomercial.

Long before he was sick, he had insomnia. He just couldn't sleep. I really think that he just had one of those minds that ran nonstop and he couldn't shut it off.

So he'd be up all night thinking of ways to entertain himself. One way was shopping on cable TV. He'd watch these infomercials and buy the damndest things. Of course he had the ability to make it all so funny.

I remember I was in Spokane, Washington, on business and he calls me and says, "Nick, guess what I just bought? The Flowbie!"

Of course, I'm thinking two things: It's in the middle of the night back east and what the f*&*# is the Flowbie?

So Jimmy starts in just like the guys who sell that stuff, using the announcer's voice promoting this incredible little barbering device, it trims, it cuts, it shapes! "And oh," he says, "I also went with the SnackMaster. I'll be making LeeAnn's lunches with this little kitchen magician!"

I'm laughing like hell, but knowing that he's being funny but not kidding.

And then he closes with this line, "Oh, Nick, I was going to make this a surprise, but on the SnackMaster, I bought you one too. Bon Appetite!'"

YOU'RE ON!

CHARLIE BRYANT remembers V's radio call-in show.

We had been in Fayetteville one spring evening. Jim was speaking to a local Wolfpack Club gathering. After his talk and about fifty personal follow-up conversations we stayed and had a few drinks.

When we finally started driving back to Raleigh, Jim realized that he had forgotten his 11:00 P.M. radio sports report that he did for WPTF radio. We whip into a 7-11, or one of those little fast gas places; he grabs a *USA Today* from the back seat of my car and starts reading.

"Hell, baseball." he said, "I can do this standing on my head."

He gives the sports page a quick read, races in, gets a bunch of quarters, and calls the station from a pay phone outside the 7-11. Bam, he's live on the air.

I'm listening to him on the car radio. I can see him out there and he's got the paper, holding it up to the lights over the gas pump, reading and commenting on spring training—who has the pitching and who has the hitting—just like he'd spent a day of research on it.

Pretty soon two young guys who are filling their cars with gas come up to me and say, "Hey, isn't that Jim Valvano?"

I said, "Sure, why don't you go over and ask him for his autograph?"

So Jim has the *USA Today* under his arm, the phone cradled between his shoulder and ear—still on the air live, and he's signing autographs!

This was the way he coached, the way he lived. He was always living in the moment... helping life along, making things happen!

POSTGAME POSTMORTEM

JIM REHBOCK remembers the day V was laid low by poor officiating early in his career at NC State.

As far as down times go, I remember him after [a] loss to Virginia. They had Ralph Sampson, and we got that horrendous call when Whittenburg got tackled at mid-court by Jeff Lamp. The ref calls jump ball. Lamp jumps up and shakes his fist. Virginia wins on that call.

But that night in the locker room, he was so good about that loss. He said, "Nobody died, this is just a game!"

He was upbeat with the kids and the press.

Then we got into the postmortem all-nighter up in his office, and it was a bit different. He was really pissed at the officials.

So the next day we're getting ready for practice and I'm really not looking forward to it. We've got a big game coming up in a few days. But right before practice Jimmy and his assistants—Marty Fletcher and Ray Martin—are sitting around in his office.

And he jumps up and says, "These kids don't need to get back in the Coliseum right now, we need a day off!"

I was in the training room getting ready to tape. They called me and said, just leave a note for the players. So we wrote a big note on the blackboard:

PRACTICE CALLED OFF
GO HOME–STUDY
SEE YOU TOMORROW.

I went up to the basketball office to see what was going on.

Well, he'd won his first ACC game prior to that against Clemson so someone had given him a couple of bottles of champagne. So he calls over to Two Guys [a restaurant near campus] and tells Mike, the owner, "I'm sending over one of my managers and I want two large pizzas with everything you can humanly possibly put on it."

Gary Bryant comes in later with these huge pizzas and we sat up there that afternoon with Coke cups of champagne and ate pizza… and laughed. He liked his wine and the food, but he loved to laugh. He just entertained us for the rest of the afternoon with all his New York one-liners. When we left we felt great.

I don't know if he felt as good as we did, but that was Jimmy. He knew how to live better than anyone I've ever known.

IN DEAN'S DOME

LES ROBINSON, who succeeded V as NC State's coach and at the time coached at The Citadel, remembers not only how much fun Valvano was but how he—somehow—always managed to be a step ahead of everyone—including, in this case, Dean Smith.

I used to love to sit with him at coaches' meetings. It was like being in the 9th grade, in the back of the room, laughing and carrying on. Back in about '84 or '85 we were in Chicago at a meeting and this was just a couple of years before the Dean Dome was built.

So we're sitting there and V says out of the clear blue, "I guess you know the North-South doubleheader [UNC and NC State played The Citadel and Furman] is about over. It will be dead in about a year or two because Carolina is going to build a coliseum. When it's up they aren't going to go to Charlotte and play this thing. You're going to have to come to Dean's building if you want to play him. They're only about five million away from having the money to build it."

A couple of coaches start listening in, so V, who really liked Dean, goes into his Dean impression. "Here's how it's going to happen," he said. "Dean picks up the phone and makes a call and says, 'This is Dean Smith. I need about a million and a half bucks to complete my building. Now that doesn't guarantee that your kid will be able to get into my camp.'"

We're laughing but I thought V was kidding about the North-South. It was a nice profitable event for The Citadel. I knew Carolina was going to get a building but I didn't see it ending the North-South.

Well, we're laughing like hell at V's impression of Dean one minute and about ten minutes later the meeting broke. When I came out of the men's room, there's Dean.

He says, "Les, I just wanted to let you know that we're building a new facility at Carolina so we won't be doing the North-South in Charlotte anymore."

That's how V was, very funny but very smart. He was always ahead of everybody.

V

CUTOUT CUTUPS

Frank Weedon remembers a V joke that he and his accomplice weren't quite cut out for.

Sam Esposito and Jim always had something going, great friends, and just a lot of kidding and carrying on. Somewhere, I don't know where, Tommy Abatemarco and Jim got this life-size cutout of Ara Parseghian, the famous Notre Dame football coach. So they wait until Sam leaves for the day, unlock his office, and set Ara up just inside the door.

The plan was for Jim and Tommy to come in early the next morning and wait to hear Sam scream when he opened the door. So they get in early and get set up in Jim's office and wait. Finally they hear the scream, but it was a few octaves higher than they expected. They had scared the maid. She went racing down the hall and hid in the bathroom.

Now while Jim and Tommy are at the door coaxing her to come out, Sam comes in with his morning paper and coffee. He goes into his office, sees Ara flat on the floor, steps over the cutout, sits down, and opens the sports page.

BUS LAUGHS

Dr. Don Reibel remembers bus rides where V did 300 miles of stand-up.

I remember one for *The Guinness Book of World Records*—the longest stand-up comedy routine. This was on a bus trip to Clemson. We had the whole team on the bus and some of the guys from the Athletic Department. When we got on the bus the kids usually gravitated to the back with their boom boxes and headsets and listened to music. [The coaches and staff] all sat up in the front near the driver.

Well, by the time we got out of Raleigh and on I-40, V just started. He went into the funniest, most informative, interesting monologue you've ever heard. He talked about his neighbors in MacGregor Downs, a lot of yuppie jokes, he told golf stories, did some of the Pam jokes. She was All-Mall, the only words that weren't in her vocabulary were "Attention, K-Mart Shoppers." Then [he] did an entire monologue about kids he grew up with in New York.

For five hours, he quoted poetry, Shakespeare, fired off one-liners like a stand-up comic. We were spellbound and he just didn't stop. In fact it went on until we were in the outskirts of Clemson, South Carolina. And when the bus finally slowed down he slowed down, and not before. It was amazing.

V JTV

Don Shea, a former WTVD-TV sports reporter, became a great friend and valued employee of V's. Shea recalls some of the numerous products that were a part of V's multi-faceted company, JTV Enterprises.

In JTV Enterprises, V was into a lot of different things. He did the [Jim Valvano] Cookbook, sold the JTV clothes [and] tailgate portable tables for football games, he had the little locker room towels for players to wear when the press did postgame interviews. Oh, there were the college sports yearbooks, the TV spots for Hardees and Mountain Dew, the commercials with his mom for a New York pasta called Ronzoni. And of course, everyone remembers the Nike Unitards, the one-piece body suits that his players wore. He did the sports on the CBS morning show with Phyllis George, the *Lighter Side of Sports* with ESPN. Of course, there were the local radio and TV shows which I handled and marketed.

Then someone came to him with the statue idea. And this was a biggie. He hired a guy to manage it for him.

The deal was that they would make life-sized iron statues, and then sell numbered replicas. The first one was Aristides, the first horse to win the Kentucky Derby. They produced Julius Erving and Walter Payton. In concept it was good. V's company would present the life-sized statues to Churchill Downs, for instance, and then we'd make miniatures and sell them for $2,500 a piece and split the profits with the people in the Kentucky Thoroughbred Association or the Chicago Bears (or Walter Payton). A good concept but in my opinion it wasn't marketed very well. We were supposed to get mailing lists from the co-operating partners, and frankly a lot fell through the cracks.

So the first one was Aristides, and we were going to have this great unveiling at the Derby. It was cast in Pittsburgh, and it was a very expensive venture. Believe me this sculptor was doing fine work—hundreds of photographs—and the funding for all this was all coming out of Jim's pocket. It was iron or pewter, and we had the model shipped to Churchill Downs and had to hire this moving van and case this thing.

Jim's getting a little antsy because, again, he's footing the bill. He was selling things at Belks, and he was doing everything. But this one was all his, and so the first one was key. We got it situated at Churchill Downs—it was beautiful—and we invited Julius and Walter Payton to go to the Derby, again this was all on Jim. There were a lot of people who formed a line who were good at spending other people's money—namely his! He didn't get as much support from the Kentucky people [as] we thought we'd get.

So the next project was Julius Erving and that statue would go outside the Spectrum in Philadelphia. Julius was great, and I don't know what he charged. Then I went to Chicago to do Walter Payton and the statues were so good. And it was really starting to roll but Jim, and rightly so, was seeing a lot of money going out and he'd say, "Hey, they're killing me. I just keep writing checks."

There was so much written and conjectured about all the money that Jim Valvano was making, but he was a businessman and a risk taker, and I can tell you this, when all was said and done the statue business was a losing proposition. And all the money that was lost belonged to Jim Valvano.

Perception is reality and the perception was that this guy was just tonning it [making a ton], using his name and OPM, Other People's Money. The fact is that a lot of people cashed in using Jim Valvano's money, and the statue business was a good example.

V MY VALENTINE

BEV SPARKS had the honor of replacing Frances Lewis when V's long-time assistant retired. Bev recalls the Valentine's Day when V's new assistant almost bankrupted the frugal coach.

Coach Valvano was on the road a lot, and he came in one morning from the airport, and I reminded him that it was Valentine's Day. He thanked me profusely and told me to call a florist and take care of all the Valvano women.

Fallon's was a florist that we dealt with, but their line was busy so I called another one. And every time I'd think I had the order in, the owner—who seemed to be impressed that this was for the Valvanos—suggested another add-on.

"How about some candy with the yellow roses for Mrs. Valvano?"

I'd shout in to Jim, who, of course, was on the phone. "Want some candy with the roses for Pam?"

"Sure!"

"Would you like a little teddy bear with the flowers for LeeAnn?"

"Sure, whatever!"

This went on and on and we finally got the order in. Well, in about a week the bill came. Now you have to know Jim. He was very generous with his time and talent but the man knew how to watch a dollar—sort of a Jack Benny in a Nike sweat suit.

I opened the bill and after I'd recovered, I walked in and said, "How did the Valentine's order go over... did they like the flowers?"

"Oh, great... good job... they loved it!" he said.

I said, "I'm so glad. Here's the bill."

You had to be there. I never heard his voice sound quite like that. He didn't read the bill he screamed it—"$868.00!"

I was Jim's assistant for a number of years after that, and he never, ever, forgot Valentine's again.

THE OTHER GUARD

BOB LLOYD recalls Lorenzo's dunk as being a basket that changed the pecking order that had—until then—lasted a lifetime.

At Rutgers Jimmy was really a great player; he averaged fifteen points a game, but because I scored a lot more and was an All-America, he was always referred to as the other guard.

So the joke was that Jimmy was the other guard and my brother Dick was known as the All-America's brother. Now, just seconds after Jimmy's NC State team won the national championship with that famous dunk by Lorenzo Charles, the phone rings at my house.

It's my brother.

He says, "Bobby, only one downside. I didn't mind being the brother of the All-America guard. But this has changed things. Now I'm the brother of the other guard!"

CRUISIN' FOR PIZZA

LARRY GROSS recalls a picture postcard of a story from one of V's Celebrity Cruises.

One that he told us that we just loved was the one about this Celebrity Cruise. He was one of the big deal celebrities, and he'd been partying all night with the guests.

So he's headed back to his stateroom about 2:00 in the morning. He realizes that he's really starving because he's been drinking all night. So he passes this room service tray in the hallway, outside someone's door, just down from his room. There's one untouched slice of pizza on a plate and he nails it. And just as he starts eating it, the door of the room opens and the guy is staring at him.

V looks up and says, "Hi, I'm Jim Valvano, Italians just can't pass up a slice of pie!"

CHEMISTRY LESSON

MAX PERRY, who played and coached with V, recalls a few of his more memorable half-times.

I remember that we were playing East Carolina at home, and they had a guy who wore the Clark Kent black, horn-rimmed glasses, looked like a professor. He probably couldn't run the hundred in fifty years, but he could just shoot the hell out of [the ball] and just was lighting us up from the corner.

V was trying to get guys to go out and get him, and for some reason they just wouldn't, and wham! he'd nail another one. So now this was normal Coach V stuff.

At half-time the door just bursts open and V comes in and says, "Will somebody tell me who's going to guard the goddamned chemist?"

ONE STOP SHOPPING

RAY MARTIN recalls a V Christmas.

One of my favorite V memories might surprise some people. It's of one of V's happiest days. And this one doesn't involve all the wins and the great games that took us to that national championship.

It was a quiet day in December, right before the holidays, and V wanted to get Pam something very special for Christmas. So I went with him to Cary, and he started shopping, and finally he found this mink coat. And man, you should have seen him—of course, the price was killing him—but he was so proud of that coat. He knew she wouldn't expect it, he knew it would surprise her, and V loved surprises.

So all the way back from the shopping mall he's going on about the coat and how he can hardly wait to see her open it on Christmas morning, to see her face. I mean he's delighted.

I thought I've never seen this man happier.

Wrong!

When we got back to his office there's this great big crate that's been delivered with his name on it. Now, this gift is for him, and he's like a kid at

Christmas–forget Pam and the coat–now he gets to open it to see what he's got. It was a bushel of crabs from Johnny Rhodes, a friend of his who owned the Gullyfield Restaurant in Myrtle Beach, S.C.

Man, V goes nuts he's so excited.

"Get the beer, call in the guys!"

He gets on the phone and starts calling everybody in the Athletic Department. And in they come, Espo, Tanner, Tarantini, all the coaches... for V's Christmas Crabs and Beer Party.

It's funny what you remember but I'll never forget that. He was excited about giving and he was excited about getting, and he could hardly wait to share it all. He had some happy days but that one–as small as it may seem–was one of them!

CAREER ADVICE

RICH PETRICCIONE recalls being a "career example" for one of V's players–ABC TV's Terry Gannon.

V had a head for figures, knew every dime he ever made and where the next ones were coming from. But this attention to the numbers and the bottom line wasn't always about him.

I remember visiting V at NC State when Terry Gannon was a senior [in 1985]. I was coaching at Iona at the time, and so I'm in his office and V says, "Oh, Pet, I'm so glad you are here, stay here, don't move!"

Terry Gannon is in the outer office talking to someone and he gets Terry to come in. Terry had told V that he wanted to be a coach.

So V introduces me to Terry and he says, "This is Richie, he's one of the smartest kids I ever had. He was a great manager and a great guy and now he's a coach at Iona. Richie, tell Terry how much money you make!"

So I say, "I make $16,400!"

And then V turns to Gannon and says, "Terry, that's what I'm f#*%ing talking about! And you want to be a coach? You can do a hell of a lot better than that!"

ACTING LIKE A DRIP

JOHN SAUNDERS remembers the night he wanted to put a wringer around V's neck for leaking the name Delta Faucet.

The first few times that we were in the studio together, Delta Faucet was our sponsor. Now every studio show at ESPN is sponsored, but back then there [hadn't been] sponsorships for shows; there were commercials [before], of course, but it wasn't the Delta Faucet Half-Time Report or the John Deere Report. Delta Faucet was one of the first [of this type] we had at ESPN, so it was very important to the sales department that the very first words that came out of my mouth were, "Welcome to the Delta Faucet Half-Time Report!" Now, there wasn't any extra money for me, but if it wasn't said by me, then we had to do what is called a "make good." How we handled it was important.

So when Jim was first working there he says, "Delta Faucet? What's Delta Faucet? I've heard of Delta Airlines and Delta Dawn but what the hell's Delta Faucet?"

So I say, "Well, that's our sponsor. A company that makes bathroom fixtures."

He goes, "Well, is their stuff any good?"

Of course I say, "I think it is... but they're our sponsor!"

He says, "Wait a minute, you don't really know if their product is good but you're going to say their name and try to get people to buy it?"

I'm like, "Yeah, that's my job."

So now he's really on me and he says, "Well, what if I say it?"

I tell him, "You can't say it! I've got to say Delta Faucet!"

Now, he's going nuts, "You're telling me that I can't say it? Well I'm going to say it."

I'm like, "You can't!"

And he's, "I'm going to say it."

Sure enough the red light goes on and we're looking at each other and he kind of chuckles and I say, "Welcome to the..."

And he shouts, "Delta Faucet Half-Time Report!"

Everybody working the show is just cracking up.

He was amazing!

V

BY GEORGE

WOODY WEBB recalls V the storyteller. V shared this CBS classic, which led to the demise of The Morning News *anchor Phyllis George.*

V was a very interesting and intelligent client. We'd meet up in his office (Case Athletic Center) and discuss his case. But while we were making our [legal] plans there was always something going on. Along with the stories, we'd play darts, toss a football, and eat popcorn (which he kept in this big black trash bag).

It was very rare that we talked about basketball. The thing that I found so appealing about him was that he was a very intelligent guy. I find that most people who have a good sense of humor are intelligent, and he was certainly that. These were the kinds of exchanges we had, him telling me about a historic moment in TV. Of course, he was there as a witness.

This was when Jim was on the *CBS Morning News,* doing the sports in New York. He loved Phyllis George [former Miss America and anchor for the show], was just crazy about her. He said she was just the sweetest, most engaging personality. And he'd go in and kid her and she'd laugh. Well, he was waiting to do his sports spot, watching the show the morning that Phyllis got in trouble. And the incident may have led to the end of her CBS career. That morning they had a woman on the show [Cathy Webb] who had accused this guy [Gary Dotson] of raping her. Years before it had gone to trial and the guy was found guilty. He went off and served five years time. Then later she recanted and said he really didn't rape her—that she really didn't know who [the rapist] was.

So the guy is out of jail and Phyllis had both of them on the CBS early show. Now V's watching this from behind the cameras and Phyllis George says to this guy something like, "Well, now that you all are here and things are smoothed over, how about a hug?"

And here's V back there in the wings watching this and he said everybody just gasped for air. "Oh, my God, this guy has just done five years for a rape he didn't commit and Phyllis asks him if he wants to give the woman who sent him to prison a hug!"

RED CARD

GEORGE TARANTINI recalls V coaching his first soccer match.

This was my first or second year as the NC State soccer coach and we're playing Carolina. All of a sudden V appears before the game and he sits on the bench. Now, I'm playing Carolina, and it's not like basketball or tennis. I scream during the game—nobody listens, but I scream. So I'm up and down the field shouting at my players. This is a big game, and it's zero to zero, and now it's like the middle of the game and here he comes.

He knows nothing about soccer, maybe never even seen a game, and he says to me, "Listen to me. Number one, you've got to understand the game is about runs, like basketball, they make a run, you make a run. Just relax, wait for your run!"

I said, "Jimmy, you don't understand—there are no runs in soccer, they score, that's one run and you are done."

But he wouldn't listen, he keeps telling me, "No, no, no, there will be runs!"

He's the expert, he knew about everything.

Finally, he turns to me at the end of the game—there had been no runs—so he says, "You know, George, the problem with soccer? There's no runs, it's a communist game!"

WEAK ARM WEAK MOMENT

RAY TANNER shared an office with head baseball coach Sam Esposito. Sam was V's Yoda and so Ray was there—in person—for one of the more infamous times that V, the mentee, came calling on the master.

V was such a ball buster, but the one who could really nail him—and did—was Coach Esposito. Those two had a very special relationship; V really looked up to Coach Espo, who was a great coach, athlete, and an ex-major league ballplayer.

V had been asked to play in the North Carolina Hall of Fame charity baseball game. He had been asked by [broadcaster] Bob

Costas. Now, Mickey Mantle—V's hero—was going to manage one of the teams. So V was all pumped up about this and came by and asked Coach Esposito if he could tune up his game by working out with our team.

There was a lot of good-natured fun, with Espo letting him know that he didn't think he could play, but finally Coach said, "Okay, if you want to come out to practice tomorrow, be my guest."

So V shows up at Doak Field, wearing a uniform and everything. The players are pretty excited about this. I wasn't, because it was my job [as a coach] to work him out. I must of hit a hundred ground balls to him, and he jumped around pretty good and made a couple of plays, and wasn't bad. His arm was suspect, but he bounced around out there pretty good. So after a while Coach Esposito calls time-out and waves the whole team to the mound.

V comes trotting in real cocky and says, with the entire team leaning in, "What do you think?"

And Sam looks up and says, "I think you throw like f*&*%ing old broad. That's what I think!"

Oh man!

Now I had to throw batting practice to him. And I'll tell you what—I may not have been the best college baseball player in NCAA history, but I could and still can throw some batting practice. I can lay them in there. And no surprise, V wasn't exactly busting down the fences. So, of course, it's my fault. I can't find the plate. I'm a horseshit BP thrower.

All this ended the following Monday morning in Coach Esposito's office. V had played the game and met Mickey Mantle, and so now here he comes into Espo's office. Coach Espo is at his desk and he sees V but pretends he doesn't. He's writing something and won't look up.

All of a sudden—and to this day I don't know how he found out—but Espo says, "0 for f*&%ing 3!"

And V goes, "How did you know?"

And with his head still down, Coach Espo says, "Because you can't play. I told you that Friday!"

GRANTED!

Ken Swartzel, now head of NC State's Department of Food Science, recalls the day that V helped him close on an important university grant.

I was a young assistant professor at the height of the Valvano years, and I had put in a grant proposal to an organization out of Chicago called Dairy Research Incorporated. We were doing some of the first aseptic packaging of milk at NC State, and this was a request for funding to test the shelf life of aseptic packaging here in the College of Agriculture and Life Sciences. Like all funding agencies, they do site visits. They came down from Chicago to take a look at our facilities, and so I thought, well, at least we made the short list for the funding.

This was a look-see for a fairly major award, probably in excess of $100,000, which was a lot of money. The visit was on a Tuesday morning; we had to visit the pilot plant that afternoon. When it was time to go to lunch, I asked if they had a preference. They wondered if we had a university or faculty club. I said, "Well, we have one but we wouldn't want to go today. It's Tuesday, the Tip Off Club meets, and Jim Valvano, our basketball coach, will be there and it will be packed. We won't be able to talk."

They looked at me and said, "Valvano will be there? Do you mean we could meet Jim Valvano?"

All of a sudden the research was the furthest thing from their minds. So we went to the Faculty Club early and got a good table, and then here he comes, just walked in and took over the way he could, and he was so entertaining. Well, they were thrilled. And later when we did our walk-through of the pilot plant all they could talk about was seeing Jim Valvano.

So I didn't know what to think. Did they like the research or were they just in a good mood because of seeing Valvano? The next morning I got my answer. They called from Chicago and told me that I'd gotten the grant. Our science and research was deserving of that award. But I think we also have to understand the role athletics can play in a university. And to this day I don't know if it was my research or just the starry eyes of the guys from the granting agency getting to meet Jim Valvano.

PACKING IT IN

MIKE WARREN remembers one of those moments that a player and coach should never have.

After V got fired, I remember the saddest scene that any player could witness with his coach. I was riding around one Sunday morning and just happened to go by the parking lot behind Case Athletic Center. This was probably the worst I'd ever seen him. He was loading up his car. I didn't know if I thought he'd be there or what, but I just drove by, and there we were.

He had the big Lincoln Town Car that Pam used to drive, and Larry Gross was with him, one of the soccer coaches, and they were packing up that car, and it looked like a homeless person's car, everything he owned was in it—all this stuff piled in the back—game balls, awards, furniture, just piled in this car. It was the saddest thing to see him experiencing this, almost like he came there with nothing and built a program that won a national championship and now here he was loading up his car and was right back to where he started. All by himself.

When I pulled up, here he came carrying his last box out, just a boxload of shit. And he walked over, and he said some things to me. He was bitter, and understandably so, but he never said, this SOB or that SOB. He never blamed anyone personally, at least in front of me!

But I do remember this, what he said was, "Mike, just remember how your university treated me. And you just never know how things in life are going to shake out!"

Then he walked to the car, and he got a letter out of one of the boxes and he showed it to me. It was the handwritten letter from Dave Didion, the NCAA investigator, and it was on NCAA stationary. I stood there and read it and it said—and I'm paraphrasing here—it said, that after investigating V's program, if the investigator had a son [and] if there was one coach that son could play for, it would be Coach V.

That was one of the strangest days that I'll ever remember. I'd never seen him so sad and to see that car loaded down. But what he said stuck with me. I'm a graduate of NC State and it is my university, and I'll always be embarrassed about the way my university handled the separation with Coach V.

TAMING THE CAMERON CRAZIES

JIM REHBOCK remembers V duking it out in Durham.

Maybe it was just Duke or the Cameron Crazies or the New York connection, but the Duke students loved V. Everyone told Jimmy how horrible Cameron was to play in. Even Lefty Driesell called him and warned him, and Lefty was a Duke graduate. Lefty said he hated to play there and used to take his team out to mid-court so he could hear.

Now at this time during the time-outs Duke had a group that may still be there called BOG—Bunch of Guys! They would literally try to get into the huddle, right in the coaches' and players' faces and scream so you couldn't hear.

So Jimmy gets this idea and he asks the basketball players to ask the [NC State] football players to come to Cameron with him, to sit behind our bench to keep the kids out of our huddle while he's trying to talk. Back then you could give them a travel shirt, so we took twenty football players, dressed them in travel shirts, and sat them behind our bench. We loaded them on the bus and then lined them up and sat them there as a buffer. So we had the football players there blocking BOG—so we could hear.

But the first time Jimmy walked into Cameron and the Crazies cut loose on him—instead of ignoring the kids—he went right up into the stands, talked to all of them, carried on with them. One kid gave him a huge inflatable champaign bottle, and Jimmy took it, tipped it up like he was drinking, and from then on it was a love affair, the Cameron Crazies and V.

𝒱

A BUILDING RELATIONSHIP

DICK SHERIDAN, NC State's football coach during V's tenure, remembers a very special relationship, one that began on shaky grounds.

I was hired by the athletic director, Willis Casey, [at] the end of December of 1985, before the 1986 season. Willis retired that spring and so there was quite a debate as to who my new boss might be. The coaches were very supportive of Jim Valvano. I didn't know Jim well but they all wanted him to be the AD and after talking with them and listening to their reasoning–that he would be a coach's AD who had great vision–that was enough for me.

It wasn't long before I knew that he was everything the other coaches said that he'd be. He was a coach's AD. He had the ability to cut through things and see the big picture. He was a visionary. My relationship with Jim started out kind of rocky. I was dealing with his assistants–Frank Weedon and Kevin O'Connell–and they still had the Willis Casey philosophy of saying no to just about anything that cost money.

I wanted to do some ground work at Weisiger-Brown Athletic Facility and at Carter-Finley Stadium. I wanted to put shrubbery around our offices, build a berm to break the sound, put in some ground cover, things like that. Well, they said no to the expense, so I just went ahead and did it anyway. When Jim found out he said, "I thought we hired a football coach, not a damned landscaper! And what the hell's a berm?"

So there were a few rounds back and forth. Football coach vs. the new AD. I was very upset about the condition of the College Inn where our players stayed. The condition was horrible. So Jim and I agreed to have a meeting. Typically a meeting might last, what, an hour or two? This one lasted five hours. My point was simply, "You hired me here at NC State to change things, and I can't do that with people continually saying no. This is my first season and I don't want it to be my last season." And this wasn't Frank Weedon's and Kevin O'Connell's fault. They had worked for Willis and he had programmed all his assistants to say no to coaches when it came to spending money.

But by the end of that meeting Jim was convinced that I had a plan, one that was best for the program, the department, and the university. So Jim called his assistants in and said, "You've been nodding your heads no. I want you to start nodding yes!"

He was incredibly supportive of everything that the football program did from then on, and I appreciated it and I appreciated him. That was the way he was–all I had to do was show him what I was doing and why.

Later, as our relationship evolved, I had two opportunities to remember what he'd done for me and the program and act accordingly. The first came when I was offered the Georgia head coach's job. This was a big decision for me and when I turned it down he and Kevin O'Connell met me at the airport with a new set of golf clubs and a new tennis racquet. The next day at a press conference his little girl, LeeAnn, presented me with a bouquet of roses. That was his style.

He was committed to so many things that would bring the program to where it's headed now. My commitment to him after turning down the Georgia job was to try to bring our football program at NC State to the Georgia program's level. And we were on the same page. I was ready to meet with architects about the stadium when the book *Personal Fouls* hit the news. All the trouble that followed brought those initiatives to a halt. During that time [Jim] Morrison, the head coach at South Carolina, died and South Carolina came to me and offered me that job. South Carolina was my alma mater, but I saw what Jim was going through and felt I couldn't leave NC State. I felt like I'd be running out on him. So I turned that offer down. He had been so supportive. I stayed for him.

We became closer as the pressures increased—media, Board of Trustees, Board of Governors—to step down and give up his job. He had asked to speak to the NC State Board of Trustees to tell his side of the story. They said no. So he asked me if I would do it. This was a great honor. I went to Chancellor Monteith and said that I'd like permission to speak to the Board of Trustees on Jim's and the Athletic Department's behalf. I was told no.

I don't want to open a lot of old wounds, but I was shocked that I wasn't allowed to do that. But the fact that Jim asked me to represent him was, and remains, one of my greatest honors. And then years later—when he was sick—he asked me to introduce him at the ten-year celebration of the 1983 championship basketball team in Reynolds Coliseum. That was even a greater honor. That was the most difficult thing that I've ever been asked to do because I felt like what I said was so important. It was, to my knowledge, the first time he'd come back to NC State. The celebration of the '83 team was a great moment in the history of the basketball program.

I remember how emotional I was talking to the people who knew him and loved him. I wanted my words to be representative of those people's thoughts—the love, respect, and appreciation of all the people there. I forget my exact words but I talked about Jim through the good times and bad times and where fantasy met myth. I know that I expressed our gratitude for all he'd done for the university and the program. He had prevailed and the love was still there for him—that day and forever.

RERUN

TUBBY SMITH, coach of the University of Kentucky, learned how it felt to win a national championship and when he did, he remembered V's run for the hug.

I got to know Jimmy when he first got the job at NC State. I coached high school ball in Raeford, North Carolina. Harold Thompson played for me, later played for V at NC State. V was always very supportive of other coaches, and his friend Pat Kennedy offered me an assistant coach's job at Florida State.

Now, when V was at the Final Four in '83, when all the attention was on him and his basketball team, he sees me and he hollers out, "Tubby, you gotta go to Florida State and help my friend out!"

That was Jimmy.

And then years later when I was fortunate enough to win a national championship, I recalled Jimmy and how he ran around that court looking for someone to hug. And you know, I almost did the same thing myself. Because I sure found out how he felt!

HEDGING YOUR BETS

DAN WHITE remembers V's inability to pass up a good line.

This is a V story with Garry Dornberg. Garry was the radio color man who hosted V's radio show. Garry was really very heavy, about 300 pounds at the time. And on the team bus when we went on road trips, we always had a cooler of drinks. We'd stop at McDonald's and buy burgers, and everybody would get a couple of burgers and fries.

So one time we stopped and we were handing out these bags from McDonald's, and Garry got Super-Sized pretty good—a big bag of burgers. We start handing out the drinks, and when it comes time to ask Garry what he wanted, I hollered at him and he shouted from the back, "Make mine a Diet Coke!"

And V looks back at Garry and that big bag of burgers and says, "Hey, Garry, you're kind of hedging your bets, aren't you?"

V

SLIDING HOME

FRANCIS COMBS, former NC State athlete and member of the WPTF radio basketball broadcasting team, remembers the day when the Pack beat Wake Forest at the buzzer and he slid home with V.

The game was in the Greensboro Coliseum; this was while Wake Forest's new arena was under construction. For some reason V asked me to give him a ride home after what turned out to be a really big win. So anyway we did all the post-game interviews and finally got out of there, and we're barely out of Greensboro and V sees a Burger King and tells me to pull in, that he's hungry.

The restaurant was packed. There was a long line of cars in the drive-through, and just as I was getting the car in line, I heard the door pop open. V just jumped out and ran to the Burger King playground. He started running around playing on all the equipment, up and down the sliding board, swinging from the Jungle Gym, bouncing up and down in one of those trampoline ball pits.

Pretty soon horns were blowing. The place was full of NC State people heading home after the game and here's their coach, once again, giving the fans their money's worth. With V you just never knew. I really don't think he knew what he'd do next either. And that's what made him so special. He could go from a last-minute pressure-packed huddle with the game on the line to sliding down sliding boards and swinging from Jungle Gyms—and never miss a beat!

48 HOURS

One of the best writing assignments I ever had was covering the CBS crew from 48 Hours cover NC State's basketball program. At the center of this piece was the most quotable coach in the country–V.

In 1988 Jim Valvano gave permission to two crews to cover the Wolfpack in a unique way. The primary crew was *48 Hours*, a new CBS national TV show that followed interesting subjects for a 48-hour period. The secondary crew was me. When I found out that V had agreed to open NC State's doors to *48 Hours*, I went to the coach and asked if I could cover the big timers covering State (the program would end with us playing Duke) for our alumni magazine.

V, of course, said, "Go for it!"

The CBS crew was as big time as they could be–and acted it! The producer was a Harvard law graduate who had produced for *60 Minutes* and *The CBS Evening News*. His reporters were some of Dan Rather's best–David Dow, Peter Van Sant, and Bernard Goldberg. For forty-eight hours I chased CBS chasing V.

The most memorable scene, among many, was shot in front of Case Athletic Center. From the moment Bernard Goldberg set foot on the State campus, he'd been earning his living by trying to break V down on the issue of dollars.

V was playing him and playing right along, literally. They actually played one-on-one against each other in Reynolds. And I remember V walking up during a conversation between Goldberg and his fellow reporter Van Sant.

Goldberg: "I played Valvano yesterday. I didn't do well. I was in his face, I was really in his face."

Suddenly V leaned in and began talking to Van Sant as though Goldberg wasn't there. "Bernie did something I couldn't believe. The score is tied. He throws the ball up against the glass, then slams right over my head. That shocked the hell out of me!"

Moments later Bernard, ever the bird dog, was trying to rock and shock V again. The microphones were on, the cameras rolling, and he had V pinned up against his red sports car there in front of Case Athletic Center badgering him about the money issues again. He wanted to know, with all his outside interests, just how much loot V was pulling down a year. Thrust and parry, it was getting pretty hot and heavy. Then suddenly V dropped to his knees on the pavement and began to bow to Goldberg (and the camera).

"Bernie," he shouted, "I'll give it all back. I'll give it all back. I don't deserve any of it!"

As the cameraman and crew howled with laughter V made a triumphant exit up the ramp to go into his office. Goldberg took one parting shot. "Coach, one more question. In 1987 when you were filling out your income taxes. What was the figure you put . . . "

Now here came V again, "Taxes? Oh my God, taxes! That's it, I knew there was something. I've got to get my '87 taxes done!"

LAST CALL

GEORGE TARANTINI remembers the night that they got an early last call.

Jimmy loved Sam Esposito, they were really close. But Sam was Sam, a real creature of habit; he had his routines and he didn't break them. He didn't go out a lot, and he had his routine—dinner, a few beers, he'd watch ESPN at 6:00 in the evening, then off to bed... early.

So one day Jimmy says to me, "You know, we've never been invited to Sam's. Let's go over there and just drop in on him."

So we go get beer and a pizza, and we go to Sam's and knock on the door. So it's about 6:30 in the evening and here we are—uninvited—with the pizza and the beer, me and Jimmy. We talk for a few minutes and have a beer and all of a sudden Sam looks at his wife, Noreen, and says, "Okay, that's enough!"

Now Jimmy is a guy who is going to be up every night almost until sunrise, and it's 6:45 in the evening.

And so Jimmy says, "What do you mean, that's enough?"

And Sam says, "Time for ESPN and bed. I'm going to bed!"

Jimmy can't believe this: "Six forty-five and you're walking out on your guests?"

And Sam just says, "That's the routine, Jimmy, that's the routine."

And he gets up and walks off to bed, with us sitting there looking at each other with our beer and pizza.

So we pick up and go off to the car.

Now Jimmy is in the car and he just can't believe it. He's the athletic director, Sam's boss, and he's sitting there in Sam's driveway saying, "I can't believe it. That's the routine! Did he just kick us out?"

THE TOY

LeeAnn recalls how much fun it was to be on the road with her dad.

My dad acted like a dad, but he was also a little kid at the same time. He was so much fun. And we really had a lot of special LeeAnn and Daddy time.

When I was real little the basketball games were a great memory. Because even though he was committed to basketball and winning and everything, I used to be with the cheerleaders for the games, had a costume, and I'd run across the floor and give him a kiss. He'd tell me that I was the good luck [charm] and the only reason they won. If it was a school night and I didn't go and they lost, he'd say it was because I wasn't there with the good luck kiss. It was such a special thing. He made everything seem like it was about me, even though it really wasn't because the basketball was his job. But if I was there, I was his good luck charm.

Mom used to say to me that when he'd lose a game he'd be devastated. And I was the little kid so I was the only one that could make him happy. So Mom would come wake me up if I was in my room sleeping after he'd lost a game and she'd say, "LeeAnn, go to your daddy!" And I'd run in and jump on him or give him a hug. And he would get in a better mood.

I remember that when I was nine, he had a speaking engagement in Boca Raton, Florida, so he decided that he wanted to take me on a trip with him, by myself, for my birthday. We stayed in this beautiful resort and he gave his speech and then we played video games the entire night. That's all we did. We stood in the video arcade and played Pac Man and Gallagher all night long. I think that one of the reasons he liked to play me was because I was really good and sometimes I'd beat him. He just loved the competition. That night we played so long that when we wanted to go in the hotel's pool it was closed, locked up.

So now he said, "Well, I promised you that we'd have a good time, so you get in your swimsuit anyway!"

So we snuck into the pool. We're the only ones in there and we heard someone coming. So now I think we're going to get into big trouble.

He said, "Go under water and hide!"

Now this was like a big deal to me. Then when I came up and they were gone, I thought we'd really fooled everybody. But what really happened was that he'd cleared it with the management before we went swimming. He was just trying to make it a bigger adventure for me, more fun.

"Hey, someone's coming, get under the water!"

That's the way he was about everything, so much fun!

It's sad that we didn't know each other when I was an adult, but at least we didn't have to go through my awkward adolescence where kids and parents sometimes go through trouble. We were just big playmates together!

PRACTICE, PRACTICE, PRACTICE

Bob Guzzo remembers V, ever the amiable host, making a few bad turns with a Sports Illustrated *reporter.*

Sports Illustrated came to do the big story on Jimmy, I think just after he'd won the national championship in '83. I don't know what they found when they visited most big time coaches, but here at NC State they got V. He chatted them up in his office then went to Amedeo's restaurant for a long lunch topped off with a couple of bottles of wine.

When the afternoon started to wind down, the reporter finally said, "Don't you have a practice this afternoon?"

V checked his watch, said, "Oh, yeah!" and so now he and the reporter head over to Reynolds Coliseum with V giving him more conversation all the way. When they walk into the Coliseum it's filled with chairs and a PA system for a concert to be held that night.

The reporter says, "You're not having practice?"

And V, never missing a beat, says. "Well, if there aren't a bunch of guys running around in short pants when we get to Carmichael [a backup facility for practice], I guess you're right!"

Most coaches would be devastated. Big time magazine and the coach doesn't even know where he's practicing.

Not V, he was just that cool.

FORWARDS AND GUARDS
GO LONG

MAX PERRY remembers an early encounter of the third (down) kind.

When V gave his first talk to the team, we knew how serious he was about winning. He'd given us all his goals, including winning the national championship.

So about three or four days later a bunch of us are playing touch football over at the College Inn. We'd gotten a keg of beer and all of a sudden we see his car pull up.

Now we're thinking, "Hell, we're in trouble!"

He had just given us this basketball is a serious business speech and here we are jacking around playing football, the last thing a basketball coach is going to want to see his players doing. I'm thinking, we're done.

He gets out of his car and says, "I gotta know one thing!"

Pregnant pause!

"Whose team am I quarterbacking?"

Of course he just took over–big QB take-over guy– drawing up plays, giving us pass patterns. He talked the whole time, nonstop talking. We knew right then that things were different with this coach. And we were right. They would never be the same again.

CHINESE FIRE DRILL

PAT KENNEDY, then an assistant coach at Iona, recalls a Valvano drill that most basketball coaches didn't practice.

The thing that was so incredible about Jim Valvano was that he had this childlike innocence and he brought it out of all of us. Only great comedians would be like this. This was at Iona, and we would be driving in Manhattan, right downtown, going to maybe scout a high school basketball game. We drove these old shit cars and he'd stop at a light on Fifth Avenue. So maybe it's V and Jimmy Gurtner and me, maybe Tommy Abatemarco.

V would just all of a sudden shout, "Chinese Fire Drill!"

Here's how it worked. Whenever he called one, I'd have to put the car in park, and we all had to jump out, run around the car and then try to pile back in the same door as fast as we could.

Grown men, representing Iona College, running around the car. New Yorkers don't make eye contact and it's almost impossible to make them laugh. But believe me, whether it was Fifth Avenue or Broadway, Jimmy's Chinese Fire Drills never failed, they always got a laugh.

We, including V, were all very serious about basketball and winning. But we were still little kids when we were around him. Things like V's Chinese Fire Drills wouldn't let you grow up!

CRÈME DE LA CRÈME

ART KAMINSKY recalls V and one of those New York nights.

There was nothing more fun than to be with Jim. And the later it got, the more fun it got. NC State was playing in New York, and so we went out after the game to, as he put it, " have some fun."

Understatement!

I remember that it was a really eclectic crew: sports writers, some Gombahs, and we all drove up to Arthur Avenue, a real old Italian area, one of the areas in the Bronx that was largely unchanged. It was Italian at the beginning of the twentieth century, and it's still Italian now. The guy who owned the restaurant was obviously a friend of Jim. It was probably past closing but he kept it open for us and we must have gotten there about midnight.

We ate and drank for four, five, maybe six hours, I don't know how long. It was just one of those special nights where Jim just got funnier and funnier and crazier and crazier. And the pièce de résistance came sometime after dawn. Jim had just done everything you can imagine to entertain us, to make us laugh.

He had no topper… we thought.

So now he orders strawberries and whipped cream, two bowls of whipped cream. And then to put the lid on this incredible night, he just dove head first into the whipped cream. He had come up with a great closer for what had to be the funniest night of my life.

HIT OR MISS

JIM REHBOCK recalls the games within the game.

He was such a competitor and he just wouldn't lose. He'd figure out a way to change the rules if he had to, but he was going to win. He'd do that with the kids in his basketball camp. He'd be playing H-O-R-S-E with them, and if it looked like he was going to lose—right in the middle of the game—he'd change the rules.

Creative things like, "Oops, I forgot it's Tuesday, gotta use Tuesday's rules. You have to hit two jumpers to win."

Or if the kids were wearing Carolina Blue basketball shoes on NC State's court and the kid is shooting the lights out against Jimmy, then that means that kid has to give up two letters. It didn't matter how old the kids were. They could be seven years old and couldn't reach the net on a shot.

He used to do things like that to me with the NC State team. We did a lot of conditioning with the team before the season started and then tapered off when the season got going. So they didn't do a lot of wind sprints during the season.

I remember the very first year and I'm sitting on the sidelines and he says, "Reebs, come on out here!"

He has the players standing around the foul line waiting to see what his latest is. Now, I'm not a basketball player. I'm one of those guys if the ball hits the rim, I'm happy.

So he says, "Here's the deal, if Reebs hits two foul shots, you guys don't have to run."

So now he wants them to run and the heat's on me.

"Here," he says, "I'll rebound for you."

He did that to me every year that we were there. If I hit it half the time I was lucky. And the kids would be on me. And of course, he loved it and knew exactly what he was doing.

KING OF THE COMPS

Dr. Jerry Punch, ABC and ESPN NASCAR and football analyst, remembers seeing the evidence and the confirmation that V was truly the King of the Comps.

This story starts in a famous steakhouse in Birmingham, Alabama, called Michael's where Bear Bryant used to eat. We were in there one day and I looked up and here's this great picture of Dick Vitale, Gene Bartow, and Jimmy V, all sitting in the restaurant. The waitress came up and saw me looking at the picture of Dick, Gene, and V.

She said, "Hey, do you know what the caption of that picture should be? 'Who picked up the check? None of the above!'"

Having worked at ESPN, I had heard that V liked his comps. So now I'm back in Bristol, Connecticut, at this hotel across the street from the ESPN studios. It's a place where ESPN people stay when we're doing studio work. Now one of the jokes was the food in this place, and the punch line was the comp breakfast. When you checked in you got this little coupon which most people immediately put in the trash. The deal was that you had to be downstairs between something like 6:30 and 6:45 A.M. The coupon was worth about $3.50 and most people would rather have a free tour of downtown Bristol than eat in that restaurant. So I had an early production meeting and I go down to get a cup of coffee and here's V sitting in the restaurant in his Nike sweats. He's eating the comp breakfast.

I'm thinking this guy sneezes three times and he makes six figures, and he's eating the comp breakfast? I walked over and the whole time we were talking, I couldn't keep my eyes off his plate. All I could see was this huge mound of catchup. So I'm thinking somewhere under his red sauce is the worst breakfast in America. V was smiling and eating away and I'm remembering that picture I'd seen of him with Vitale and Bartow in Alabama the week before and I'm thinking that waitress was right: "Who picked up the check? None of the above!"

V was the King of the Comps!

SINCERELY THE AD

Bruce Poulton, the chancellor who promoted Jim Valvano to athletic director at NC State, recalls the circumstances that led to that decision.

People need to understand that Jim had a very sincere side to him.

I remember the day he came to me confirming the request made by his fellow coaches and said, "Yes, I would like to be athletic director."

I said, "Well, Jim, if you want to be the AD that's fine, you can become a candidate but you can't be the coach and be the AD, can you?"

And he said, "Sure, no problem!"

We went around on this, and of course, I knew him so I'm thinking, what is he really up to here?

I said, "Jim, you don't think I'm going to pay you an AD's salary on top of your coach's salary, do you?"

He said, "Oh no, I don't want any more money."

So this led to my question regarding his motive. And he reminded me that the other coaches thought he could really help them by getting behind their programs and giving them support. And it turned out that way. I had had a number of those coaches come to me and say they wanted Jim to be the AD. The coaches were unanimous, and when I talked to them, they knew that he had a sincere desire to help them build their programs and build the athletic programs at NC State. That was the reason that I made that decision.

I will say this: that was a very questionable decision on my part... to give him two major roles like that. I've always wondered if maybe he had so much responsibility as the athletic director that some of what I call his "sins of omission" were because he just didn't have time to pay attention to whether a player was selling his extra pair of Nike shoes.

Jim wasn't that big of a cop anyway. One of the reasons that he wasn't was because he realized that there was a real discontinuity between a coach who was making hundreds of thousands of dollars from shoe companies—just to have the kids wear their shoes—and a player who had an extra pair of shoes and couldn't sell them. But anyway he was—there is no question—very sincere, he had that side to him. And I believe that he was asked by the coaches to take on the AD's job, and he accepted it because he thought he could help them.

I know that he didn't take a dime more for taking on all that responsibility.

GRIN AND BARE IT

JEFF RULAND remembers what it was like to play golf with a guy who knew how to make the game fun.

Before my freshman year, I used to come up and work [an alumnus's bar], and V and I would play golf. Man, was he something, really funny.

After I retired from the NBA I took up golf and I'm about a 12-handicap now. But back then I could barely get the ball in the air. We'd wind up only playing a couple of holes because I couldn't play at all and he wasn't much better. But we entertained ourselves by just driving all over the course in the cart like wild men.

So one time he drives over this hill and I'm down there with my shot, thinking, "Where the f*#&@ is he?"

Then all of a sudden he breaks out of the trees in the golf cart, and he's bare-assed naked. This was just to get a laugh.

I'm thinking this guy is going to be fun to play for, and he was... one of the funniest guys you'll ever be around.

V

FAT FRIED

ERNIE MYERS was one of V's secret weapons, filling in for Dereck Whittenburg in '83 when Whitt went down in the Virginia game. Myers remembers V the disciplinarian.

The national championship experience was a once-in-a-lifetime thing, and now I realize that it was so much better because of V. He knew how to treat you, and the celebration after that win couldn't have been better. We felt like rock stars and he just sat back and let us enjoy the moment.

He said, "This is what I was talking about, this is what it's all about."

But there were plenty of times leading up to that moment when it was time to be serious. He was very serious about winning and we knew that we had better be.

Today, people in New York ask me about the championship and ask me about what V was like. I tell them that he treated us like men, he didn't baby-sit us. We knew what we had to do, and he got us ready for the game, and man, he could be tough. Everyone knows how funny he was, but I remember this one time that he was funny but he didn't mean to be. We had to keep our heads down so he wouldn't see us laughing. He had this thing about diets, he was always on one; the popcorn diet was the one that he was usually on, where he'd eat nothing but popcorn.

So we lost about three games on the road in '82-83–maybe Clemson, Virginia, and Georgia Tech–so he started looking at us and decided we were all fat. At State we ate at the training table in Case Athletic Center. But when we were on the road, we could eat anything we wanted; we'd just sign off on it. So the guys would eat like crazy. He knew that, and he put two and two together and decided that we couldn't win on the road because we were loading up on the food and getting fat.

So we're on the road getting ready to play a game and he calls this meeting. We don't know what's coming, and all of a sudden he just goes off on us: "Do you know the reason we're losing on the road?"

No one answered because we didn't know why.

Then he says, "Because we can't get up and down the court; you guys are eating eighteen million calories at McDonald's–too many damned fries–that's why we're so sluggish. You can't get up and down the court. You're playing the game in slow motion. I'm taking away your food privileges because you guys are fat."

Now, we had a lot of guys on that team, and really none of us were fat! So we're kind of looking at each other, checking each other out, seeing who's fat. And the more he dishes it out, the funnier it gets. But he was serious, and man, he loved to make people laugh–but not when he was serious. And we're fighting back the laughter. We couldn't look at him, knowing that, man, if he catches us laughing, it's going to be a whole lot worse than missing our next meal at McDonald's.

When you were losing he was just like any other coach. He was going to be our worst nightmare. When we'd lose, sometimes we'd get off the bus back at Reynolds, no matter what time it was; we were going into Reynolds Coliseum.

He'd say, "Lace them up, we're going to practice!"

He'd run it out of us. And you really could see a complete change in his personality from when he was winning and losing. You didn't want to be around him because he was such a competitor that he just couldn't stand to lose. You could see it in his face, like "I gotta win."

He used to say to us, "I've got more energy in my little pinkie finger than you guys have in your whole damn bodies!"

And it was true! He was a winner and he made us winners.

THE WALLS COME TUMBLING DOWN!

RAY TANNER recalls the day that a one-on-one interoffice competition became an earth-shaking event.

The office set-up in Case Athletic Center between basketball and baseball back then was this: V had the whole top floor except for the end office and that was where [baseball] Coach Esposito and I were housed. Coach Esposito and I both had a desk in that one office.

Now this was when V was [just] coaching, not [also] the athletic director. He would always come to our office just to get away from the phone and things. We'd close the door, and it was his chance to shoot the bull and relax for a while.

We had a hoop that we hooked behind that closed door and a Nerf ball, and what we did was play H-O-R-S-E and other games in there. It was usually me against V. He called me Thick Man. And being an ex–third baseman, I reminded him that through the hips is where the hitters get their power. Anyway we'd shoot from different spots in the room, and he was always changing the rules, because it wasn't that he wanted to win–V had to win!

Every game you ever played with him, it was structured, weighted his way. But we had a great time. And one day we decided the hell with the H-O-R-S-E–we'd go one-on-one. Well, pretty soon we were really going at it. With him giving me a lot of Thick Man conversation, trying to move me away from the basket, and me trying to take advantage of my, I guess you could say, "Thickness" to go to the hoop.

As I was making my move to the hoop, he caught me with a hip and drove me into the wall. And the damned thing split. The sheetrock started coming down on us, and I mean the entire wall almost came down, sheetrock flying, dust, it was scary. Coach Esposito was just sitting behind his desk looking at us like we were a couple of eight-year-olds.

Now V was the one who hipped me into the wall but, of course, the first thing he did was blame me for being so thick, "Hey, wide-ass, look what you've done!"

Now we were scared because Willis Casey, our AD, was about as tight as they came. So we had to come up with a story. No problem. By the time the dust had settled, V had the story. Coach Esposito had just innocently slammed his office door, and the damned wall, probably inferior construction, had come down. V even added a little touch that the university should be glad that we weren't hurt because the whole thing might have ended up in an ugly lawsuit.

SAVE THE LAST DANCE FOR V

JOHN SAUNDERS remembers the night that he and V covered the Big Dance.

We're in the studio covering basketball and we had gone off the air. It was Jim, Dick Vitale, and me. Vitale's acting like a fool and he's dancing around while we're on a commercial break. So Jim and I start dancing.

Now Jim leans over to me and says, "Okay, we're going to do this until we get on the air and then we're going to stop!"

So he says to Dick, "Hey, we might as well do this on the air. Basketball's Big Dance, everybody getting fired up!"

So sure enough as soon as they cue us and the red light comes on, Jim and I stop dancing and Vitale keeps going, and of course, Vitale starts screaming, "They were dancing, baby! They let me down, they were dancing, they were dancing!"

Jim and I just looked at Dick very seriously, like he was crazy. Jim loved to tweak Vitale!

MOUNTAIN MAN

ED McLEAN recalls the day when he had to deliver the news about scheduling, knowing that V might just kill the messenger.

This is hardly news, but coaches don't like to play good small programs, and they just won't ever play a small program that might beat you at their place. It's just death, and they won't do it. When Jim came to NC State there was an agreement in place, a contract with Western Carolina. At that time they had a pretty good program. It was a four-for-one agreement. They had come to play us four times at NC State, and we'd agreed to go play them at Western—a one time deal—to dedicate their new building. The payback game up there was in 1986.

Nobody wanted to tell Jim this. It was on the schedule, and I was responsible for the schedule, and I kept telling Frank Weedon, "You better tell Jim about this game at Western, because I think he just assumes that it's here!"

Jim had never been to Cullowhee; it's way, way up in the North Carolina mountains. He knew I'd gone to school at Western and played for them. And when we'd played them here, he'd been all over me about being a mountain man and having one leg shorter than the other from living in the mountains, things like that. Frank kept putting off telling him. When he finally did and Jim finds out that he has to play Western up there, it suddenly becomes my fault. I had nothing to do with this contract. I think it was between the administration of the two schools and the university system, because it was centered around the dedication of that new arena at Western.

By the time we played that game, I was dreading it. We had to fly into Asheville and then bus up the mountain to Cullowhee. Oh man, you should have heard him. There was one motel in the little town called Sylva, way up on a hill. We checked in there.

First thing, no cable TV. Jim had to have cable. He stayed up all night, the man never slept. He did not want to be there. Now I'm just praying that we don't get upset.

Then we go to the new building to practice and they're real proud of their new building so they take us for a tour.

And Jim says to the guy, "I've got good news and bad news for you. The good news is that you have a beautiful building here. The bad news is that nobody's ever going to see it!"

When we finally played the game, it was really close. We got them at the end, but I mean it was a nail biter, and when we finally did get out of there it was still hell to pay. I've come down that mountain many times, but I don't remember a longer trip than that one. He stayed on me—Mountain Man, the guy who scheduled Western Carolina—all the way back to Raleigh!

COMING HOME TO ROOST

DERECK WHITTENBURG remembers V as a recruiter and the day he and Sidney Lowe said no to the coach they'd eventually play for.

This was at the Boston Shoot Out, a big AAU tournament played at Boston University. You talk about ironic. Sidney and I were playing for DeMatha High School [D.C.] and we'd played a New York team in a double-overtime in the first game and won. The Shoot Out was trying to set it up for a Boston high school to win, so they had the two best teams play in the first round of the tournament, Washington, D.C., and New York.

Well, that didn't work; we won a great game [against Boston] in the finals, and we were in a hallway outside the gym.

Sidney and I were just standing there and here comes this wild Italian guy and he's screaming, "I love you two guys," and he grabbed both of us by the neck. "I love you two guys, why don't you come play for me. Iona College!"

I said, "What the hell is I own a college?"

And Jimmy said, "No, Iona College. I've gotta have you two guys, you've gotta come play for me! I want to coach you two guys."

I said, "Nah, we're going to NC State!"

In a year we were playing for him. [Coach] Norm [Sloan] left and Jimmy came to NC State, that was our sophomore year. And he not only coached us, but our senior year he coached us to a national championship.

STICKY SITUATION

Dan White remembers the half-times in the locker room when things got sticky.

There were some pretty spirited locker room talks at half-time with V. Sometimes you'd just want to go hide, get the hell out of there. But I only ever saw him like a deer in the headlights at half-time once, and this was, I believe, a Wake Forest game.

We had this Gatorade-like sports drink, sweet and sugary and real sticky. Anyway V was pissed off, and he takes this cooler full of the drinks and kicks it and knocks it over. The lid flew off and this stuff went all over Coach McLean. Then Coach McLean was so mad that he kicked it and threw his clipboard against the wall.

Now Ed was the X's and O's guy, and he'd diagram the plays at time-outs and half-time, that was his job. He'd make the suggestions, and then V and the other coaches would react. He was a real genius as far as X's and O's.

But Ed's clipboard was across the room where he'd thrown it and he was just covered with this stuff that V had kicked. So he'd thrown his clipboard and after he threw it he went and sat in front of one of the lockers. He was just steaming.

And V was, for the first time that I remember, just stuttering. His eyes were so big, he couldn't talk because he'd never seen Ed get that mad.

V didn't mean to do it. But Coach McLean wouldn't get up for his X's and O's, and that was the only time that I ever saw V kind of shaky.

Oh, the players?

They were all trying to keep from laughing. Here's V trying to get their attention, pretending that he hadn't just kicked these bottles of crap all over his X's and O's coach.

V

THE INTERVENTION

One of V's favorite indoor sports was shooting the bull with the other coaches. He'd leave his office to hide from the phones, drop by one of the offices, coffee up, and hold court. The subjects discussed in these think tanks ran the gamut—from how to break a match-up zone defense to marriage counseling. FRANCES LEWIS remembers.

Just about every morning when Jim came in he would go around and socialize with all the other offices. About 10:00 one morning, he was down in [assistant athletic director] Bob Robinson's office and Sam Esposito was in there with George Tarantini. So Jim buzzed me from down there and asked me to go into his desk and bring a letter to him. I thought this sounded a little funny but I took the letter to him. And when I got into Bob's office, Jim jumped up and locked the door.

Man, did they give me a fit. This was an intervention. My husband had died and time had passed and now I was going to marry Bill Lynch. And my surrogate sons, Jim being the ringleader, weren't sure that this was a good idea.

Now I loved those guys, but marriage counselors? Jim was pretty sure that Bill was marrying me for my money, that he was a golddigger! But I had an ally that they didn't know about. Father Donahue was Jim's priest. He used to hang out in Jim's office because, I think, he was trying to get Jim back in church.

So I said, "Listen, guys, I've already checked with Father Donahue and he said that Bill Lynch is as fine a man as he's ever known. And that if I had the opportunity that I should sign on the dotted line."

Bob Robinson… was a former Air Force officer and he was quick to present the fact that retired military officers [e.g., Lynch] don't necessarily have a lot of money. But what pushed them over the top on this issue was when I told them that I knew Bill's broker. Bill's father had been a shipbuilder and Bill had inherited a sizable amount of stock. This brought on more discussion. Some "how do you knows," and a few "well, maybes."

Finally Sam Esposito said, "Jim, I think she's done her homework. Leave her alone!"

And that was it. Jim Valvano and his review board reluctantly agreed to allow me to marry Bill Lynch. And by the way, with their blessings, Bill Lynch and I have lived happily ever after.

GENTLEMEN, START YOUR ENGINES

JIM POMERANTZ, an NC State University Sports Information writer during the V years, recalls the then-new coach's early radio days.

The first call-in radio show that Jim did for WPTF radio was just Jim, me, a microphone, and a telephone. We went on the air, this was back in about 1980 or 1981. He just started talking and we waited for the phone to ring. About fifteen minutes into the show we still hadn't gotten a single call.

So I wrote him a note telling him that I was going to go out of the studio, phone in, and ask him a question. He gives me the okay sign. I go out and call and throw a big country accent at him, but the question didn't have a damn thing to do with basketball; it was a NASCAR question.

Now Jim had just touched down in NASCAR country, which to him was another planet. I asked him what he thought of Darrell Waltrip, who had been in a wreck the Sunday before with Richard Petty. Darrell had half the race fans in the state down on him.

Jim takes my question and doesn't miss a beat. He goes on for about five minutes ad-libbing like crazy, saying how he likes Waltrip and thinks he's a pretty great guy, that racing is racing and accidents come with the territory. This was all we needed—it was like someone had said, "Gentlemen, start your engines!"

The phone started ringing off the hook with calls—angry NASCAR fans, but calls—and the Jim Valvano radio show was off and running.

THE LIGHTER SIDE

His guest appearance on V's TV show, The Lighter Side, *was one that* ROLLIE MASSAMINO *can't forget.*

I don't know how many people will recall the TV show called *The Lighter Side Of Sports.* Jimmy emceed this crazy show. So I go down there to be on the show and I brought my daughter; she was about twenty-two at the time. And so it's me and my daughter. Jimmy flew in for the show and the Hawk [co-host Ken Harrelson, former Boston Red Sox star] came in. We went on, and I was going to play the piano and Jimmy was going to sing. We were in one of the big casino hotels in Atlantic City. And oh, did we laugh and scream and had one hell of a time.

Something happened, he was screwing around while I was playing drinking beer or something, and they just decided not to air the thing. But oh, it was funny. But to him this TV show—the reason we were all there—was just the warm-up.

Then we go to a bar in one of the casinos for a drink, me, Jimmy, and my daughter. Well, he had a 7 A.M. flight in Philadelphia, and so he just decided that we'd stay up, make a night of it.

I played the piano in this bar, and he was dancing on the bar, and we were laughing our heads off. His whole game plan was well, no need to go to sleep, and we didn't want to gamble, so he said, "Hey, I've got an early flight, let's just hang out all night."

We went to eat and then the music, me playing and him singing and dancing with my daughter, and we just carried on for the rest of the night. And he really couldn't sing. He thought he could.

But Jimmy's begging the guy to stay open: "You gotta stay open. I've got an early flight!"

Well, we stayed there until about 4 in the morning and so we take him back to Philadelphia and drop him at the airport, and then he runs into one of my assistants at the airport catching an early flight. He [the assistant] asks Goofy where he's been.

Jimmy says, "Oh, I was out with Rollie. Your boss—he kept me up all night!"

AD DELIBERATION

*Former assistant athletic director **BOB ROBINSON** remembers the day that he and the coaches nominated V for the position of athletic director.*

Here's the real story of how Jim Valvano became the athletic director at NC State. A lot of people looked at his ego and thought it was his idea. I can assure you that it wasn't. Chancellor Poulton had a meeting with the Athletic Department in the Weisiger-Brown Building. I know that Jimmy was away and I think the team was playing at Florida State.

This was after Willis Casey retired as the AD. All the Athletic Department was there. And Dr. Poulton told us flat out that there was no one on that staff that he was considering hiring as the new AD. And it got very quiet in there.

Someone stood up and asked, "What would you think about taking a coach, someone with a dual responsibility?"

Other coaches asked some questions, and then I said, "Dr. Poulton, this room has hundreds of years of experience in the athletics business. If we're going to have an input on the hiring of the athletics director, how are we going to handle that?"

He said, "Bill Simpson, the university secretary, is handling the applications and anyone in this room can talk to Bill about who they'd like for that job."

Several of the coaches went right to Bill Simpson's office to express their concerns.

When that meeting was over we all knew that Frank Weedon (senior associate athletic director) was the logical choice. But the coaches and Charlie Bryant (head of the Wolfpack Club) met in one of the offices and we decided, Frank included, that the only person who had the juice for consideration was Jim Valvano. He had the experience—he'd been both basketball coach and AD at Iona. We didn't want someone from a smaller school coming in and revamping what we knew was a very successful program.

The next day some of us were in Sam Esposito's office talking about this and Jimmy walked by.

Charlie Bryant said it again, "That's who we need right there!"

So when Jimmy stuck his head in the door, Charlie said, "If we recommend you, would you take the AD's job?"

I'm not sure of the time frame, how much he discussed it with us, but after he'd thought it over, he said, "Well, if that's what you want, fine!"

I remember that the team was getting ready to go to I believe Hawaii for the Holiday tournament, and Charlie Bryant came to me and said, "Bob, write up a recommendation, all the facts that we know about Jimmy. We need to make this a formal proposal."

I still have a copy of it at home, it's about eight or ten pages. It outlines Jimmy's experience, etc. We circulated it; all the coaches signed in support of Jimmy. Dr. Poulton reviewed it and then made his decision.

That's how Jimmy got to be AD. Not because he went out and asked for it. We wanted him to be our boss. With him we knew what we were getting. And to be frank, we were afraid that an outsider would bring in his own team. Frankly, in many respects, he did an excellent job. He took care of his coaches, wasn't partial to basketball, and had tremendous vision for the entire athletic program. A lot of the new facilities in football, baseball, and basketball were things that Jimmy initiated, including the new arena. He had them on the drawing board but unfortunately was never given a chance to finish what he'd started.

RANGERS REPORT

FRANK WEEDON remembers V on one of his landmark nights.

We went to a Texas Rangers game. This was 1985; we were in Dallas for an NCAA meeting. It was [former athletic director] Gene Hooks from Wake Forest; the athletic director from Lehigh University; Billy Hunter, who was the AD at Towson State [and the old Baltimore Orioles manager and shortstop]; and V and me.

So a pretty good group. Of course we were comped on the tickets through some connection of V's. We pull into the Texas ball park looking for a place to park when the attendant recognizes V and says, "Hey, right over here!"

He waves us all the way up to the front line... right next to the stadium. V smiles and nods.

We take our seats—prime—right behind the Texas dugout. Now this is the part people who know me may not believe, but I volunteered to buy the first round of beers. When everyone is served, the guy sitting next to me—who no one knew—reaches in his pocket and pays the vendor.

"I just want to be able to say that I bought Jim Valvano a beer," he says.

Big smile from V again.

Then, about two innings into the game, here comes a guy with a video camera—we thought it was a tourist—he squats down and points the camera at V and all of a sudden there's V up on the big Jumbotron in center field. Now everyone is applauding. V is being V telling all of us that we should travel with him more often if we want to go first class. No sooner than he says that and here comes Bobby Valentine, the Texas manager, looking over the dugout.

He saw V on the Jumbotron and he says, "What are you doing here? How about coming down to the locker room after the game... my guys would love to meet you."

And then, just when we thought we'd seen it all, a young man comes up and hands Jim a note. We thought it was a request for an autograph. Oh, no, the Texas Rangers play-by-play announcer has seen him on the Jumbotron and wants V to come up and announce an inning with him. So up we go and while V is in announcing—by the way, he did three innings not one—we are ushered into the owner's box and sit with the old gentleman who owned the Texas Rangers.

Here's how it ended. V finishes his radio work and comes in and sits with us—takes a seat right next to the team's owner. V's still full of himself from his radio stint and is managing now, expounding on moves he'd make. Suddenly an umpire's call goes against Texas and V slaps the table and spills Coke all over the owner. Now it looks like his perfect night has finally gone bad. V's apologizing to the old gentleman saying that we'll leave. But as the owner is wiping Coke off himself he's begging V to stay, saying that just having V there has made this the most enjoyable game of the year for him.

From that time on, anytime baseball would come up around V, I ran because I knew what was coming, "Frank, tell them about V night at the Texas Rangers game!"

$$\mathcal{V}$$

NY HOMECOMING

Don Shea, who produced V's TV show, recalls a TV homecoming for Jimmy V, one of his finest days.

When he came in '80, we went back to play a holiday tournament in the Garden, and State beat Iona and then St. John's. I was producing his TV show so we decided to go to his old neighborhood in Queens where the A line went right over his house. It was really something: all the Italians who lived in these walk-ups came out to see him. They talked about the tradition where the younger kids had to live at the top in the attics, and as you got older you moved to the lower part of the flat.

Then we went to Seaford High School, and he sat in his old desk and he talked about his Aunt Marion, who when he visited would let him stay up late and watch TV, give him whatever he wanted to eat. He reminisced about the teacher who had influenced him the most, his old English teacher. Then we went and had Italian ice cream.

And when we went back into the neighborhood, people were spilling out of the houses saying, "Rocco's son is back in the neighborhood!" We had the cameras rolling and that was our story for the *Jim Valvano Show* for that week, and of course, we never topped that one. I'll tell you this, he had many great days but that was one of his best. You could see it in his eyes and in the looks on the faces of the families and friends where he'd grown up. He was a returning hero—like a magnet—to those people. Quite a day!

TEE FOR TOMMY

V went total dichotomy when it came to generosity. He could be both giving and incredibly tight. And it was funny because the stinginess heightened in certain areas. The treasure trove of comp clothes that he had stashed in his office fell into this "hands off" category. He used to warn coaches, managers, any who might see something in, say their size, to keep their hands off his stuff.

I learned this lesson the hard way. I was in Vero Beach, Florida, writing a story for NC State's alumni magazine, following Tracy Woodson, an ex-NC State baseball player who was in spring training with the LA Dodgers. The piece was aimed at telling our readers what it's like for a rookie hopeful to experience making a major league club. During my week with Woodson and the Dodgers I had a number of occasions to talk to Dodger manager Tommy Lasorda. Lasorda was a great friend of Jim Valvano's.

Turned out that Tommy liked free stuff too.

This was just weeks after V and the Wolfpack had won the 1987 ACC tournament so I took Woodson an NC State ACC Champions T-shirt. I left it in the locker room, and following that day's ball game Tracy came over to me and said, "Tommy wants to know why you didn't bring him a T-shirt. He says V's been promising him one!"

I went back to NC State and called V. He was out of the office. So I told Frances Lewis, V's secretary, that Lasorda was griping about a T-shirt that V had promised. I said that I'd be glad to buy it and ship it to Tommy but that I thought maybe V would want to send it personally.

Frances said, "Oh, I'll take care of it!"

So she went into V's office and picked out one of his shirts and fired it off Federal Express to the Dodgers.

About a week later V came back to his office and did a quick inventory and saw—we would later learn—that he was short a one-of-a-kind ACC Championship T-shirt. Nike or some company had made it just for him. When V found out that Tommy Lasorda was now strolling around the Dodgers locker room in his prized shirt, well, needless to say, "it" hit the fan!

$\mathcal{V}$

FINAL DAYS

MIKE WARREN remembers his coach going through the agony of Personal Fouls

When all the stuff was going on with *Personal Fouls,* I had graduated. But I supported V. I'd still go to practice when I could and support him in anyway that I could. I was close to him and I told him that I'd like to talk to Chancellor [Larry] Monteith [who succeeded Poulton], to represent the players' point of view. So I got a meeting set up with Chancellor Monteith. It was obvious why I was there. But before I could say much at all the chancellor starts talking and about forty-five minutes later I'm still listening and haven't said anything.

So I figured that he was going to boot me out, but I said, "Well, I appreciate what you've had to say but at the same time I came here to give you the players' side of the story, to tell you a little bit about what we think about the guy."

Then I told him that having been around V for five years plus that I was there as kind of a spokesman for everybody. He let me talk then, and I got about ten minutes in [before] he cut me off. I was out of there.

I knew then that V was done. That was when he'd asked to talk to the Board of Governors and had offered to work for a dollar a year. So as soon as I left Chancellor Monteith's offices I went over to see V and I told him. This was the first conversation that I had with him like two adults talking, not just player to coach. It was hard because I was delivering a message that I knew he needed to hear and at the same time I knew he didn't want to hear it.

I just said to him, "Coach, you're done with this guy. He didn't want
to listen to what I had to say and I don't think he wants to listen to what
you have to say. I think he has his mind made up. Whatever's going to
shake out is going to shake out."

I don't remember what V said, but he was very upset. At the
same time he was very strong and resigned to what the outcome was
going to be.

$$\mathcal{V}$$

COAT OF ARMS

*GEORGE TARANTINI remembers two great friends—V and Sam—and the
threads that held them together.*

Jimmy loved Sam Esposito. And Sam, very smart, a great athlete, and he could just wear Jimmy out. They were so funny together.

I'll never forget one day Jimmy says that in a Chicago newspaper poll Sam was named the best schoolboy athlete the city ever
produced. You'd never hear anything like that from Sam, an ex-
major league baseball player, University of Indiana point guard and
quarterback, great handball player and golfer. But very modest and
Jimmy really respected him.

But Sam would just wear Jimmy out; he'd say, "V, you never played
anything, you played for your father in high school, your father's friend
in college [Bill Foster]."

This would really get to Jimmy, who was a good athlete. Sam could
just work him, knew what would get to Jimmy.

Now, Jimmy was very possessive about his stuff, all the comps,
maybe Nike T-shirts, hats, clothes. Whatever was his was his and nobody else could have it. So Sam knew this. And one time Sam had to get
an award at a football game at Carter-Finley Stadium and he needed to
borrow a raincoat to wear that day.

Jimmy loaned him his coat, an old raincoat. So Sam wore it out on
the field, got the award, and then never gave it back to Jimmy. So Jimmy
wants the coat.

Sam says, "You've got too many coats."

It wasn't a new coat but this just drove Jimmy crazy. This went on for years, the argument over the coat. Whenever they would start on this I would say to Jimmy, "It was an old coat, why don't you just let it go?"

But Jimmy [was] always with Sam, "Where's my coat? You stole my coat!"

Finally Jimmy, who hated to lose, just said, "Okay take the coat. Pam always used that coat to take out the garbage. So I don't want that shit coat anyway, you can keep it!"

Sam said, "Thanks!" He still has the coat!

TURKEY SHOOT!

Former Virginia coach **TERRY HOLLAND** *recalls a UVA "Turkey" who wanted two prime seats in Reynolds Coliseum to see the 1983 NCAA champions play. V obliged him.*

Our teams played some remarkable and memorable games. On one occasion a good friend of mine, Paul "Turkey" Hodges, from Turkey, NC, in Sampson County had asked for tickets to our game at NC State in the 1982–83 season. Turkey owned and operated Calico Jack's Marina on Harker's Island and he bragged to the "regulars" there that he was "going to Raleigh to see this year's national champions play." We had him right behind the UVA bench and won a very close game, mainly because Dereck Whittenburg, after scoring 27 points in the first half, broke his foot in the second half of that game.

Of course, later in the season, when Whittenburg recovered and NC State completed its miraculous march to the national championship, Turkey's buddies on Harker's Island never let him forget, and V never let me forget, that back in January of that season Turkey had indeed been to Raleigh to see the "national champions" play– N.C. State.

GOING SOUTH

Les Robinson remembers his early meetings with V, back when Les was coaching The Citadel.

We used to play the North-South doubleheader at the Charlotte Coliseum. The Citadel and Furman would play NC State and Carolina back to back in these games. I had my coach's TV show at The Citadel and so my producer thought it would be a good idea if I interviewed V while we were in Charlotte. We'd played State the night before and lost and were getting ready to play Dean Smith and Carolina that night.

So on the air I said to V, "Coach, in a couple of hours we're going to play your big rival, Carolina. Do you have any advice for me?"

Carolina was loaded then–this was the early '80s.

V said, "Les, isn't that your blue Citadel bus out in the parking lot?"

I said, "Yes."

And he said, "Well, when you get your players loaded up on it in a few hours you're going to head down Route 77 and when you get to Tyvola out near the Charlotte Coliseum you can either head north to the Coliseum or south back to The Citadel. Tell the driver to head south!"

INSIDE THE LOCKER ROOM

Dr. Don Reibel remembers being in a very special place at a very special time–the NC State locker room before the national championship game.

This was the pre-game speech in Albuquerque and everybody thinks that we're going to hold the ball until Tuesday, which is what V told the press. Nobody thinks that we even deserve to be there– Dave Kindred with *The Washington Post* had written that lead to an article, "Elephants will drive in the Indy 500, etc, etc. before NC State beats Houston."

Here's what really happened in that locker room. I'll never forget it because I was privileged to be one of the few who was right there and saw it and heard it. After the X's and O's came the pre-game speech to top all pre-game speeches. He told those players, "There isn't a single sports writer that thinks we can win this thing, nobody thinks we can, but we can and we will and I'm going to tell you how!" And he's just going on and on and the players were so enthralled they weren't even thinking about that crowd, that national TV audience, that national championship. They were hanging on his every word and he went down the line, right through the top six or seven players, and told them individually what they were going to do that would win that championship.

He didn't ask, he told.

"Sidney, you are going to have the game of your life, you won't have a single turnover!"

"Cozell, tonight no Phi Slamma Jamma. You are going to be the greatest player this crowd has ever seen. I want you to stay between Akeem and the basket, no dunks, don't front him, don't allow a single dunk!

"They think we're going to hold the ball. We're going to go out there and shove it up their tails. Whitt and Terry, when you get open you're going to knock in the Js. No hesitation, take the shot, take it to them."

Then he turns to Lorenzo. "Tonight you are going to get every rebound that comes off that rim. It's going to be just like back in Brooklyn when you were stealing hub caps. I expect you to get every damned one of them."

He laid a personal challenge on every one of the players then he said, "Now, if you do what I just told you, we'll be back in here in a couple of hours with a national championship."

When they left that locker room they didn't think they could win a national championship, they knew they could. And of course they did. To those of us who heard that speech it sounded like he'd rehearsed it a hundred times. But I'll guarantee he probably didn't even know what he was going to say until he got into that locker room and said it. When it came to motivation, V was the master.

ME NO TONTO, KEMO SABE

Monte Kiffin, NC State's football coach in V's first years at NC State (now the defensive coach of the Tampa Bay Buccaneers) was probably best known during his tenure at NC State for dressing up as the Lone Ranger and riding into a student pep rally. Before Monte mounted the white stallion he had an even "better" idea. TOMMY ABATEMARCO, *V's assistant coach, recalls.*

Monte Kiffin is the football coach. So we're in Sam Esposito's office about 7 in the morning. It's V, Espo, and me, and Monte comes in and I'm just real quiet sitting on the sidelines listening to this, but Monte says, "Jim, I've got this great idea. We're playing Carolina [in football] and I'm going to ride into the pep rally on a white horse as the Lone Ranger."

Jimmy's just kind of dumbfounded looking at him.

Then Monte says, "Here's the capper. You're going to come in on a pinto with me; you've got the dark skin and the dark hair, you'll be my Tonto!"

V just sat there with this look. And when Monte left V said, "That guy is going to get fired at the end of the year, and so if he thinks I'm going to be his Tonto, he's crazy!"

Sure enough Monte rode in on a white horse and then, just like V said, he got fired at the end of the year. Of course, he's hardly the Lone Ranger now. Monte's one of the hottest defensive coaches in the NFL.

CAR 54, WHERE ARE YOU?

DEE ROWE, *the legendary head coach at UConn, remembers V and the case of the missing state vehicle.*

We used to get these state cars, old Chevrolets or Fords, and that's all we had to recruit in, they didn't even have radios. I remember coming home in the middle of the night and Jimmy with his head out the window singing to stay awake. We'd be out every night scouting, so you'd drive home and return the car to the motor pool.

I don't know what happened–Jimmy must have forgotten to get one of the cars back on time the next day after one of these trips. We had this associate director of athletics who was responsible for the cars. He came out in the midst of practice, a very tough guy, and was all over Jimmy. He couldn't find state car whatever the number was. Now, everybody knew that this wasn't exactly the kind of car that anybody would want to take or even be seen in for that matter. Of course, Jimmy just turned it into a big joke. "Car 54, Where Are You?"

All of us at that practice were in hysterics and for years, that was one of our big laughs together, "Car 54, Where Are You?"

ALL WET

LeeAnn remembers the fun it was to be Jimmy V's daughter.

Daddy always made everything a game, a big adventure. We had a beach house in Emerald Isle and when we went down there all my dad and I would do was play miniature golf at Jungle Putt Putt. And I re-member one time that we were about to go to dinner and we were all dressed but he'd promised to take me to Jungle Putt Putt.

So before we went my mom said, "You have to keep her clean. We're going out to dinner!"

So we got there and they had these little bumper boats, rubber tires that flew around in the water and you bumped into each other. Well we got in those boats and I got drenched.

My mom was so mad, "I told you not to get her dirty."

But the funny thing was what my dad said: "Hey, she looks just like she's had a bath!"

QUASI-COACH

Jim Rehbock recalls the day he got a little too much air time.

Oh, he was a needler and... he never forgot. In my early years with him I realized that even though I was on the bench not one of those 12,400 people in Reynolds had bought a ticket to see me. So I'd sit on the end of the bench calm, cool, and collected. I did that for a number of reasons—I had to watch the game for injuries and so I couldn't let myself get wrapped up in the win vs. loss thing. Also I knew that I was one of those fans who tends to get excited, a screamer, and so it took some mental discipline.

But there was one game where Jimmy beat Carolina for the first time and this was at home. It was '83, the championship year. Jimmy used to always like to have his defense in front of him the second half, rather than his offense, because he wanted to make defensive changes late in the game. So it was important which basket we chose to defend first—and last. He wanted to be in position to make verbal contact with Sidney. Dean was onto him, and when he could, he always made sure when they came to our place that it was the other way around.

Anyway I'm supposed to be this stoic person, and in this Carolina game he wanted to change defenses—we had been pressing and he wanted them to fall back into a half-court defense—so he's waving, Dick Stewart is waving, Ray Martin is waving, and so I'm up now and I start waving.

Bad luck.

Channel 5 shoots the bench, and that night on TV you see everybody on the bench waving.

Well, after the game we go up to his office and he sees this on TV. And here I am coaching, waving the team back, and he says, "Rheebs, you coached a hell of a game tonight!"

I LOVE A PARADE

There were plenty of times that V found his players in the wrong place on the court. MIKE WARREN remembers the day that he caught three of his guys way out of position.

This was like '84 and we were playing Georgia Tech at home on a weekend, a day game, and it was just one of those beautiful days you can get in North Carolina in January or February, 60 degrees, sunny, like spring. Terry Gannon and I were living in an apartment off of Avent Ferry Road and one of the guys that we knew had a white Cadillac Eldorado convertible, one of these big old tank things, early '70s, maybe late '60s model. It was so pretty out and we're not playing Tech until like 1:00. We'd had our pre-game meal so we decided to go for a ride in the caddy, top down. Now this is a big game that we're about to play, but we've got our buddy chauffeuring us, and Terry and I are sitting up on the back seat, like we're in a parade.

[Then] we decide to go to the College Inn and pick up Lorenzo. Now it's the three of us perched on that back ledge, and we've got a driver, and so he takes us for a tour through campus. We're waving and carrying on and so we end up taking a turn down the hill toward Reynolds Coliseum and we're laughing and carrying on and we're okay because we're still within a few hours of game time. Well, Terry looks back as we're pulling down the hill from Reynolds Coliseum and who's in the car behind us?

V!

And he's got this look, "I'm going to kill you." So we're trying not to make eye contact and we tell our driver to go left toward the Student Center. Fortunately V goes right toward Reynolds and Case Athletic Center. Now pre-game we're waiting to hear from him. We're really making ourselves scarce in the locker room, nobody making eye contact with him. Then, short of that dunk in the championship, Lorenzo pulls off his biggest bail out. He scores about 32 points that day and we beat Tech at the buzzer 68-67.

After the game V comes up and says, "Hey, Lorenzo, let me know what time the parade starts before the next game; I'll drive the float!"

REINCARNATION

DAN WHITE remembers the one night that V would have rather been Danny than V!

We were out in Denver, this was '85, and we beat Alabama and were going to play St. John's to go to the Final Four. Garry Dornberg, the announcer, and I decided to celebrate by going to the dog track. Well, we were on a roll because I hit the Trifecta and won three or four hundred dollars. So I'm a college guy and this made me rich. V heard the story and to add fuel to the fire I also got lucky and met a girl out there. So I was really riding high.

Well, the next morning I get on the elevator and here's V; he says, "Hey, heard you hit the Trifecta last night. Then Dice [assistant coach Ray Martin] tells me that later he sees you with a babe on your arm! I'll tell you what, when I die I want to come back as a f*&*ing basketball manager. You drink, play the dogs, chase broads, and occasionally bag up a basketball or two. You sons of bitches have it made!"

CUTTING TO THE CHASE

TERRY GANNON remembers a meeting with V following his senior season to discuss the Gannon future.

This was going to be the big one. I knew that V would have a number of thoughts and so I was looking forward to about an hour or so of discussion as to whether I should accept an offer to go to Europe to play basketball or maybe get into coaching here in the States. So I walked into his office at the scheduled time and he's on the phone.

V looks up, puts the caller on hold, and says, "What?"

I said, "Well, I'm trying to decide whether to play basketball in Europe or... "

And V says, "Look, you're short, you're white, and you're slow. Who the hell do you think you are... Walt Frazier? Get on with your life!"

And then, without missing a beat, he picks up the receiver and goes right back into the phone conversation.

If he'd have sat and weighed the pros and cons with me who knows what I'd have decided to do. But when I walked out of that office I knew what V thought... my future wasn't going to be as a professional basketball player, and of course he was right.

Oh, V was the guy who got me started in broadcasting.

DUELING GREENVILLES

RUTH CURLEE, the long-time secretary for NC State's Wolfpack Club, remembers the details of one of V's version of Planes, Trains, and Automobiles–the follow-up to V's going to the wrong Greenville.

I happened to be in the office late one evening waiting for a Wolfpacker to come in with his membership payment. The phone rang. It was Dave Hoffman calling from Greenville, North Carolina, where he'd been waiting to take the new coach to a meeting in Tarboro.

Dave said, "Guess what, Ruth? I just got a call from Jim. He's in Greenville, South Carolina, not North Carolina. He flew to the wrong Greenville."

So we had to come up with a plan. Dave would go on to Tarboro and hold the Wolfpackers who were waiting to meet their new basketball coach. Somehow, Jim would fly back into Raleigh from Greenville, SC, and an assistant coach would pick him up and take him to Tarboro. They were going to try to make it all by 9:30 P.M. in hopes that Dave could hold the crowd.

In the meantime I talked to Charlie Bryant and he wanted to know if there was anything I could do. Well, I started calling Wolfpackers in South Carolina that I knew had planes. It was after 5:00 now but I reached Mr. Wells, with Daniels Construction Company in Spartanburg, SC. He said, yes, they had five airplanes. So I asked him if he'd do me a big, big favor. The answer was yes. Now I was trying to find Jim on one phone and calling on another to find out if Tarboro had a lighted airstrip. They did.

When Mr. Wells's driver finally pulled into the Greenville-Spartanburg airport–to take him to the private plane–there was Jim wearing his red jacket and telling everyone that he was the new NC

State coach. But of course, they couldn't have cared less. He's telling everyone that he's in town for a Wolfpack meeting, still no reaction. The driver wasn't even sure who he was. But he and the pilot showed up with, I guess, a map to Tarboro and a fifth of Wild Turkey. Well, you had to hear Jim's version of the flight.

He was scared to death, but, as he said, "I flew in on a Wild Turkey."

When he finally got to the Holiday Inn in Tarboro, the cocktail party had been raging on–from dinner until the flight touched down. There were 330 Wolfpackers flying pretty high. Now here comes V on the wings of the Wild Turkey. So it was quite an introduction of our new coach. And of course he really wanted to impress his new fans, and the one thing that I'll say, having been around him for all the years that followed: he was a genius. But there was one subject at NC State that he didn't pass, and that was geography.

$\mathcal{V}$

BACKSTAGE BOBBY

V wasn't easy to surprise. He either knew what was coming or thought he did. This time there was no denying it: the look–of utter shock–gave him away.

When NC State won the national championship I was working in the Public Relations Office. The call came from Chancellor Poulton–who was with the team in Albuquerque–to ready Reynolds Coliseum for a celebration. We won the championship on a Monday night; the team was arriving late Tuesday afternoon. That Tuesday was wild for our PR office, for campus security, and for our facilities people.

I had the pleasure of working several events when the president of the United States visited Reynolds Coliseum, and the draw for the highest office in the land wasn't even close to this one. A stage was set in the southern bay of the Coliseum. Carpenters constructed a make-shift wooden corral in front of the stage for the press. The folding chairs placed on the floor along with the Coliseum's regular red backed seats probably brought the seating up to about 15,000.

The media were alerted. And by 3:00 P.M. we were "sweating" the fire marshals because we couldn't have shoehorned another fan in the building if they'd have been slipping us $20 bills. There were more fake press credentials offered up than you'd find at your average Stones Concert!

"I'm with the *Beaver Lake Weekly!*"

Around 3:30 P.M. we got the word that the plane had landed and that the team bus—led by a police escort—was inching its way down Route 40. When they finally arrived, the place was rocking—network TV, national press, and again, more fans than you'd legally want to see in any university building. It was a great show to say the least. The players walked out on the stage—Sidney and Dereck wearing cowboy hats—souvenirs from the trip west. As the players talked and the raucous crowd cheered, I had my V moment.

There was a large black backdrop behind the stage and for some reason I walked out of the press corral and behind the curtain. There was V. All by himself. He didn't know it, but he was about to see Reynolds Coliseum in a first-ever one-of-a-kind state. I remember that he looked sick. Which he was: he'd had a high-grade fever the night we'd won the championship. I waved and gave him the V for victory sign. He laughed.

"Wait till you see what's out there!" I said.

He laughed knowingly. "Hey, I've been here a few times," he said.

Just then they pulled the curtains open and he looked out into that wild mob of people. V couldn't believe it! Then, before he went on stage he turned back to me, shook his head, and returned the V sign.

HAIR CUT!

JOHN FEINSTEIN, a Duke grad who grew up to become the author of Season On The Brink *and numerous other bestsellers, remembers the one that V used to tell to illustrate just how difficult it was to coach in the state of North Carolina during the Dean Smith years.*

Soon after V became the basketball coach at NC State in the spring of 1980 he walked into a barbershop near campus on Western Boulevard. The barber, an older man, a guy Valvano guessed had probably been cutting NC State hair for forty or fifty years, peered at him as if he recognized Jim.

"Aren't you the fella who replaced Norm Sloan as basketball coach?" he asked, as Valvano settled into the chair.

"Yes, as a matter of fact, I am," Valvano replied.

"Well," the barber said, "all I can say is, I hope you have more luck than old Norm did.."

Valvano couldn't help himself. "Now wait a minute," he said. "Didn't old Norm win a national championship here? Didn't he go 27-0 one season while he was here?"

The barber paused, scissors in the air to think about that for a minute, "Yeah, I guess he did," he finally said. "But just imagine what old Dean Smith would have done with that team."

PRACTICE MAKES PERFECT

KAY YOW remembers V as a coach who cared about everyone's team.

Over the years we coached together there were mix-ups, of course, over the use of practice courts. And I remember that something was being held in Reynolds Coliseum and so we were to practice in Carmichael Gym. Well, Jim and I were scheduled for the same court space at the same time. We walked in and they were there, the guys were practicing. In two days we were playing UNC and so my practices were really critical. We were just a day or two from our biggest game of the year.

So Jim comes over and instead of saying, "Hey, good luck, we've got the court!" He says, "Who are you playing next?"

I say, "North Carolina!"

And he said, "Well, I'll tell you what, our next game is important but it isn't Carolina. Give me forty-five minutes and the court is yours!"

That is the way he was, and there were other times that this happened. I remember once on a Saturday morning where he just said, "Okay, we'll share the court. You take half and I'll take half the court, how will that be?" It wasn't what either of us wanted but the bottom line was that if there was a conflict he was always fair. It was never, "I'm sorry, that's your problem!"

With Jim it was always a shared problem. That was a side to him that people need to know. Because in certain places men's basketball is just going to hold a higher trump card. But Jim just wasn't that way, and this was after he'd won the national championship

BLACK MONDAY

FRANK MCCANN, V's neighbor and golfing buddy who stood by him throughout his illness, recalls the horrible day that he discovered V had cancer.

He'd just come back from Europe; he was doing the color commentary for the World Football [League]; that was a hoot in itself—he had a couch on the 50-yard line and did the interviews from a couch. It was wild, but he went with a cold, and he couldn't shake it, and he had a pain in his groin and he came back with the same symptoms, the pain in the groin.

He came over to my house and we were having hamburgers and hot dogs and I said, "Jim, how many people do you know at Duke? Just go in Monday and get this all straightened out and get it over with."

He said, "Yeah, yeah!"

I thought it was just a bad cold and that he was run down—he was always run down; he was doing everything.

Then on Monday he went to the doctor and we got a call from Pam or our friend Mike Martin's wife, and they said, "You have to come, it's serious, Jim has cancer."

So we jumped in the car—I had just retired from IBM and it was a Monday morning—and we went to the doctor's. We went to a doctor on Glenwood Avenue in Raleigh and there were X-rays and they could see the black stuff and it was surreal because what do you say, what do you talk about? Finally they came out of the office and the guys got in one car and the girls got in another and it was the strangest fifteen or twenty minute ride that I've ever been on in my life. It was watching the world collapse around a person, just collapse because here was a really bad prognosis. I think it was maximum five years. He talked a little bit. It was the classic cancer scenario, denial, then why me? What did I do? Mike Martin and I were trying to pump him up, whatever we need to do we'll do it to beat this thing. But he hadn't gotten to the point where that had any meaning because he was still in the denial stage.

But the thing I remember most was how sick I felt for him, Pam, and his family, and that's what cancer does, it attacks the family, everyone around him.

So when we got back home Jim hadn't had a cigar in a long while but he said, "Screw it, I'm breaking out a cigar."

We always smoked cigars and so he is going to light up a cigar. I knew that even though it was early, this was a defining moment in the process, because he'd laid off the cigars for a long time.

Then he just stopped and said, "No, I'm not going to smoke it!" And he didn't.

It was like, "Okay, I'm not giving up," that he was ready to fight.

WORDS TO LIVE BY

MIKE FINN, by then the sports information director for Georgia Tech, recalls one of V's last talks directed at players. This was after a shootaround before a Georgia Tech–Florida State basketball game, and it was the first time that Bobby Cremins realized that he was about to lose an old friend.

Bobby Cremins asked V to address the Georgia Tech team. V, of course, had nothing planned but suddenly it kicked in and there was the raspy voice… and it was V being V.

"Guys, what would you do if you knew you only had one year to live? Most of you know I have cancer. And the doctors told me I might have about a year or so. I decided, in addition to whatever responsibilities I have with my family, the one thing I wanted to do with my life, the one thing that was most important to me, was to be affiliated with college basketball.

"So I told the people at ESPN that I wanted to do college basketball as long as I was able to. I told them as long as they could prop me up and roll me out and my voice doesn't fail me, I would do it.

"That's how much I love this game. This game is a great game. And I think my message to you guys is that. Sometimes I wonder why you guys don't play harder every time. It won't be that long before you'll have to hang up that uniform for good and you won't get another chance. You just don't have that many games left, and you cheat only yourself when you don't give it your all.

"Or maybe there's a day like today, where you have a tough practice day. When it seems like you can't do anything right. I know I heard some of your names called out a lot today. When these days happen, don't get down. Don't get discouraged. Players tend to get myopic, while a coach is always looking at the long term. Don't just see that Coach Cremins is always trying to correct you. Listen to why he's trying to correct you. He sees only the best you can be, while as a player you only see what's in front of you. Remember what a great game this is and that you're lucky to have the opportunity to play it.

"You don't get that opportunity for long. And if I had my wish, the best is to play this game. Playing, then coaching, then watching. Bobby and I, if we could still play, would be playing. The reason we aren't is somebody told us that we weren't good enough to play anymore.

"So if you can't play, you coach. And if you can't coach, you watch. Anything, just to stay close to this game. So I guess what I'm trying to say, is that when you experience some adversity, when things aren't going right, think of me. Think of Jim Valvano. Remember that I'm someone who's got it a lot worse than you do. And be thankful that you can still play this game. No matter how many difficulties you might experience, find a way to fight through it. Find a way to love this game.

"As a child of the '60s, in college we would always play this game of 'What if you only had a year to live, what would you do?'"

And then V gave them the answer to that question . . . and it wasn't the same game he'd played with his friends in the '60s. It was the answer to the game of his life. He said, "When all is said and done and you look in the mirror, you have to be accountable for you. You've got to get your priorities in line with the true love of your family and friends and the man upstairs!"

LAUGHTER TURNS TO TEARS

FRANCES LEWIS recalls a day that she'd loved to forget. For years the man had made her laugh and now the laughter turned to tears.

He made me laugh thousands of times but he only made me cry once. He called me one morning and wondered if it was okay to come over to my house. I thought he wanted to talk to me about accounting with his business and so he came over and we went up and sat down in my little office. We went over a few things and then he got up to leave and I was walking him to the door and I sensed that something was wrong.

When he turned around he had tears in his eyes and he said, "Frances, I've been definitely diagnosed with cancer."

I just couldn't speak.

But then I said, "Jim, promise me one thing, that you'll seek the finest, most reputable doctors in the country. And please, please, don't procrastinate."

He promised me that he would do this. You see, he hated going to the doctor. Pam and I used to beg him to go. I remember the time Pam called asking me to look on his calendar and make a doctor's appointment and make him go.

I said, "I'll do the best I can."

So I started telling Jim on Monday that I'd cleared his calendar. I said, "I made you a doctor's appointment for Thursday afternoon."

He said, "You can just forget it, throw that in the trash can."

I said, "Pam and Dr. Manley want you to go. Dr. Smith's expecting you."

Then I just went back to my desk and I told Pam what I'd done. Finally I just kept bugging him and he did go.

I don't know if that was the beginning of his problem or not. I got the impression that it may have started as prostate cancer and then went to his bones. I'm not sure and I'm not sure that he even knew because he was reluctant to go to doctors. I'm a cancer survivor myself, so I'm very much in favor of checkups. I won't speculate about Jim's situation, but a checkup saved my life!

$\mathcal{V}$

PARTING SHOT

Graham Wilson, president of PRStreet, the agency that handles all the media for the Jimmy V Charity Golf Tournament, recalls one of V's final credits.

This was when V was sick. And one day he was coming through MacGregor Downs where he lived and there was a little boy on a bridge who had just caught a fish. The kid had the fish on the hook in one hand and a camera in the other and was trying to take his own picture.

V pulled over, got out of the car, took the camera, and snapped the kid's picture.

When he handed the camera back to the little boy he said, "Now remember, when that picture's developed, be sure you get the photo credit right. On the back I want–PHOTO BY JIM VALVANO!"

BIG TIMER

V had a very strong affection for his managers. And Rich Petriccione at Iona remained a very close friend until V's dying day. Here Pet, as V called him, remembers his old boss, sick now but still acting like the big timer he'd always been.

The first time I saw Jim after he was diagnosed was when he came up to New York. My wife works at Sloan-Kettering and so the minute I heard about his cancer I called him and asked if he wanted to go to Sloan-Kettering. We started to do some arranging but someone at a higher level had already made sure that he got an appointment.

So he was in Sloan-Kettering for some testing and my wife, Mary, and I were going to go visit him. We're walking up and down some avenue in New York and I said I have to take him a gift, bring him something. We went into a bookstore and bought him the book *When Bad Things Happen To Good People*, which is by a rabbi.

So I bring him the book, he opens the book, and he goes, "Oh thanks, Pet. This guy just called me a few minutes ago!"

I said, "What do you mean this guy just called you?"

And he says, "The guy who wrote this book. He's a great guy. He's on the Washington Speakers Bureau with me and he just gave me the whole book over the phone!"

I laughed and said, "f*&% you, Valvano. I can't do anything for you anymore. You are such a big timer!"

𝒱

MAKE-A-WISH

DICK VITALE remembers the impact V had on a cancer victim long before he was diagnosed with the dread disease.

It was ironic. This was in 1992. I got a call from the Make-A-Wish Foundation telling me about this youngster named Mark Kelly who had cancer. Mark wanted to spend a day with me, which was flattering. Well, during that day Jim Valvano [who was working a telecast with Vitale] found time to spend with this young man, autographs, conversation. Then later he helped us get Mark a researcher's job at ESPN.

This is the irony. Now Mark Kelly is cancer-free and working at ESPN. And when you think about it, here's Jim Valvano—who that same year started to have back pains—the person who impacted his life at a very important time. I remember being on the set with Jimmy—this was that same year, '92—and he was complaining of really bad back pains which, of course, was his cancer. Jimmy would be so proud of the fact that Mark Kelly, this good-looking kid, is now cancer-free and working at ESPN. That's just the way Jimmy was.

And you know, when Jimmy first had symptoms, we just thought it was something that he'd shake off. Then when he found out that it was cancer, we had a number of very tearful phone calls. I can remember seeing him in so much pain, once in his hotel room, he was watching the *Frank Sinatra Story* on TV, and he was in so much pain that he just started beating on the wall of the hotel room.

Then later, I remember standing on that stage next to him at the ESPN ESPY Awards in amazement. I had seen him that day at the hotel, so sick and so weak [that] we had to literally carry him up on to the stage, and I just didn't know what he'd do, or if he'd be able to do much of anything. And then he gave that incredible speech that not only captivated millions, it was the beginning of the Jimmy V Foundation, the charity that has raised millions of dollars to fight cancer.

One of my last promises to Jimmy was this. I told him that whenever I spoke to anyone I'd tell them. Whatever you do, don't forget to call 1-800-4-JimmyV. And because of that 1-800-4-JimmyV, he is still so very much alive and still making a difference.

V DAY

Jim Rehbock recalls a bittersweet day at V's house.

I had already resigned at NC State and I was in physician's assistants school. Our old athletic director, Willis Casey, passed away and at the memorial service for Willis, Mark Bockelman from Sports Information said, "Have you heard about V?"

I talked to Jim about twice a month on the phone [or] at events or something. It wasn't like at NC State when we were on a daily basis, but when Mark said, "He's getting ready to announce that he has cancer," it hit me like a ton of bricks. I couldn't tell you what they said at the memorial service for Willis because that's all I could think about. I left that service and went straight to Jimmy's house.

All his golf buddies were there and they were just having a great time—Frank McCann and the guys from MacGregor Downs. But then they all had to get their wives for dinner. Pam and the girls weren't there and so suddenly it was just me and Jimmy. And we sat in his living room and we just didn't say a word, we just sat there and cried.

Then Dick Sheridan and Kevin O'Connor came in from our Athletics Department. Now this was just before they announced it on *Sports Center*. We had the big-screen TV on and we watched ESPN make the announcement and of course he was joking about it and trying to make fun of it—saying things like at the end he'd be taking shark enemas and IVs of coffee grounds. He was doing this for all of us. But I remember that he was so worried about which picture they were going to use because he always made fun of his nose. He said that he was really hyper about ESPN using a decent picture of him, if they put him up there. Of course they did and they were very solemn about it and he just kept making jokes left and right.

After the announcement his place became Grand Central Station, the doorbell ringing and the phone ringing. I stayed there and answered the phone and he just held court. People started coming over and to tell you the truth it was such a parade, maybe ten, fifteen people there in the room. He was holding court—basketball, NC State, ESPN, Vitale—had people in stitches.

I'd say, "Do you want to talk to so and so?"

He'd say, "No, take a message. I'll call them back."

A lot of his coaching buddies called—some he'd take, others not, just because he wanted to talk privately with them.

Bob Staak was just dying to talk to him and V just didn't want to talk to him until he could really spend some time with him. The food started showing up, we ate, drank, we had the damndest time and it was typical V—whenever there was a tough situation this is how he dealt with it, turning the biggest negative into a huge positive.

BROWN BOAT

There are very few times that I can remember looking back and saying, "Wow, that was a moment. That was something very special." This rarity occurred the day Valvano's friend **Frank McCann** *showed me his home video of Brown Boat. Now I'm no film critic but I can say without reservation that this video is one of the best V moments ever recorded.*

In defense of "Steady Cam" Frank, the videographer, his VCR player was having trouble the day he played it for me. But the content was riveting. The story of Brown Boat begins with one of Jim Valvano's final ten goals when he was suffering from cancer.

He wanted to put an oil painting on canvas. So he sent his friend McCann off to buy him easel and canvas. Of course, they were too small for The Master, and so off McCann went again. When the proper canvas and easel were in place, V began his work of art.

He was in tremendous pain at the time and couldn't sleep, so when the Valvano house lights went out, V painted. In due time he had put on canvas a reasonable facsimile of the picture that appeared on the box that contained his oil paints–a small body of water, a beach, a light house, and a brown boat. Throw in a few sea gulls and some sand and–well, you've got the picture.

What McCann's incredible video captures is the artist's unveiling of his work. V invited a group of close friends to his home for a black tie event (many wore shorts and golf shirts but all were in black tie). The artist met his audience decked out in tam and sunglasses. To watch this video is to see the ghost of Ernie Kovacs. It begins with a brief interview with the artist, who shares his thoughts on the inspiration for his soon-to-be-revealed work.

V looks into the camera and says, "I was influenced by Monet, Renoir, and of course, the late, great, Earl Scheib!"

The moving picture (sorry, Frank, I do mean moving) follows the artist as he interacts with his audience. A golfing buddy in Bermuda shorts seated on the couch suggests that if the artist should decide to do nudes, he would be willing to model.

V responds, "I couldn't afford to buy enough paint to put that body on canvas."

Then the artiste goes to his painting–which is draped for its unveiling–and addresses the audience, taking a shot at everyone, including Angelina Valvano, his poor defenseless mother.

He describes his life as a starving artist, "And my mother is with us this evening. Many of you are not aware but she worked as a maid to support our family until her green card ran out. At this time she was–unfortunately–run out of the country leaving us motherless."

V addresses the fact that most of the classics were put on canvas by artists whose talent came from pain, and then places himself squarely in that category.

"Every night as I would come to my canvas and prepare to work my loving wife, Pam, would come by before retiring for the evening and say, 'If you get any paint on this carpet, I'll kill you!'"

There was a brief moment for seriousness where V talks to his friends about his illness, thanking them for their support and love. And just as he has them all set up, caught in the sentiment of the moment, he stops and works one of his favorite jokes into the monologue. This is a joke within a joke because everyone in the room has heard it a million times (he does this to them all the time) so the booing begins. For years, catching them off guard, he has slipped the joke Timbuktu into conversation. So here it comes again.

He's mid sentence on a totally unrelated subject, "Why that reminds me of the story... "

The audience's protest does not deter the artist.

He continues:

"There was a contest to name the best poet in the world and it came down to the great Ogden Nash and one lone, unknown poet, a man who had somehow survived the competition. The crowd could not believe how far the unknown had gotten in the competition. The judge of the contest said, 'Whoever provides us with the best poem which uses the word Timbuktu shall be named the Greatest Poet on Earth.'

"Ogden Nash stood and said,

> *As I look upon this strange land,*
> *And gaze upon the burning sand,*
> *A caravan came into view,*
> *Bound, no doubt for Timbuktu.*

"The crowd went nuts in awe of the genius, and when they subsided, the unknown poet stood, looked to his audience, and said:

> *Me and Tim a huntin' went,*
> *Met three ladies in a tent.*
> *They was three, and we was two,*
> *So I bucked one, and "Tim Bucked Two."*

When V (probably for the last time) had slipped his favorite joke to his friends once again and deflected the boos, he suddenly flipped and was an artiste again. The cloth was pulled, the work revealed, and amid much oohing and aahing, the artist now described his creation in an impromptu Q & A session.

FRIEND: Is the boat coming into the beach or going out?

V: I don't know, what do you think?

AUDIENCE: Is that just a glitch there in the sand, a mistaken drop of oil paint from the artist's brush, or some kind of symbolism?

V: Or is it bird shit? You tell me!

And on it went, raucous laughter, V playing the role of the pained artist going back and forth with his friends, raising hell, creating havoc, having fun.

As I watched the video of this incredible performance, I turned to Frank McCann and said, "How much longer did he live?"

V died approximately one month after the unveiling of Brown Boat. And as the tape played out I became even more aware of just how witty and how much fun this man had been. But the overriding thought was this: He couldn't beat death but he surely deflected it by living life right until the very end.

JACKIE MASON

PAT KENNEDY, who at the time was coaching basketball at Florida State, recalls meeting his father's hero—who delivered a line that Kennedy could hardly wait to share with his friend V.

Now Jimmy gets diagnosed with cancer and Richie Petriccione and I fly into New York City to see him. Jimmy's at Sloan-Kettering, and we spent most of the night with him. It was a very difficult night. So when Pet and I leave we go to P.J. Clark's, one of the city's famous old watering holes—the traditional bar, guys serving beer in the white aprons. We're crying in our beer about Jimmy, sitting there drinking and talking about life. Suddenly the door flies open and this guy comes in and he's got an entourage following him. It's Jackie Mason, the old Jewish comedian from the *Ed Sullivan Show.* Later he did a TV sitcom called *Chicken Soup.* Mason was on Broadway at the time in a play called *One Man's World.*

So I'm thinking, "Okay here's my dad's hero, I've gotta do something. What would V do if Jackie Mason walked in? Well, he'd jump the guy, right?"

So I hit Jackie Mason with the story about my dad, I tell him that I'm the basketball coach of Florida State, that I'm a great friend of Burt Reynolds [a Florida State alum]. Then I finish off my pedigree by telling him that I'm a close friend of Jim Valvano.

That's when he nailed me with a classic Jackie Mason line. "Oh, and I should know him?"

When I told V that story the next day, oh man, did we laugh. I used that line on him right until the end.

"Jim Valvano. I should know him?"

𝒱

AS TIME RUNS OUT

GARY SMITH's "As Time Runs Out" was published by Sports Illustrated *during V's final days. The cover story is considered by many to be one of the most powerful pieces in SI's history. Smith, who has written for* Esquire, Rolling Stone, Washington Post Magazine, *and* Life Magazine, *looks back at this interview with fond and insightful memories.*

Jim Valvano and Dustin Hoffman stand out as my two most fascinating interviews. They were the most full of life, full of humor, and full of intelligence. Both of them would be pacing around the room with extemporaneous thoughts leaping into their heads, blurting them out. They were invariably funny, smart, and also underlayered with emotion. It was hard to miss (as a writer) with a guy like Valvano. You just wanted your pen to keep up with it. It was particularly incredible to see a guy do that as he was facing death. God, to be able to do that in that scenario was pretty startling,

Before I approached him, I have a vague memory that he'd given us the green light through the editors. And despite any reticence that his family may have had, he'd come to the point where he wanted to address some issues in his life. He knew he was staring down the barrel of death and I think he was looking for a format to deal with some of these things.

When addressing all the controversy and the scandal, he found that line in between. He didn't absolve himself nor did he lie there and take all the arrows of blame. He wished he'd done a number of things differently yet almost in the same breath he relished what living that way and making the choices he'd made brought him. Life is a mixed bag. It's [his life] probably what some people might see as a contradiction. But he was kind of knitting these contradictions together so you could see that this was all a part of a human being.

As to his regrets, what jumps into my mind was Father's Day when he was finally home for the first time. There was nothing planned for him and [he talked about] the emptiness he felt. But then looking back through the lens approaching death, looking back, he realized he had no right to be hurt that day. He'd never been home for Father's Day; he'd probably been off somewhere giving a Father's Day speech or accepting a Father-of-the-Year award. So he was just realizing that you have to pay consequences for choices you make.

Of course one of his great stories was about the day he came into the house and his wife, Pam, yelling upstairs, "Girls, come on down, your father's in the living room!"

And one of the girls shouting back, "What channel?"

Jimmy, of course, then booming upstairs, "Here, live, right here!"

I interviewed him at his home, and then we hit the road and went to Tallahassee, Florida, where he did his first college game following his illness. We talked there and after the game in Tallahassee, we went on to Sarasota to relax a little bit and hook up with Dickie V[itale]. And so that's where we did most of the interview.

I remember him telling me how much he loved those midnight sit-arounds with the other coaches after games, where he'd end up standing on a chair with a lamp shade on his head or singing Sinatra. And I remember after that game (in conversation) the acceptance of his reality and the love of his wife. There was also the underlying sadness. He had to go back to his hotel room (after the game). He was totally worn out and he had to go back there and eat cold pizza in front of a TV while the boys went out and had beers—the broadcasters and coaches, that frater-nity that he'd headed for so long.

I can't forget sitting at a hotel in Sarasota at poolside, a gorgeous day. He cried openly, not even making any attempt to hide it as he talked about his love of his wife. Everything had been built upon the proposition of his having his run and then paying her back; payback time was vanishing in front of him. He was telling me about the Ozzie and Harriet life that he wanted to live with the kids, grandkids, and Pam.

But you wonder if he might not have ended up in his own restaurant some day, smoking a cigar and holding court for half the night. Hope-fully he'd have found some time to do some of both, but it was pretty hard for him not to have lights on! Very few people burned the candle like Jimmy V did. He was one of those people who didn't learn to say no to himself, didn't learn the wisdom to say no. It's great to say yes, but a wise man also learns to say no.

When I remember that interview I also think of images–lights on, camera's on, action! That's the V everybody knows, but then at the end there were other images. He was going out in his pajamas to feel the grass and putting his arms around a tree just to feel the bark. His feeling was vanishing and he was realizing how fast he was going and how much he missed and trying to grab for it before it was gone.

He told me about the things that had whipped by him. He hadn't slowed down enough to drink in life. There was just something about him that would accelerate and exaggerate everything. It was like God had turned up the dial on a human being about five or six notches above everybody else.

When you work at that speed you miss some things, details can go right past you. And that was where at the end, the last couple of months, all the things he missed along that warp speed ride were suddenly occurring to him. Clearly among them was [that memory of a player who once asked him why winning was so important] as a young coach that his Johns Hopkins players were crazy for thinking that the trying was the thing that defined the person and not the result. And it was like a thunderbolt hitting him late in life, the realization that he was going to die and the result was unavoidable. So how could you define yourself by the result? Everybody dies, so looking at life through those lenses, everybody is a failure.

But it was the fight that he put up until the end.

That's what defined him!

LAST TELECAST

FRANK McCANN, who now heads the Jimmy V Celebrity Golf Classic, recalls one of life's lessons that he learned from V–The Hug.

When he was sick, whenever the lights came on or the mike was on, he just changed. I took him to Duke for one of his last TV broadcasts. He was extremely sick and you could see it in his face, and as we entered the building, as he walked in the door, the sea of people just parted. He walked through and out on to the floor and people just stood and started clapping.

After that a friend of ours, Jim Yonkers, took him down to Florida State for a telecast. Then I took him to Bristol, Connecticut, to ESPN for what would be his last telecast.

Jim Yonkers had told me about taking care of him; he said, "Don't think it's going to be easy."

So I said, "Well, I'll just be with him."

"No," Yonkers said, "the disease is so complex that it is attacking him in ways that his body is changing all the time, and being in the dead of winter he has no resistance."

He was always cold. In Florida Yonkers had him under a ton of blankets and said that it just didn't do any good, that he had to cradle him in his arms because he was so cold. When Jim Yonkers told me that, it got me.

I digress here, but I have this personal reticence. I am an Irish Catholic from New England and of course, Jim was an Italian from New York. New England people are very private and I had just never ever hugged another man, maybe not another person except my wife. That was just the way I was. Of course, Jim was the opposite. What Jim did from the time I met him until the time he died was he had this thing where he was teaching me to hug people. And it's amazing. Now I'll hug anybody. It's one of the gifts that Jim gave me.

So now I have to take him to Bristol and I know that I may have to hold him in my arms because of what Jim Yonkers had told me. I was still in training and at that time this hugging thing still made me very uncomfortable. So we fly to Bristol and when we get to the hotel it's so cold, maybe about 0. I put the temperature in the room at about 90 degrees. But the wind is blowing and Jim is very uncomfortable and finally gets to sleep. He has to rest before his broadcast. So I was running at the time and I had been sitting with him and he was sweating like crazy in the room. But now he's finally asleep so I decide to go out for a run. I grew up in New England but you forget how cold it gets up there.

Well, I go out in my T-shirt and running shoes and shorts and step out in that weather. It was bitter cold and I got out there and just kept running, thinking about Jim, trying to get it out of my system, and I got lost. I thought I was going to die. I knew I needed to get back to him and it was scary. Finally found my way back to the hotel and he was still asleep.

Then when he woke up, he couldn't get warm. He was shaking and what Jim Yonkers said happened to me. I had to just cradle or hold him. And it was probably one of the saddest times I've ever had in my life. Here was this incredible vibrant person so full of life, shaking like a leaf. And I'm holding him—this non-hugger—trying to keep him warm.

Finally he settled down, we got him dressed, and I said, "Jim, can you make it down the stairs?"

And this was the clue that the end was near.

He said, "Better get a wheelchair."

The ESPN studios were right across the street and when we finally got him downstairs, I pushed him out the front door and he stood up and said, "Frank, I can't do it!"

I called over to the studios and told them that I was taking him home, that he couldn't do it. I had met Chris Fowler earlier and he knew that I was planning to go to the ESPN store when Jim was on the air and get a souvenir hat. And the next morning when we went down to the lobby to wait for our cab to the airport there was a package with my name on it.

Pinned to an ESPN hat was a note from Chris Fowler that said, "Frank, I know that you couldn't make it to the store. Take care of Jim!'

PRESIDENT ON LINE ONE

PAM VALVANO remembers a presidential—one way—call.

When Jim was sick it was incredible the people who called or wrote to wish him well. Dustin Hoffman, Johnny Carson. One day the phone rang and they told me it was the White House calling. Fortunately I'd been warned that President Clinton might call or I'd have hung up thinking it was a crank call.

Jim was really out of it at the time but I took the phone to him. He was in bed and I told him that it was President Clinton. He popped up and started talking. I don't know what the president said—not much I'm sure, because Jim dominated the conversation. He had a lot to say about the need for more cancer research and this was just the way he was. He didn't give the president a chance to offer up a lot of sympathy. He had the President's ear and he was going to take advantage of it–get his points across on behalf of future research.

LAST REQUEST

DAN PATRICK, ESPN's Sports Center *anchor, remembers V and their very touching farewell.*

During the last year that Jim worked at ESPN, my father had died of cancer. So I purposely stayed away from Jim because I didn't want to relive that. I didn't want to go through that again with a friend, so I hid out. It was toward the end of the basketball season and he was sitting in the ESPN newsroom, and I walked over to him because I knew he wasn't coming back to ESPN again, and I apologized to him.

And he said, "Why?"

And I said, "Well, I purposely stayed away from you because my dad died of cancer and I didn't want to relive that."

And he said, "How long did they give him to live?"

And I said, "Six months."

And then he started crying and then I started crying.

And I remember saying, "If I have a hard time saying goodby to you, it's because I don't know if I'll see you again and in some way I'm saying goodby to my dad."

He said, "No, I understand that."

I said, "You always made me laugh," and he said, "Well, I can't make you laugh now."

And then he said, "Do me a favor, when I finally do go, just say something funny on *Sports Center* about me."

When he died I didn't say anything funny. I just told people that's what he wanted me to say, something that would make them laugh and bring a smile to their faces!

CHESS MASTERS

FRANK McCANN remembers that while V was fighting cancer that there was a war on another front–the one that V and McCann waged against chess master Garry Kasparov.

I used to accompany Jim to Duke [Medical Center] when he was having chemo. And to while away the time we started playing chess. And as soon as we started Jim bought one of these electronic chess sets. At the time they were kind of revolutionary, this was early '90s. It was a Garry Kasparov model, and so Jim and I and Jim Yonkers used to always play against Garry Kasparov. Now this game had sixty-four levels. We're on level one and the three of us–as a team–are trying to beat Garry Kasparov.

So "Team Valvano" came at this game with widely different philosophies. Jim Yonkers has a seize-and-destroy mentality. He takes everything he can without any thought of the consequences. I'm the conservative one, thinking through every move, looking ten moves ahead. Jim's in the middle and of course, looking for an edge, even against a computer game. Well, it's three-on-one and Kasparov and his game is just beating the crap out of us. And we're only at level one. With Jim– who always got to make the call for our move, of course–this was interesting to say the least. He was so into it.

Jim would say, "Hey, we're playing Garry Kasparov on level one. On level sixty-four as soon as you make a winning move, Garry Kasparov flies in from Russia, knocks on your door, comes in and makes a final move, and leaves the winner!"

So we can't beat Garry Kasparov on level one and we're playing him three-on-one, and Jim is getting really frustrated. Well, one day we're at Jim's house and we beat Kasparov on level one. It was unbelievable. This was a Tuesday afternoon and he's up high fiving, running around the table in his pajamas. We thought we'd won the NCAA's, the NBA championship, and the world chess championship all in one.

That was Jim Valvano, his competitiveness, his orientation to goals, and his sense of fun in everything he did. And this was very close to the end–when anyone else would have been in bed feeling sorry for himself, Jim Valvano was going after Garry Kasparov at level one!

𝒱

INTO THAT BRIGHT LIGHT

There were many "moments" in V's life. MARK BOCKELMAN recalls one for the ages.

V's return to Reynolds Coliseum for the 10-year celebration of the '83 championship was incredible. After a pre-game celebration, V was scheduled to call [that day's NC State–Duke] game for ABC with Brent Musburger. Of course at the time he was very sick, taking treatments to fight the cancer. He was sequestered off in one of the offices in Reynolds to prepare to cover the game. One of my jobs as sports information director was to stay in communication with V and the family, then take him out for the celebration.

They didn't want to bring him out too early considering the crowd and because physically he was hurting. And that's what I remember. It was the first time that I'd seen him in a while, and he was sitting there going over his notes before the game.

I was so pleased to see him and he started to stand up and it struck me that he was in pain and I said, "Jim, don't get up. It's my honor to see you again."

He said, "Mark, I do this for my friends."

And that was a personal moment for me. But what I remember most about that day and being back there with the family was that they were all very excited about that day.

The celebration was designed to have him walk out on the court where he'd—for the first time since he'd left the university—see the fans and his former players again. Just a very emotional moment. Of course Reynolds was standing room only and then there were all his players lined up along the sidelines and at mid-court along with his friends from athletics—everyone from Charlie Bryant to Dick Sheridan.

So my duty was to, along with Pam, bring him from the ROTC offices behind the bleachers and out onto the court right where the visiting team normally came out. As we were coming by the steps to the Duke locker room door, Mike Krzyzewski came out and they had what I would describe as a very special moment, very private. In the background you could hear V's team being introduced over the PA out on the court and there was Mike and V and it was really a moment.

But the one that really got me was after Coach K had left and while they were still introducing V's team. All of a sudden I saw Jim's attitude change and it was the first and only time that I can say that I ever saw him look like he might be nervous. He was always on and could be kind of fidgety but this time there was a look in his eyes and he turned to Pam and just before he made arguably the greatest speech of his life, he said, "Pam, I don't know what to say!"

I'll never forget that.

And Pam patted him on the arm and said, "Jim, you'll do fine!"

When he stepped out on the court the spotlight was shining down on that corner and he and Pam walked out into this brilliant light to thunderous applause. It was magical and I get chills every time I think about that. They just disappeared into that great bright light to this unbelievable noise and emotion. After going down the row and spending a moment with each player he spoke to the crowd. He lit the place up to levels that made that spotlight pale in comparison. He wrapped the '83 championship into the history of the program, shared the incredible ride that he and the team had enjoyed, and then took us all off the hook emotionally by addressing his illness with the promise to Never Give Up!

As he spoke I couldn't help but think what he'd said to Pam, "I don't know what to say!"

NAMESAKE

Confronting the fact that his friend would die gave JOHN SAUNDERS *a new lease on life.*

He had called me and he wasn't feeling well and this was before he'd gotten the MRI or had been diagnosed. He told me that he knew he had cancer.

And I said, "Jim, come on. You do not. You have a virus or something."

So sure enough he goes through the tests and he had cancer. So he came up to Sloan-Kettering (in New York City) and he was in an apartment, and the first day he was there I went down and went to Sloan-Kettering with him for his chemo treatment.

When I got to the apartment, I remember him saying, "Why me?" which was natural. So we got to the hospital, and when we got off the elevator at the floor where he was going to be treated, here comes this little kid with no hair. And then here comes another one pushing the little iron pole with the IV. Now we're walking past rooms with kids in them and by the time we got to the room he was going to we'd passed about maybe eight kids.

I saw his attitude change. He went from "Why Me!" to "We've got to find a way to beat this disease! This is killing me and killing these kids."

His daughters were there, and when he was in getting his chemotherapy, I saw how his daughters comforted each other, how LeeAnn, who was only eleven or twelve, how much she leaned on her sisters.

At that point my wife and I had one daughter, and my wife had wanted a second child, but I didn't. I really didn't think I was the father type, and I didn't think I'd be a good father for one child. But when we had the one child, I fell so in love with her and realized how much that she'd added to my life that I couldn't imagine having enough love left for another one.

But I looked at Jim's girls and I thought, "My God, what if something happened to me, and my daughter would be left alone with no brothers and sisters?"

So we went back to the apartment, and when it came time for me to go I hugged everybody and I didn't say anything to them, but (this was a time when I didn't have a cell phone) I pulled off the road and went to a pay phone.

I called my wife and told her what I'd just experienced and said, "I think we should have another baby!"

And she started to cry a little bit and said, "Well, I'm pregnant!"

So that was like a little miracle. We decided to name our child, boy or girl, after Jim. And when we found out that it was going to be a girl we named her Jenna Tiana Vanessa Saunders, JTV!

The capper on this one is that Jim lived to see the day that she was born. And on the day she was born, Jim worked [on ESPN] that day and I watched him from the hospital. Well, they announced that John Saunders's wife had just given birth and that the little girl was named after Jim Valvano. And Jim had a cigar on the set and he was twirling it around, acting like a proud poppa.

I'm thinking this is great, he looks really good. So after the next intermission Jim's not on the set. I call ESPN and ask where he is, and they say, he just got too sick. He had to leave.

So Frank McCann was with him, his friend from Raleigh. I called the hotel and Frank says, "John, he's just awful!" So I went right to the hotel and he was shaking, just freezing, throwing up, and really, really sick!

And all I could think was, this is the same guy that I just saw on the air? That was one of the most amazing things about his battle with this disease, what a great actor he was, just to make people think he was fine. At the ESPYs, an hour before that show started, I was in the hotel room with him and he couldn't even walk; we had to take him down there in a wheelchair. Then he got up there and just mesmerized everyone with one of the greatest, most moving speeches ever.

That was Jim.

MEANINGFUL COACH SPEAK

DERECK WHITTENBURG recalls a most memorable message from Coach Dean Smith.

I never publicized my relationship with Jimmy, never talked about it. But I was the only player who was asked to be a pallbearer at his funeral. I don't think anyone can realize what that meant to me. All the things that I've accomplished, the honor of having the family ask me to carry their loved one, that was the ultimate honor.

I remember that we were at Jimmy's funeral and we had taken the casket out of the church. I had been pretty strong the whole time but when we were finally outside I broke down a little bit, not balling, but I was in tears. Sidney had his arm around me and was telling me that it was all right! And the most unbelievable thing happened.

As we were getting ready to go to our cars, I saw Dean Smith kind of looking at me and very quietly he said, "You know what, Whitt, he really loved you, he talked about you a lot!"

All I could say was, "Thank you, Coach!"

But that was so touching and it's something that I'll never forget. I can still see Dean's face and hear him saying that. As a player, sometimes you never really see the other coaches up close or hear what they talk about. But that was such a classy thing to say, and it still means so much to me because it came from Coach Smith and he was telling me how Jimmy felt... about me.

SINCERELY YOURS!

DEE ROWE recalls the love in the streets for "James" that he saw on the way to the cemetery. He then sums it all up in a personal letter to Pam and the kids.

I was a pallbearer at Jimmy's funeral. I just loved him, he was magic and I recall that I rode to the cemetery with Mike and Mickie Krzyzewski and that it was quite a way from the church to the cemetery. Along the streets as we rode by, it was incredible, the signs, the waving, the tributes that these people paid to Jimmy.

It was absolutely overwhelming.

The emotions were so overpowering. He died in the spring and it wasn't until the following fall, just about the time when the [basketball] season was ready to start, that I got to the point where I could sit down and write to Pam and the family, to tell them how I really felt about James.

I wrote:

Dear Pam and Family:

Forgive me this belated letter, the time has never been right. I have long struggled with this maybe thinking that Jim's only away on a trip. It's all a very bad dream. Someway, somehow he'll think of a way to come back. I think I've thought of him every day since he first told me that he was sick. It didn't end with his final peace. Now the balls are bouncing (the beginning of basketball season again) and it's time for a new season, a new dance and for the first time Jimmy won't be a part of it. The reality is setting in but I can't and don't want to believe it. James gave me something very special back twenty-five or so years ago. He was such a breath of fresh air, he always made the glass half full, he went to the top. He lived his dream and somehow he always managed to let me share a little bit of it. In spite of the bright lights, the glitz, the glamor and the fast track, he never forgot the old coach from Worcester. I will never stop celebrating his life, no one ever had a greater passion for life or his game. In his final race he, more than anyone I've ever known, taught us the true meaning of life, why we coach. He fought to the end, never giving up, telling his story for all of us to hear. His last year he truly found the person he was meant to be. I will take time out every day to laugh, to think, to cry and to love and to remember James, his courage, his lessons and his friendship. He touched us all in his own way and he made so much sense. Now the pain is gone and his spirit will live forever in all of us. His last year was such a terrible struggle and yet a very special mission. And your love and incredible support made it possible for him to complete that mission. The heartache will never go away but I hope that the good things that you had together will give you the strength, inspiration and courage to go forward.

After my visit to Duke [Hospital] I put together this personal tribute to Jim, thinking of what he'd said to me a year ago in June. I wanted very much for you and the family to have it. The timing could never be right but as we begin our first season without him I felt that I shouldn't wait any longer. We had a relationship that maybe few could understand. I watched from afar as he ran his wild and crazy race though life and just always wanted to be there for him. Sometimes he would call and sometimes he wouldn't, but he always knew that I was there. I loved him dearly and will forever cherish our special bond. Please know that you, James and the kids will always be in my thoughts and prayers.

Love, Dee

WISE AND FUNNY TO THE END

PAT KENNEDY recalls a final meaningful moment—one full of wisdom and fun and... so typically V.

We were in the hospital room at Duke and Jimmy was getting pretty incoherent. There wasn't much time left. He was on morphine and would go into these deep sleeps. Well, he popped up one last time when we were there. The daughters were at the end of the bed and he saw the girls and all of a sudden this came out of absolutely nowhere.

He said, "Girls, remember what Yogi Berra said!"

And we're all up on our toes now to hear and then he says, "Girls, Yogi said, 'If you don't know where you're going, you'll never get there!'"

Then he talked to each daughter and outlined her future in life.

He started with Nicole and said, "Nicole, you're brilliant and you can be a brilliant scientist, a brilliant pharmacist, you can do anything that you want to do. You are one of the most brilliant young ladies that I've ever been around."

Then he went to Jamie, "Jamie, you're the most loving, most beautiful daughter that anyone could ever have. There will be great things in your life, you'll be a great teacher, an even better mother."

Then to LeeAnn. "LeeAnn, you are so talented. You can sing, dance, you could be on Broadway." So he goes through each daughter.

And then he says it again, "But remember what Yogi said, 'If you don't know where you're going, you'll never get there!'"

Then he went back to sleep. He died two days later.

BONDED

MIKE KRZYZEWSKI and Jim Valvano had a unique relationship. Were they friends? For years, not really! But they were at the end. Mike Krzyzewski remembers how their lives' paths crossed over the years and then how these two high-profile coaches bonded at the end.

A lot of people may have known Jim better but I think overall I had a unique way of knowing him. First of all we competed against each other as players and secondly we competed against each other away from the ACC. Then we coached against each other here in the ACC. When he went to TV we developed a closer relationship and then the last four or five months of his life we developed an incredibly unique relationship.

We were both really ethnic oriented—he was Italian, I'm Polish. Jim was from New York, I'm from Chicago, we were city guys. We both ended up having three daughters, so there are some amazing similarities; it's almost like his family tree started in Italy and mine started in Poland but it's the same type of fruit in the tree, the same roots and leaves. For the last four to five months of his life the fact that we had so much in common created an environment of total trust—candor in our conversation isn't [a] strong enough [description], this went even deeper than that. So much so that when I came he'd kick everybody else out of the room. And the two of us, it was almost like we were brothers at war. And when we got together, what we talked about, well, it was like if anyone else had been there, they wouldn't have appreciated the conversation.

So it was a fraternity of sorts but it wasn't even a coaching fraternity. It was all those things combined—the playing, the coaching, the similarities in our backgrounds—that made those last four or five months so incredibly open. And I'm sure in our relationship that there were times when we hated each other, because you're competing, so you make fun of one another, you get angry with one another.

But ultimately we respected each other. And when he got out of coaching we really ended up liking each other more than we thought we would. Then the last months we realized that we should have been doing this—having this relationship—a long time ago.

The nights and days that I was there, probably about three times a week, were so emotional. Emotions could be busting a gut laughing or crying. I'm sure we were so loud sometimes—crying and laughing—that people wondered what was going on. But what we were was being totally honest with each other, being totally frank. I had so many moments with him that were from incredibly funny–Jimmy doing an imitation of Lenny Wirtz, the official–to him giving me advice as to why people don't like me.

Then there were moments about the game and coaching. But the thing that blew me away, the most incredible thing, and I can't say what night it was, but we were talking about death, and the way we got around it was using basketball as the metaphor. We were talking about how to win games and he was saying that he'd do just about anything to win, he hated to lose. He'd use a triangle and two, a box and one, and he said, "That's kind of what I'd like to do with this cancer. I want everybody around me to do anything they can to win. They've told me that this cancer, you can't beat it. So I'm willing to try anything. And all the things that they've done [the doctors], the triangle and two, the box and one, subbing five guys at once, none of this has worked. And in their world these doctors haven't ever won against this type of cancer. So I'm willing to experiment with whatever they have, if they want to try it, they can try it on me."

There were all these obstacles there that equated to losing and it frustrated him. He'd get very emotional about it, because he wanted to try anything, and he'd say, "What the hell do I have to lose?" He was very acceptant of the reality that he was going to die soon. But he wasn't on his deathbed at this point, he was very lucid here and on top of his And this was it, his last recruiting, he was absolutely recruiting. And I didn't know who he was going to recruit but he was clearly, "Okay, we need a point guard, a power forward, someone to come off the bench."

That night when I left the hospital as I was walking to my car I was thinking–in the way that you talk to yourself when you think–and suddenly I just stopped and there was a bench and I sat down there and thought about what I'd just witnessed. And what I was thinking was, that didn't really happen, this guy is dying and he should be filled with self-pity or whatever the emotions are that you have when facing death. But instead he had just come up with one of the great ideas of all time.

What I realized was that he'd found a way to win. And now the Foundation is great and getting better, funding millions of dollars in research. But I couldn't believe that he could be thinking of that at that time in his life. So I kept finding out just how much more unique this guy was during those hospital visits. To me that was the most extraordinary thing that a human being could ever do, to face death and to come up with a way to win. And as a coach that's what you are always trying to do, turn a loss into a win, a bad run into something good. And he did the ultimate, the last loss, which was his life, and he turns it into an amazing positive. When he did die I was sad. But there was a part of me that just didn't feel he was dead, because he created something positive that will be there for the ages.

THE LAST CARD PLAYED

Pam Valvano remembers finding V's last and lasting goal.

Jim was so goal-oriented. He used to write his goals on these little 3x5 cards and I'd find them in his pants and coat pockets when I was taking his clothes to the cleaners. This was for our entire married life—"Be a Division I Coach," "Get an NCAA Bid," "Play the 9:00 Game in the Garden," "Win a National Championship."

When he was sick, I found the last card, and it said, "Find a Cure for Cancer!"

And it's been ten years now, and I know that he's the only one who wouldn't be surprised at the success of the Jimmy V Foundation For Cancer Research. Millions and millions of dollars have been raised, thanks to him and to all of his friends. And I know that he's probably looking down right now wondering why we aren't doing something. I know he'd have some suggestions—but he'd be very proud of the impact that this charity is having in the fight against cancer.

And like so many of his accomplishments it all started on one of his 3x5 cards.

STORYTELLERS' WHO'S WHO...
BACK WHEN THEY KNEW V

Tom Abatemarco–Assistant Coach, Iona and NC State
Joyce Aschenbrenner–Assistant AD, UNLV
Thurl Bailey–Player, NC State Basketball
Fred Barakat–Head, ACC Officials
Mark Bockelman–Sports Information Director, NC State
Jim Boeheim–Coach, Syracuse University
Linda Bruno–Administrative Assistant, Iona
Charlie Bryant–Head, NC State Wolfpack Club
Gary Bryant–Manager, NC State Basketball
Lorenzo Charles–Player, NC State Basketball
Francis Combs–Reporter, WPTF Radio
Chris Corchiani–Player, NC State Basketball
Bobby Cremins–Coach, Georgia Tech Basketball
Ruth Curlee–Administrative Assistant, NC State Wolfpack Club
Vinny Del Negro–Player, NC State Basketball
Walt Densmore–Player, NC State Basketball
Dave Didion–NCAA Investigator
George Dixon–Admissions, NC State
Lefty Driesell–Coach, University of Maryland Basketball
Sam Esposito–Coach, NC State Baseball
John Feinstein–Author
Nora Lynn Finch–Assistant Director, NC State Athletics
Mike Finn–Sports Information, Georgia Tech
Roy Firestone–TV Personality
Bill Foster–Coach, Rutgers Basketball
Bill Foster–Coach, Clemson Basketball
Terry Gannon–Player, NC State Basketball
Jim Graham–Commissioner of Agriculture, North Carolina
Jeff Gravley–Reporter, WRAL-TV
Mike Gray–Host, *Almanac Gardner*, WUNC-TV

Larry Gross–Coach, NC State Soccer
Bob Guzzo–Coach, NC State Wrestling
Terry Holland–Coach, Virginia Basketball
Sarah Sue Ingram–Sports Information, NC State
Ed Janka–Director, Nike Coaches' Clinics
Jay Jennings–Cameraman, WRAL-TV
Art Kaminsky–Agent and Attorney
Pat Kennedy–Coach, Florida State Basketball
Tony Kornheiser–Writer
Mike Krzyzewski–Coach, Duke Basketball
Frances Lewis–Administrative Assistant, NC State Athletics
Bob Lloyd–All-America Guard, Rutgers Basketball
Sidney Lowe–Player, NC State Basketball
Mike Lupica–Writer
Jeff Mann–Administrator, NC State
Jim Marchiony–Sports Information, Iona
Ray Martin–Assistant Coach, NC State Basketball
Rollie Massamino–Coach, Villonova Basketball
Frank McCann–Friend
Ed McLean–Assistant Coach, NC State Basketball
Cozell McQueen–Player, NC State Basketball
Ernie Myers–Player, NC State Basketball
George Nixon–Manager, NC State Basketball
Dan Patrick–TV Announcer
Tom Penders–Coach
Max Perry–Player, NC State Basketball
Rich Petriccione–Manager, Iona Basketball
Jim Pomerantz–Sports Information, NC State
Bruce Poulton–Chancellor, NC State
Dr. Jerry Punch–TV Announcer
Jim Rehbock–Trainer, NC State Basketball
Dr. Don Reibel–Doctor, NC State Basketball
Harry Rhoads–President, Washington Speakers Bureau
Johnny Rhodes–Restaurateur
Bob Robinson–Administrator, NC State Athletics
Les Robinson–Coach, Citadel Basketball

Dee Rowe–Coach, UConn Basketball
Jeff Ruland–Player, Iona Basketball
John Saunders–TV Announcer
Don Shea–Administrator, JTV Enterprises
Dick Sheridan–Coach, NC State Football
Dean Smith–Coach, University of North Carolina Basketball
Gary Smith–Writer
Tubby Smith–Coach
Beverly Sparks–Administrative Assistant, NC State Basketball
Bob Staak–Coach, Wake Forest Basketball
Dick Stockton–TV Announcer
Ken Swartzel–Food Scientist, NC State
Ray Tanner–Assistant Coach, NC State Baseball
George Tarantini–Coach, NC State Soccer
Jerry Tarkanian, Coach, UNLV Basketball
Joab Thomas–Chancellor, NC State
Mike Tirico–TV Announcer
Jamie Valvano–Middle Daughter
LeeAnn Valvano–Youngest Daughter
Nicole Valvano–Oldest Daughter
Nick Valvano–Older Brother
Pam Valvano–Wife
Dick Vitale–TV Announcer
Mike Warren–Player, NC State Basketball
Woody Webb–Attorney
Frank Weedon–Administrator, NC State Athletics
Dan White–Manager, NC State Basketball
Dereck Whittenburg–Player, NC State Basketball
Graham Wilson–President, PRStreet
Alex Wolff–Writer
John Wooden–Coach, UCLA Basketball
Kay Yow–Coach, NC State Women's Basketball

JIM VALVANO'S LIVING LEGACY

THE V FOUNDATION
FOR CANCER RESEARCH

It's been more than 20 years since Jim Valvano led NC State to the most unlikely NCAA Championship win in tournament history, and more than 10 years since Jim Valvano lost his life to cancer.

Jim's stature as a Division I head basketball coach and later, as an analyst for ESPN and ABC Sports, put him in the forefront of the college basketball world.

His speech at the 1993 ESPY Awards made him a vanguard in the fight against cancer.

The deep sense of purpose by which he lived his life continues to inspire others to sustain his quest. From Cinderella basketball coach to crusader for cancer research, the spirit of Jim Valvano will never give up until triumphant.

THE **V** FOUNDATION®
for Cancer Research

Current statistics indicate that one out of every two American men and one of every three women will develop cancer in our lifetime. Every single day, approximately 3,655 Americans will be diagnosed with cancer and more than 1,500 people will die from the disease.

The good news is that 8.9 million people are alive today as a result of progress in cancer research. Over the past 30 years, the five-year cancer survival rate has risen from 38% to 62%

The V Foundation for Cancer Research funds essential cancer research to help locate the causes and develop the cures for the over 100 diseases that are cancer.

The V Foundation was started by friends of Jim Valvano. They have enlisted their friends and have been joined by many others – celebrities, individual as well as corporate donors, volunteers, event organizers both large and small – all of whom realize that every single donation, no matter the size *will* make a difference in this quest.

You can help award grants to deserving, talented researchers. No gift is too small. To learn more about the Foundation, its programs and people, please visit our website www.jimmyv.org.

Help make Jim Valvano's final dream become a reality–that victims will become survivors and that the disease that claims so many loved ones will devastate no more.

The V Foundation for Cancer Research
100 Towerview Court
Cary, NC 27513
1-800-4JimmyV   1-919-380-9505
www.jimmyv.org

V